An Introduction to West Indian Poetry

This introduction to West Indian poetry is written for readers making their first approach to poetry in English written in the Caribbean. It offers a comprehensive literary history from the 1920s to the 1980s, with particular attention to the relationship of West Indian poetry to European, African, and American literature. Close readings of individual poems give detailed analysis of social and cultural issues at work in the writing. Laurence Breiner's exposition speaks powerfully about the defining forces in Caribbean culture from colonialism to resistance and decolonization. This book will be invaluable on courses in literature, history, Caribbean studies, cultural studies, and post-colonialism.

Laurence A. Breiner is Associate Professor of English at Boston University, and has held visiting appointments at the University of Pennsylvania and the University of the West Indies. He has published articles on Caribbean literature in a wide range of journals, and essays in *West Indian Literature*, edited by Bruce King (1979), and *The Art of Derek Walcott*, edited by Stewart Brown (1991).

AN INTRODUCTION TO WEST INDIAN POETRY

LAURENCE A. BREINER

CAMBRIDGE
UNIVERSITY PRESS

PUBLISHED BY THE PRESS SYNDICATE OF THE UNIVERSITY OF CAMBRIDGE
The Pitt Building, Trumpington Street, Cambridge CB2 1RP

CAMBRIDGE UNIVERSITY PRESS
The Edinburgh Building, Cambridge CB2 2RU, United Kingdom
40 West 20th Street, New York, NY 10011–4211, USA
10 Stamford Road, Oakleigh, Melbourne 3166, Australia

© Laurence A. Breiner 1998

First published 1998

Typeset in 11/12.5pt Baskerville   [CE]

A catalogue record for this book is available from the British Library

Library of Congress cataloguing in publication data

Breiner, Laurence A.
An introduction to West Indian poetry / Laurence A. Breiner.
p.   cm.
Includes bibliographical references and index.
ISBN 0 521 58331 4 (hardback). – ISBN 0 521 58712 3 (paperback)
1. West Indian poetry (English) – History and criticism.
2. West Indies – Intellectual life.
3. West Indies – In literature.
1. Title
PR9212.B65   1998
821–dc21   97–42231   CIP

ISBN 0 521 58331 4 hardback
ISBN 0 521 58712 3 paperback

Transferred to digital printing 2003

With gratitude and admiration,
this book is dedicated to the faculty,
staff and students of the
University of the West Indies:
Mona
Cave Hill
St. Augustine

Contents

Preface

This is a general introduction intended primarily for readers of poetry who are making their first approach to the poetry of the Anglophone Caribbean; it pays particular attention to the history of the literary culture, and to the literature's relationship to Caribbean, European, African, and American writing. While the book provides a grounding in the literary history of the West Indies, this is an introduction to issues and developments rather than a chronicle; its emphasis is less on the history *per se* than on the dynamics of that history. It is not a survey, or a thematic review, or an account of the cultural background. Instead the point here is to provide categories for thinking about this poetry, and to investigate the poems *as poems*, rather than as documents of social/political developments. The emphasis will be on the texts, and on what they reveal about what West Indian writers are doing when they write poetry. How are writers using the particular resources of poetry (as distinct from those of prose, drama, journalism) to address their concerns? What kinds of problem arise in the act of writing? What decisions are being made about such matters as audience, language, and strategies of representation?

Apart from oral poetry and some scattered early publications, Caribbean poetry in English begins around 1920 – long after colonization, the colonial wars, slavery, emancipation, and indenture. As a result, those are subjects for poetry only in retrospect, as they underlie the more immediate concerns of this century, among the most prominent of which are:

a critique of colonial status, developed in both political and
cultural terms;

a preoccupation with national identity and self-
  consciousness;
an exploration of multiple cultural traditions;
the adaptation of the English language (and the literary
  tradition that comes with it) to local settings and
  experiences;
a complementary exploration of local forms of language
  and of the oral tradition as resources for poetry.

These issues animate West Indian poetry up to the present
moment, and make it distinctive; for practical purposes the
book considers material up into the 1980s, the point at which a
third successive generation of poets, those born in the 1950s,
had firmly established themselves, making it possible to speak
confidently of an indigenous literary tradition. My end-point
also coincides with the beginning of what Frank Birbalsingh
calls the "fourth stage." His outline of the literary history
distinguishes the colonial period, the period of nationalism
associated with the Federation of the West Indies (1950–65), the
post-independence visions and disappointments of the "micro-
national period" (1965–80), and a "trans-national" period in
which West Indian poetry is concerned with – and often
written by – people of the "external frontiers" of a new
diaspora.[1] This period is marked by an enormous expansion of
the scope of the term "West Indian literature"; the number of
writers has increased greatly, and their positions – both physical
and ideological – are more diverse. As a result, the issues
characteristic of this period are quite different from those that
characterized the preceding decades.

Starting with an analysis of events in 1970/71 which crystallized critical issues, my exposition of West Indian poetry from
the 1920s to the 1980s is shaped by the question: "how did the
writers get there, to that moment of self-definition, and what
were its consequences?" This inquiry lays a firm conceptual
and aesthetic foundation for reading West Indian poetry
written since 1980, and in fact I have not hesitated to take up
individual poems from the 1980s and even 1990s when they

---

[1] *Frontiers of Caribbean Literature in English* (New York: St. Martin's Press, 1996), xi.

illuminate a specific point, but I have not attempted to offer an account of the ongoing "trans-national" period as such.

Functioning as a kind of overture, chapter 1 – "West Indian poetry and its audience" – begins by narrating a moment of West Indian self-recognition, a famous and consequential debate on "the function of the writer" that took place under the aegis of an academic conference in Jamaica, 1971. This marks the symbolic occasion when West Indian writers acknowledged themselves not merely as a scattering of individuals but as constituting a literature. The book thus sets out from a moment when West Indian literature became conscious of itself as a going concern, and reflected upon its "function" as a matter of its relationship to its audience(s) and to West Indian society. A look at the issues which arose on this occasion leads to an analysis of the peculiar position and function of poetry in the small, highly verbal, but not necessarily literate societies of the West Indies. The chapter emphasizes the unique position of poetry in these societies: the sociology (so to speak) of writing poetry in the West Indies, and the cultural and political roles poets play. Here and throughout the book I emphasize responses to and analyses of this matter by *Caribbean* rather than European or American scholars in order to show how the Caribbean situation looks to those who have been observing it most closely.

The next two chapters present perspectives that have for the most part been passed over in studies of West Indian poetry. In chapter 2, "The Caribbean neighborhood," a brief review of the shared history of the Caribbean Basin leads to an account of the coming to self-consciousness of non-Anglophone Caribbean poets as manifested in Haiti, in Cuba, and in the work of a group of Martinicans which matured into the Negritude movement (like "the West Indies" itself, a trans-national entity, one which included Africans as well as Antilleans). This account provides Anglophone writing with a regional context that is often ignored; it also demonstrates that parallels between these cases and the West Indian case can be revelatory of certain broad patterns of development which mark the dynamics of literary history in small colonial societies. In addition, these parallels bring to light the effect on all Caribbean writing of economic, political, and cultural conditions quite external to the region. Studies of West Indian literature rarely even mention other literatures of the Caribbean. While this accurately reflects the inattention of most West Indian *writers* to writing elsewhere in the region, even a brief account can enhance the discussion of West Indian poetry by revealing similar patterns of cultural development, similar issues (sometimes very differently addressed), and even similar poems. In the same spirit, the following chapter – chapter 3, "Overview of West Indian literary histories" – presents the separate histories of poetry in Jamaica, Trinidad, Guyana, Barbados, St. Lucia, and the smaller territories, ending with a history of the idea of a comprehensive "West Indian" literature. Besides providing the reader with a chronological framework for the detailed discussions of the ensuing chapters, this survey is included because there has been surprisingly little attention in the critical literature to the differences in the development of poetry in each of the various territories. Even such national anthologies as do exist do not include histories of the individual island's poetry.

The next three chapters focus on the issues and developmental patterns present in West Indian poetry itself, both overtly as subject-matter and more subtly in choices of medium, form, diction, and field of allusion. To put it another way, these chapters explore in detail how such issues *generate* poetry. Several shorthand expressions may require explanation (and your indulgence). The words "Europe," "Africa," and "America" in the chapter titles (and throughout) are set in quotation marks because they denote not geographic places but complex cultural pressures that West Indian writers feel and to which they respond. Where further discriminations are necessary I have made them, but it is very convenient to have umbrella terms for these complexes, and a West Indian precedent was established with the use of "Africa" in this sense as early as 1955.[2] Another shorthand expression – "Poetry" – is

---

[2] Anonymous, "'Africa' in West Indian Poetry," *Caribbean Quarterly* 4:1 (1955), 5–13.

meant to encompass everything about the metropolitan production of poetry that intimidates colonials: not just the special cachet of High Art, but everything from the potentially embarrassing pitfalls of diction and decorum to the sense that the accumulated tradition was a burden of accomplishment built on an array of trade secrets accessible only to metropolitans. The Trinidadian poet Wayne Brown uses the phrase "the filter of English eyes" in the course of analyzing early nature poetry for its manifestations of colonialism.[3] I have appropriated a distortion of his metaphor as a device for unifying these chapters, which as a result can be summarized like this: the effort of poets to remove the "filter of England" from West Indian poetry (chapter 4) was facilitated, but also complicated, by their subsequently adopting the "filter of Africa" (chapter 5). Yet even Kamau Brathwaite, often reductively regarded as an Afro-centrist, states it as a principle that "the eye must be free seeing" – that West Indian poetry should aspire to do its work without filters (chapter 6).

In these chapters I have borne in mind the value of considering a broadly representative sample of poems from throughout the region and from various periods, but my highest priority has been to emphasize specific texts which problematize or at least exemplify issues under discussion. For the particular purposes of a study like this one, unsuccessful poems are often more revealing than successful ones. Many first-rate poems (and first-rate poets) are not included here. A book on the best West Indian poetry would look quite different from this one. I have attached a date to virtually every individual poem cited, since it seems useful for a book of this kind to indicate when a particular text first became available to West Indian readers. My rule of thumb has been to indicate the earliest publication known to me that had some circulation. These dates must be taken with a grain of salt. Bibliographic research for West Indian poetry is still in its infancy, and I have certainly misjudged the availability of some texts, and missed others altogether.

[3] "The Poetry of the Forties, Part II," *Trinidad Guardian* (Sept. 20, 1970), 11.

Chapter 4, "The relation to 'Europe,'" traces the emergence
of West Indian poetry in the shadow of the literary tradition in
English: first, the dawning recognition of incongruities between
West Indian experience and the tradition, as that is apparent in
choices of diction and poetic form; then the emergence of this
difference as an explicit issue in pre-Independence texts, and its
subsequent ripening into themes (and gestures) of outright
opposition. The discussion focuses on changes in the representation of Caribbean nature, and on poetry of the 1930s, 1940s,
and 1950s.

"Africa," idealized in a variety of ways, is invoked as an
alternative tradition. It constitutes a lever by which West Indian
poets dislodge "Europe" to clear a space for themselves. The
matter of Africa provides subjects for poems, and materials for
addressing related subjects, such as race and history. Chapter 5,
"The relation to 'Africa,'" traces all these dimensions of
'Africa,'" with particular attention to the emergence of indigenous language as an element of, or vehicle for, poetry. After
some attention to forebears, the discussion focuses on poetry of
the 1960s and 1970s (the era of Independence and "Black
Power").

West Indian writers tend to understand the term "America"
as hemispheric in scope and mythic in its force. Chapter 6,
"The relation to 'America,'" considers on the one hand poets
who aspire to set aside history and its burdens and to begin
with the poetics of place, of geography and even geology, and
on the other hand poets who articulate the *fullness* of Caribbean
experience. Central here is the figure of "Caribbean man," the
imagined inhabitant of this new world, and the chapter pays
particular attention to the work of Walcott and Brathwaite.

That phrase "Caribbean man" brings up a related point:
throughout the book I have used masculine pronouns to refer
to the generalized West Indian poet. This is not thoughtless-
ness, but a recurrent reminder of assumptions that shaped both
male and female perceptions of poetry until well after Independence. It was a struggle to establish that the writing of poetry
was a serious and consequential activity for anyone in the West
Indies. That struggle was played out within the already heavily

masculinist conceptual frame of nationalism. In a setting where writing professionally was unthinkable, male writers kept reassuring themselves that writing was not just a pastime. Sometimes this involved no more than grandiose self-figuration (as prophets, spokesmen, warriors, and the like), but anxiety sometimes led them to make a point of distancing themselves from pioneering female poets, many of them affiliated with the Jamaica Poetry League, whose work was insufficiently ambitious or serious by the standards of the nationalist "struggle." It has taken the strenuous efforts of the present generation of West Indian poets to make that usage not only "politically incorrect" but also genuinely inaccurate, obsolete. A single grating pronoun economically keeps this dimension of the story within sight.

NOTES ON TERMINOLOGY

The heritage of colonialism is patent in the inconsistency of the terms by which we refer to the Caribbean area. "Caribbean Basin" is a geographical term that embraces all the islands and the bordering nations of Central and South America, but not the coasts of the Gulf of Mexico. "Antilles" is sometimes used as a geographical term for all the islands, but more usually is defined politically, so that its precise meaning depends on the nationality of the speaker. The "West Indies," used as a geographical term, would correspond to "Antilles" – the archipelago Columbus misidentified. For historical reasons having to do with the short-lived Federation, however, "West Indies" most often refers to the English-speaking islands, along with Guyana and Belize on the mainland, but excluding the US Virgin Islands and (usually) the Bahamas. There are further anomalies in the details: Dutch St. Maarten is arguably more English-speaking than nominally Anglophone St. Lucia. The term "Latin America" implies a completely different way of dividing the pie.

The crucial term "creole" is extremely unstable in Caribbean usage. Even within the narrow context of Trinidad, for example, it can refer either to black Trinidadians or to the descendants of French planters. I have tried to stay as close as possible to the fundamental meaning: "native," or "born here," as opposed to someone or something newly arrived. The connotation of priority is important but of uncertain value: when the recently arrived planter meets the next boat he may choose to present himself as "English" or as already "West Indian," but those he meets may be deciding whether he remains "English" or has "gone native." The general shiftiness of the term confirms that "creole" is an elective identity, an identity imputed or claimed, rather than inherent. To put it another way, "creole" identifies the local product *wherever* the original materials may have come from (as an "American" car can be one assembled in Mexico out of parts made in Korea). The term thus has a further connotation of "mixed" as opposed to "pure." On the basis of these connotations chapter 6 in particular explores the associations of the "creole" with processes of *bricolage* and self-fashioning.

"Creole" is also a term-of-art in linguistics, and with respect to language issues I have followed these conventions of usage: here "nation language" refers to the whole range of the creole continuum exploited by West Indian speakers. Its extremes are creole and Standard English (SE), the varied intermingling of which creates the continuum. For the limited purposes of this study it does not seem necessary to distinguish the variety of "Standards" now recognized by linguists. The term "dialect" has taken on a pejorative sense in the Caribbean, where it is understood to connote an imperfect or defective version of a standard language. In this book I use the term "dialect" to identify self-conscious instances of creole, creole used (so to speak) "in quotation marks." Each Anglophone territory has its own more-or-less distinct creole (depending on the vicissitudes of its colonial history), and so its own nation language. There is no spoken language that could properly be called "West Indian," but extensive linguistic affinities among the territories make it possible to approximate a common written language. Any such approximation is a compromise, a grapholect, rather than a language that anyone actually speaks; in no sense can it constitute a standard for the region. I should add that West

Indian writers and critics often use the terms "creole," "patois," "dialect," and "nation language" inconsistently or interchangeably; in particular many of them would identify "nation language" specifically with the speech of the peasantry and not (as I do) with the entire continuum.[4] The spectrum of linguistic usage in the West Indies is unusually broad. In speaking about the continuum I have preserved the prejudicial directional terms – "up" to *acro*lectal Standard English, "down" to *basi*lectal creole – as a reminder of the assumptions under which these writers themselves functioned.

ACKNOWLEDGMENTS

I welcome this opportunity to thank the Joint Committee on Latin American studies (ACLS/SSRC) for a grant which first enabled me to go to the Caribbean to study West Indian poetry.

Langston Hughes's translation of "When the Tom-tom Beats" by Jacques Roumain is reprinted by permission of New Directions from Dudley Fitts, *An Anthology of Contemporary Latin-American Poetry*, copyright 1942, 1947 by New Directions Pub. Corp.

Slade Hopkinson's "Rain over St. Augustine" is reprinted by permission of Peepal Tree Press from *Landscape with Signature*, copyright 1992 by Peepal Tree.

Grateful acknowledgement is made to the authors of works quoted in this book. Every effort has been made to seek the necessary permissions, but in some cases we have been unable to trace the copyright holder.

---

[4] "I don't use the word dialect anymore because it has too many connotations of things that are debased . . . I prefer the term nation language because it does not have any connotations of debasement or inferiority or colonialism." Edward Kamau Brathwaite, "Caribbean Writing Today," in *NAM Speaks* 2:3 (Aug.–Dec. 1978), 32. (New Artists' Movement, Kingston Youlou, St. Vincent.)

Chronology for Anglophone Caribbean poetry

1492–96	Columbus encounters the Amerindian populations of the Caribbean
1624	British settlement of Barbados
1655	British capture of Jamaica from Spain
1775	American Revolution begins
1789	French Revolution begins
1791	Haitian Revolution begins
1797	British capture of Trinidad from Spain
1804	Independence for Haiti
1808	abolition of slave trade by Britain and USA
1838	complete abolition of slavery in British colonies
1841–1867	indentured laborers imported from West Africa to the British West Indies
1845	first shipload of East Indian indentured laborers arrives in Trinidad; Chinese indenture follows
1848	abolition of slavery in French colonies
1869	J. J. Thomas, *The Theory and Practice of Creole Grammar*
1886	complete emancipation in Cuba
1898	end of Spanish-American War
1904–1914	Panama Canal construction
1910	discovery of oil in Trinidad
1912	Claude McKay, *Songs of Jamaica* and *Constab Ballads*, first collections of Anglophone poetry in creole
1914–1918	World War I
1917	end of East Indian indenture
1923	founding of the Poetry League of Jamaica

1929	first anthology of Jamaican poetry, *Voices from Summerland*
1930	Una Marson, *Tropic Reveries*, first modern collection of poems by a West Indian woman
1931	Norman Cameron's anthology, *Guianese Poetry: 1831–1931*; first publication of the *Beacon* magazine in Trinidad (until 1933)
1934	*West Indian Review* begins publication
1938	oil-field riots in Trinidad; labor unrest throughout the region
1938	C. L. R. James's history of the Haitian revolution, *The Black Jacobins*
1939–1945	World War II
1942	first issue of *Bim* (Barbados), beginning of BBC "Caribbean Voices" program; publication of Louise Bennett, *Dialect Verses*
1943	first issue of *Focus* (Jamaica)
1945	first issue of *Kyk-Over-al* (Guyana); George Campbell, *First Poems*
1946	French Guiana, Martinique, and Guadeloupe become part of France
1947	Independence for India and Pakistan; first complete publication of Aimé Césaire, *Cahiers d'un retour au pays natal*
1948	burning of the city of Castries, St. Lucia; Walcott, *25 Poems* privately printed
1949	first issue of *Caribbean Quarterly* (University of West Indies)
1950	beginning of "colonization in reverse": West Indian migration to England; Pioneer Press inaugurated in Jamaica; St. Lucia Arts Guild founded by Derek and Roderick Walcott
1951	A. J. Seymour begins publishing Miniature Poets series
1952	Collymore's "Glossary of Barbadian Dialect" begins to appear in *Bim*
1953	suspension of Guyanese Constitution by Britain
1954	Martin Carter, *Poems of Resistance* (Guyana)

1956	Eric Williams comes to power in Trinidad
1958	Federation of the West Indies established (until 1962); final broadcast of BBC "Caribbean Voices" program
1959	Cuban Revolution; Walcott's founding of what will become the Trinidad Theatre Workshop
1961	Frederick Cassidy, *Jamaica Talk: Three Hundred Years of the English Language in Jamaica*
1962	Independence for Jamaica and Trinidad and Tobago; restrictions imposed on West Indian immigration to Britain; Walcott, *In a Green Night*
1963	founding of University of Guyana
1965	assassination of Malcolm X in USA
1966	Independence for Barbados and Guyana; Bennett, *Jamaica Labrish*; Caribbean Artists Movement founded in London
1967	Brathwaite, *Rights of Passage*, first volume of his trilogy *The Arrivants*; Cassidy and LePage, *Dictionary of Jamaican English*
1968	expulsion of Guyanese scholar Walter Rodney from Jamaica and student occupation of the Creative Arts Centre at University of the West Indies, Mona; assassinations of Martin Luther King Jr. and Robert Kennedy in USA
1969	Walcott, *The Gulf*
1970	abortive "February Revolution" in Trinidad; first issue of *Tapia* (now *Trinidad & Tobago Review*)
1971	ACLALS Conference meets in Jamaica; publication of "New Writing 1970" anthology in *Savacou* 3/4
1972	first Carifesta (Caribbean Festival of the Arts), Georgetown, Guyana; Wayne Brown, *On the Coast*
1973	Walcott, *Another Life*; Dennis Scott, *Uncle Time*; Mervyn Morris, *The Pond*
1974	suicide of poet Eric Roach
1977	Brathwaite, *Mother Poem*

1980	assassination of Walter Rodney in Guyana; A. J. Seymour's anthology, *A Treasury of Guyanese Poetry*; *Jamaica Woman* anthology; Goodison, *Tamarind Season*
1981	Walcott begins teaching at Boston University; death of Bob Marley
1982	Brathwaite, *Sun Poem*
1983	murder of poet Michael Smith in Kingston, Jamaica
1984	David Dabydeen, *Slave Song*; Grace Nichols, *The Fat Black Woman's Poems*
1986	Michael Smith, *It a Come*; Walcott, *Collected Poems*
1987	Brathwaite, *X/Self*
1990	Walcott, *Omeros*
1991	Brathwaite begins teaching at New York University
1992	Nobel Prize for Literature to Walcott

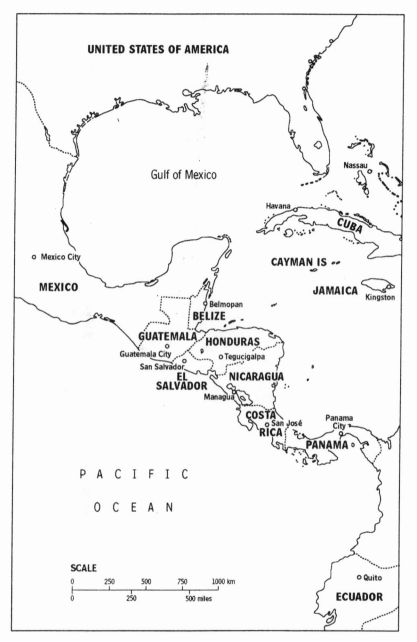

The Caribbean

CHAPTER I

West Indian poetry and its audience

In 1971, the Conference of the Association for Commonwealth Literature and Language Studies (ACLALS) provided the occasion for a galvanic West Indian event. The main theme of the conference was West Indian literature, "the enactment of national identity in poetry, fiction, and criticism." The setting, however, was shifted from the usual British university to the University of the West Indies (UWI) in Jamaica. As a result, this international academic forum (to the confusion of many of its delegates) served as the stage for a sort of private conversation, though it was as public and histrionic as most West Indian private conversation. What the delegates witnessed was a surprisingly literal "enactment of national identity."[1]

The lines were drawn up at the opening session. The panel that took up "The Function of the Writer in Society" included the most antithetical figures in West Indian literature at the time: the Barbadian poet and historian Edward (now Kamau) Brathwaite, then recently returned to the region after several years in West Africa, and V. S. Naipaul, the East Indian West Indian turned Englishman, soon to be the most renowned West Indian novelist, and happy to have escaped to the metropolitan capital. Brathwaite's keynote address rephrased the topic as a question: how does the writer develop a new sense of community for a multi-directional culture with a history of slavery, colonialism, and uncertain independence? He argued that the integrating principle must be sought in the submerged continuity of the "Little Tradition," the culture of ordinary people. In agreement with many Caribbean intellectuals he repeated that each race and group in the West Indies needs to descend into its own past before a truly multi-racial society, a creole society, can be anything more than a glib ideal. He went further than many commentators, however, in identifying the matrix of folk culture specifically with the African heritage.[2] What the West Indian writer must help to recover is "the true self which the colonized African exercised in the task of survival." Brathwaite concluded that the function of the writer is to express and articulate the people's culture in its historical depth, and give it back to them. For him, the writer properly functions in, from, and for his own society.

As we shall see, Brathwaite's position has roots deep in Caribbean thought, and it raises questions that invite strenuous debate. But in his short speech Naipaul did not take up the details of Brathwaite's proposal; instead he took issue with the subject of the session, denying that the writer can *have* a function in a society like that of the West Indies. The writer's primary function, he said, is "self-cultivation." Unfortunately West Indian society is a sterile void, and by the very act of cultivating himself the writer necessarily educates himself above his "destitute" society and so must leave it, moving to a place where he can find an adequate response to his work. (Naipaul has somewhat shifted the terms toward subjectivity here; from "what is the writer's function" to "can the writer function." As usual the novelist is somewhat more practical than the poet; a good part of what he means by "response" is economic support.)

The third panelist, the Indian novelist Raja Rao, though only a visitor in the Caribbean, had something in common with each of his colleagues. His first novel, about a peasant uprising, was published in 1938, coeval with the West Indian novels of social realism whose appearance helped to create the tradition of self-consciously West Indian literature of which Brathwaite was the inheritor. But because he writes in English, the second language of an Indian readership that shares no first language, Raja Rao suffers a kind of alienation from his immediate audience that is chronic among Commonwealth authors. He, like Naipaul, writes from voluntary exile, and perhaps as a result he proposed to the Conference that an achieved isolation was the writer's goal. He spoke of the writer's function as "self-discovery," of the "other" as the enemy of all writing, of poets as in communion with silence. In its extremity Raja Rao's ACLALS statement went beyond Naipaul, and yet it echoed the words of George Lamming, one of the bellwethers of West Indian writing but also an expatriate, who in one of the earliest position papers to come out of the region had written of the origins of art not in engagement but in silence and alienation.[3] It is a position virtually every writer, West Indian or otherwise, would at some moments share, and not merely in moments of discouragement, but whenever he wants above all to be left to his work.

All three of these views of the writer's relationship to society have supporters and opponents in the West Indies, and this confrontation of perspectives presents itself as the symbolic moment when the subject of this book became feasible: when it became possible to speak with confidence of "West Indian poetry" in terms of writers, an inventory of works, and an audience. The ACLALS Conference was the first comprehensive presentation of West Indian literature by West Indians that included fully articulated critical positions. Further, though the authority of the Conference was certainly enhanced by the cachet of metropolitan sponsorship, the success with which West Indian participants took control of its program gave the lie to the usual corollary of such sponsorship, metropolitan domination. Brathwaite's speech initiated a first attempt at the programmatic formulation of a distinctive West Indian aesthetic, and the nature of the occasion immeasurably increased the impact of his words. Published in a West Indian journal such as *Bim* or *Savacou* they would have attracted attention, but here they could literally provide the keynote for a discussion carried on by an audience of informed participants assembled from the entire Caribbean area. Indeed the presence of this particular audience was so important to the success of the discussion that it would be fair to say the most immediate impact of the ACLALS Conference was not its substance but its choice of venue; the fact that it was taking place not in a London flat, like the meetings of the Caribbean Artists Movement, or in a

BBC studio like the "Caribbean Voices" program, but in the West Indies, before a large and responsive (some of the speakers would have said "intimidating") West Indian audience.

This initial contribution of ACLALS to West Indian critical reflection was probably all but unwitting. Yet if the Conference had been held, as usual, at Leeds, a few West Indians (for financial reasons chiefly those already resident in London) would have presented themselves as a rather marginal phenomenon to an essentially British conversation. But in Kingston it was possible to assemble virtually all the important writers and thinkers (except, for financial reasons, some of those resident in London). Here they could outnumber the analysts, present themselves in action rather than by report, and make the integrity of their literature apparent not only to the world (or at least, to the Commonwealth delegates) but also to themselves. It was ACLALS, in effect, that formally introduced West Indian writers to their audience. The interplay of speakers and listeners at the conference was the first substantial manifestation of West Indian society attending to its own thoughts about literature. For writers resident in the region, the ACLALS audience constituted the revelation of a tangible public, the promise that West Indian society could and would support a self-sufficient literature.

The significance of the occasion was already made explicit in an anonymous "Statement of Position" circulated at the sessions, a document explaining "what the tension is about," and addressed to the non-West Indian participants, who must certainly have been unprepared for the course events were taking:

The simple reality of the Conference gathering centered around the fact that West Indians – writer, student, critic, intellectual – had come to this Conference with a new seriousness to insist on our literature and Art as a Sovereign part of our being . . . The day when such a Conference generates such tensions and energies in the Caribbean is a New Day, for we have come to claim ourselves in our Literature, and for that task new concerns, new conceptions and new traditions are necessary.[4]

In Jamaica that phrase "New Day" has a powerful resonance.

It is the title of Vic Reid's novel of 1949, an often exultant story of the struggle for independence, "a pioneering claim that a West Indian island could have its own national history and culture," and the first West Indian novel in which the narrative as well as the dialogue were written in a form of the actual language of Jamaicans, rather than in standard literary diction.[5] But the phrase has more than literary significance, since it refers to the end of Crown Colony status in November 1944, when a new constitution restored representative government and universal suffrage – government (so to speak) by the audience. By analogy, the "New Day" for literature meant that the center was no longer in London but at home, that the language was West Indian and not British, and that the audience would now participate directly in the shaping of its own literature.

In other words, what the Conference revealed above all was that writing had become a functioning, integral part of West Indian society for the first time in the history of the Anglophone Caribbean. As Brathwaite put it, events had now

brought the writer out of the tower, out of his castle, out of his ego. Until recently, the writer was hero, was one of the elite; his distance overseas added to the glamour of this ideograph. The reader was his pupil: told what to think; must follow if he could. But suddenly. . . all that has changed. We now have a mature contributing audience who demand to share in the artistic exploration of our terrain. Not you and me, but us. Not what is happening there, but *here*.[6]

Brathwaite had been thinking along these lines for a while, but at the Conference it was apparent for the first time that his line of thought and particularly his conceptualization of the function of the writer were not private or eccentric: that whether others agreed or not, his terms were immediately accessible. The surface of the Conference was ideological collision and psychic abrasion, but the wonder of it was discovery, illumination, clarity. Not resolution, certainly, but an unexpectedly clear and *shared* view of the alternatives – of what was at stake. The confidence and energy generated by this discovery found expression at once in the papers presented or developed at the Conference itself, many of which have since become landmarks in Caribbean criticism. A distinctive West Indian literature could be proposed anywhere, at any time, but only when an audience seemed assured could that gesture of cultural independence be meaningful, for every declaration of independence is first of all a declaration of interdependence, of solidarity. Now it had been brought home to the scattered writers of the region that their art was at last a conversation.

To conceive of isolated writers dispersed throughout the Caribbean and even England as constituting a joint venture arising from and addressing a coherent society was of course to idealize powerfully. But this was an idealization that enabled West Indian writers who remained at home – most of them poets – to envision solutions to problems that had been worrying them at least since before independence: was there an audience? Was there a literature? Was that literature distinctively "West Indian"?

It is emblematic that ACLALS begins with the poet ranged against the novelists. During the 1960s the success of compatriots who had gone to England to write and publish set in high relief the uncertainty about a serious audience for poetry. Lamming, Wilson Harris, and Edgar Mittelholzer in particular, who went to England and abandoned poetry for fiction, stood as disheartening examples, drawing all too much attention to the hard fact that a writer's choice of genre had economic and societal implications. The international success of West Indian fiction pressed poets to define the project unique to their poetry, to clarify the "function" of poetry as distinct from that of fiction. Though there had always been poets living abroad, this defining involved seeing poetry as peculiarly in and of the region; seeing the West Indies not only as the source of poetry's subject-matter and language, but also as the scene of its practice.

Before 1971 there was always some doubt whether there could be such a thing as a West Indian literature (more on this in chapter 3). If the term was to correspond to any reality two things were necessary: literary activity, certainly, but also a West Indies. Economic unrest in the 1930s and the self-reliance imposed by wartime conditions in the 1940s had fueled independence movements throughout the islands. For reasons chiefly economic and commonsensical, Caribbean leaders saw independence in terms of federation. The Federation of the West Indies (1958–62) failed as a political entity, but throughout this period political and literary figures were very close, particularly in Trinidad, Guyana, and Jamaica, and the sense of the English-speaking Caribbean as a cultural unit, which had likewise emerged in the 1940s, and came to be embodied chiefly in the university and the journals, was much more successful. It lies behind the terms "West Indian literature" and "West Indian poetry," which first come into use around 1950 and are particularly prominent in the titles of articles and anthologies during the years of the Federation.

Each island had produced its writers, but the recognition of a West Indian literature, even by its practitioners, depended on their physical proximity which, under the circumstances of those days, only London could provide. It was there that writers from different islands could discover a common endeavor, and sustain one another's work. Their *salon* was the BBC studio in which for several crucial years the "Caribbean Voices" program brought together those who had left home and beamed this paradoxical show of unity back to an audience scattered throughout the islands. By the bizarre geometry of colonialism, London was the center of the West Indies; there is no physical center to the region but empty sea, and local nationalisms have strained against establishing a center of any higher order. Hence the failure on the political and economic planes of Federation. As late as 1965 Derek Walcott, who had been working continuously in the region, took touching delight in the mere fact of a gathering of poets: "because the islands still separate us and it is a nice gesture to have us here together, because this little exchange, or just their presence, is enough to keep one going."[7] In his remarks he emphasized the importance of a community of poets in the region, and regretted the lack of "any form of circulation of poetry." For him, a sense of shared enterprise was what could give West Indian poetry strength, and as an example of what could be possible he cited the work of George Campbell, Roger Mais, and other Jamaican writers associated with the literary journal *Focus* and the Peoples National Party (PNP) of Norman Manley in the 1940s.

If the conception of the West Indies as a cultural entity was to be anything but a purely cerebral accomplishment, several conditions had to be met *in* the West Indies. Mervyn Morris puts the case succinctly:

> In the last decade conditions for the writer in the West Indies have improved. There are three main ways in which we can improve them further: by making it easier for the writer to earn substantially through his writing and to find expression here for some of his cultural interests; by offering intelligent critical interest in his work; and by enlarging and improving, through education, the local audience for his work.[8]

The community of authors themselves might provide the germ of an audience, but there is an essential need for "critics"; that is, for talkative, responsive readers. In a pinch, writers may play this role for one another, and much of local criticism in the West Indies is still grounded on this principle that writers live by taking in each other's washing. For a literature to exist as a going concern, however, there must be some commentators who are not primarily writers themselves, but critics who see themselves as having a particular role in the venture, a role that combines objective evaluation with a certain nurturing impulse. The explicit call for such critics in the late 1960s coincided with their appearance in the figures of Gordon Rohlehr, Edward Baugh, Sylvia Wynter, and Kenneth Ramchand, among others – critics who emerged in the act of calling for a criticism.[9] But what a nascent literature needs is a true audience, the secure assumption of being attended to by one's society.

West Indians at the ACLALS Conference of 1971 asserted that these minimal conditions had at last been achieved for the Anglophone region *as a unit*, even though they had not yet been fulfilled in each of its component nations. By manifesting the presence of an audience, ACLALS made it possible to approach the question the other way round: the existence of a distinct West Indian literature stood established once and for all, because in the region there were writers addressing a public whose concerns they shared. If there was a local audience, the existence of the literature no longer had to be demonstrated exclusively by the accumulation of works, and that was of value not only to the critic, but to the writer as well: it increased his sense of the legitimacy of his work, and so his confidence, while it gave him a reader he could visualize, and encouraged him to exploit the resources of West Indian language and allusion without apology.

The ACLALS Conference was not an isolated event; it was preceded by pertinent critical discussions, accompanied by such provocative publications as the *Breaklight* and *Savacou* 3/4 anthologies, and echoed outside the intellectual establishment by an upsurge of what would now be called "performance poetry," with its roots in Jamaican popular culture. Yet ACLALS conveniently marks the moment when certain distinctive features – defining a "West Indian aesthetic" in some minds – were recognized and proclaimed. The profile of West Indian poetry was transformed in the years between 1960 and 1970, and it was those idiosyncratic, characterizing changes that make West Indian poetry as an enterprise intriguing and illuminating.

If poets seemed to distance their work from fiction by grounding themselves in the local audience, there was a complementary move closer to the realm of drama. This was true even in the most trivial sense: poetry readings increasingly shared the same spaces with dramatic presentations. However, the increasing performativeness which becomes a defining feature of West Indian poetry does not result from the influence of drama. It is instead an expression of the well-attested theatricality of most Caribbean cultures, flourishing under the pressure of very limited resources for publication. Faced with daunting obstacles to literary production, West Indian poets responded with a strong incentive to explore the unique modes of access possible in a small society. It seems that poets, perhaps because in the modern world their art is more marginal, are more aware of potential media for reaching the public, and more inventive in the use of them. In any case it is already evident in the ACLALS "Statement of Position" that the conception of what is to be done is largely a poet's conception: the task is to recognize the actual state of poetry in the region, and to cultivate it, most especially through acknowledging and increasing the intercourse between high culture and folk culture. This is to be accomplished, first, by turning attention to "the basis and terms of the folk artistic sensibility, the African influences and continuities as the subject of new literary explorations, the employment of new modes of literary expression through oral resources embedded in the language," and, secondly, by taking advantage of "the press, radio in particular and TV in the dissemination of literature and art."[10] The possibility of new links to music rather than prose proved especially exciting and productive. Calypso provides a powerful model here, given its success in delivering topical political and social commentary directly to a live audience. This model revealed to poets the characteristic agility of their medium, which enabled it to address current issues before an audience of the people directly involved.

Brathwaite was the leader among those who emphasized the affinity of West Indian poetry with the "Little Tradition," as opposed to the "Great Tradition." This terminology conflates F. R. Leavis's notion of the Great Tradition of English literature – very influential in the Anglophone Caribbean – with anthropological distinctions between courtly or canonical practices and those which are popular, and often undocumented. In West Indian usage, two social strata generally viewed as distinct are here redefined as the focal areas of different, but not exclusive, cultural heritages. By reinterpreting two "societies" as a single plural one, this terminology preserves discrimination as an analytical tool, but shifts the basis of discrimination. The old view was implicitly evaluative – who can doubt that something called "High" Culture must be preferable to its "Low" alternative? But the identification of elements in society by their degree of sensibility, articulateness, or wealth, or successful mimicry of privileged models, is in this case replaced by a frank discrimination by *sources*, and thus the model is historicized. The two terms have already come to be used rather loosely to distinguish Old World from New World elements, Europe from Africa, metropolitan culture from folk culture, the Establishment from the people, the Academy from the artist. But underlying all of these narrow applications is a metaphor that identifies on the one hand the inherited structures and institutions of a society, and on the other the impulse of a people to adapt and remodel these structures to make them habitable.

In the context of West Indian attitudes and education, what was modestly revolutionary was not of course the mere use of these terms, but their parity. To set the Little Tradition on a par with the Great was to exalt it, even to fly in the face of the relation of "little" to "great," and for many this seemed necessarily a rejection of the Great (though the rejection of a tradition is a gesture more frightening than actually possible). Yet for those who worked most closely with these terms – Brathwaite, Wynter, and Rohlehr, among others – the relative values of the two traditions were of much less interest than the exploration of the West Indian writer's possible relations to the two of them. The vision of a whole plural society is at heart an assertion of optimism, of faith in West Indian resourcefulness; it was in that spirit, for example, that the partisan "Statement of Position" praised Wynter's role at ACLALS:

She showed us that what we were talking about all the time in the opposition of Africa to Europe, of New World to Old, of folk-culture versus museum-kultur, was the possibility of a new man, a new people and a new humanism emerging from these humanly rich societies.[11]

The glorification of the Little Tradition is a recurrent component of cultural nationalism, familiar not only among the European Romantics, but (as we shall see in chapter 2) among nationalist writers throughout the Caribbean. The common people, the salt of the earth, provide an obvious basis for defining national identity ("a new people"). They become a favored subject of poetry, but there is usually also much greater respect for them as producers and consumers of poetry (again, think of the vogue for folksongs and folktales in nineteenth-century Europe). Canonization of the Little Tradition entails a widening of the horizon of the term "poetry" far beyond the confines of the *Golden Treasury.* West Indian poetry certainly opened up in an unprecedented way to elements of popular culture – rural and urban, African, European, and East Indian, atavistic and creole. The change went far beyond mere subject-matter. There was widespread adaptation of traditional oral forms and also of specifically musical forms – from reggae, calypso, traditional folk music, and even the music of the churches. Moreover, the extraordinarily limber language West Indians actually use transformed or displaced the traditional poetic diction that had dominated earlier West Indian poetry. As we shall see in chapters 4, 5, and 6, there was considerable disputation about the relationship between poetry and the Little Tradition, and particularly about just what that tradition *was.* Some writers, for example, identified the West Indian Little Tradition with a submerged African heritage, a fixed quantity preserved among and therefore identified with the folk, while others maintained that it was the ongoing creole strategies of accommodation, assimilation, adaptation.

In the late 1960s, then, interest in the Little Tradition (variously and even contradictorily defined) combines with the effort to solve the problem of limited resources, and with a renewed sense of a relation to drama rather than fiction. The upshot is the cultivation of an aesthetic of performance, which (among other things) has the virtue of circumventing the obstacles to publication. Though grounded on the orality of non-literate cultures, the attraction was not merely ideological; it was not merely an alignment with newly valorized "African" traditions, or their successors among the rural folk. The wider audience for poetry in the West Indies prefers to hear, not read. There are risks associated with this preference. This might invite a mystique of solidarity with the voice of the writer, rather than critical attention to him – the communication of attitude, rather than thought. It appealed to poets, however, for the immediacy of relation to audience that it offered, and not less for the patent authority with which it endowed the performing poet, whose social function was thus clear: his responsibility was to set the West Indian person before us, dignified, articulate, and "authentic."

It is frequently observed that poetry seems to play an unusually prominent role in West Indian society since Independence. The implied comparison is with the English-speaking world, and perhaps underestimates the role of poetry in Ireland or Anglophone Africa, but the observation remains valid. To some degree this prominence has to do with preexisting conditions: the small scale of the society, the close links of many individual poets with political figures, a culture of dramaticality. But the characteristic profile by which West Indian poetry is nowadays recognized has been shaped also by the factors introduced in this chapter: the openness to popular culture and especially to music (reggae and calypso), the appeal of public performance, the enthusiastic acceptance of overt social responsibility. First and foremost however is the insistence that poetry has a "function," that it has a real, reliable basis in the society. This insistence underlies both the emphasis on the Little Tradition and the aesthetic of performance, and it arose out of consideration of the poets' almost schizophrenic relation to various audiences (both a knowing coterie and a popular audience at home, as well as an anonymous readership abroad). The peculiar nature of the audience for West Indian poetry was already under discussion, but awareness of the success of fiction, which depended heavily on a metropolitan readership, surely served as a catalyst for the assertion that West Indian poetry (in its direction as well as its assembled corpus) is distinctive and self-sufficient.

If the topic for the opening panel at ACLALS was "the function of the writer in society," the ensuing discussion made it clear that each speaker's sense of the writer's function was shaped by his prior understanding of that third term, "society." By a commonplace habit of thought, every West Indian island is regularly conceived as supporting two distinct societies: the so-called middle class, and everyone else. But a history of slavery gives sharper point to an otherwise fairly universal analysis, since here these two societies evolve in part from the social polarities of slavery. This fundamental split is reinforced by discriminations of wealth, color, and language. In the abstract, two such strata are associated with high culture and popular culture respectively. But in the actual West Indies, the habit of denying the possibility of any culture among slaves added its peculiar force to the more generalized habit (among commentators usually themselves middle class) of dismissing popular culture outright as no culture at all. So even as the two strata are acknowledged, emancipation hardly affected the consistency with which both West Indians and visitors used the word "society" to refer to the middle class alone – the only likely consumers of literature.

When Naipaul famously calls West Indian society "destitute" and opens his first analysis of it (*The Middle Passage*, 1962) with Froude's numbing pronouncement that "there are no people there," he echoes the exasperation of generations of Caribbean leaders and outside observers. To speak only of Jamaica, the litany begins with the opinion of the abolitionist James Stephen in 1831: "There is no civilised society on earth so entirely destitute of learned leisure, of literary and scientific intercourse and even of liberal recreations."[12] Marcus Garvey takes up the theme in 1930: "From my observations I am forced to conclude that Jamaica is indeed an ignorant community; it is limited in intelligence, narrow in its intellectual concepts, almost to the point where one can honestly say that the country is ridiculous."[13] Roger Mais takes up the theme at length in an article, "Why I Love and Leave Jamaica" (1952) of which this is only a sample: "There is in this country, alas, a moated tower of mediocrity, close and unassailable, and it holds such sway, it has acquired such a body of mediocre opinion about it that it is useless to try to make a dent in its smugness and its exclusiveness and its indifference to anything that does not come entirely within its limited scope and compass and influence."[14] Similar exasperation could be cited for all the West Indian nations.[15] On this point at least we find Naipaul in agreement with some of the most committed West Indian intellectuals.

If only the middle class can support a culture, and if that class is incorrigibly philistine, then the West Indies is truly destitute, and in 1971 these were the received opinions, backed up by the accumulated frustrations of the most creative West Indians. Even George Lamming, the novelist of that generation who was most attentive to the true culture of ordinary people, could occasionally slip into this inherited attitude:

If we accept that the act of writing a book is linked with an expectation, however modest, of having it read; then the situation of a West Indian writer, living and working in his own community, assumes intolerable difficulties. The West Indian of average opportunity and intelligence has not yet been converted to reading as a civilised activity, an activity which justifies itself in the exercise of his mind. Reading seriously, at any age, is still largely associated with reading for examinations.[16]

This is the second time we have encountered the notion of "seriousness" in a West Indian critical observation, and it will not be the last; for some time the burning question for West Indian writers committed to an indigenous literature was just this: "Does an audience exist here for serious poetry?" In their aspirations for a functional relationship to society, West Indian writers are speaking about a form of alienation rather less metaphorical than that in many metropolitan settings. The West Indian poet's alienation is a matter of factors like these: illiteracy, scarcity of paper, absence of local publishers, rudimentary marketing infrastructure; an audience situated precariously between a barely literate lower class for whom one book, the Bible, suffices, and an upper class whose members simply do not read books at all; the complex colonial attitude that rejects him because as a poet he is associated with the culture of metropolitan power, but also rejects him as inferior to the products of that culture, and finally disregards him in the face of a deluge of imported popular culture (music, film, television). Indeed, the actual venue of the ACLALS meetings, the Creative Arts Centre on the Mona campus of UWI, had just recently been built for the express purpose of encouraging the arts and helping to put artists in contact with an audience.[17] The responsiveness of the crowd occupying that space at ACLALS encouraged an affirmative answer, and the optimists among the critics pursued that possibility by in effect theorizing that the central terms "society" and "audience" should be more broadly conceived if they were to be applied to West Indian conditions. Brathwaite, very much an heir to Lamming, was the nominal leader of those at the Conference who, in the face of the obstacles, insisted that for the small nations of the Caribbean the term "society" could only refer to the whole population; that it was unrealistic to conceive of two incommunicative "societies" somehow coexisting on each small island – one of them beneath consideration and the other hollow. Rather the society of each island was to be seen as inherently single, if diversified, made up predominantly by the "folk," and variously subject to several cultural heritages.

This maneuver involved a rationalization of the term "society," a reminder that its center of gravity is firmly among the mass of the population, and an acknowledgment of the unavoidable significance of popular culture under such conditions, wholly apart from questions of its quality. With a few important exceptions, such as Roach, the poets active during the 1960s were generally from the middle class; the redefinition of audience is their pledge of social allegiance. It takes a step beyond the PNP poets in Jamaica with their effort during the 1940s to offer a sympathetic view of the peasantry and urban poor to their own middle class, which would be the first group to gain from independence. The new openness to elements of popular culture in the 1960s entails a broadening of the resources and scope of poetry itself, but also a kind of aesthetic suffrage, including a larger, more diverse audience in the project of poetry. This supported the turn to popular sources for poetry, and also the recognition of literary value in writers, like Louise Bennett, previously regarded as entertainers. Thus, when Mervyn Morris entitled his groundbreaking essay about Bennett "On Reading Louise Bennett, Seriously" (originally published in 1965), he was anticipating the language of his own lament that "an audience for serious contemporary poetry scarcely exists" – in effect discovering a larger audience by redefining the scope of the word "serious" to encompass a larger body of work.[18] The maneuver involved too a suspicion that such analytical terms as "mass" and "elite," "proletariat" and "middle class" can be applied only circumspectly to the analysis of small, dense, isolated, and often endogamous West Indian nations. While this projected redefinition of "society" can easily be debased into an apotheosis of the folk, often accompanied by a romantic or politically motivated rejection of "High Culture," in any more sophisticated formulation it properly amounts to a shift of emphasis, respecting the human weight at the lower end of the social scale.

The next proposition was more radical: that this whole society is the potential audience for poetry. Such an enabling vision has many precedents, of which the universality of Shakespeare's Globe Theatre is only the most familiar stereotype, and that is perhaps less illuminating than the example of an oral culture, since Brathwaite began advocating this proposition after his exposure to just such an example in rural West Africa. He had returned from Ghana in 1962 with a renewed commitment to the West Indies, and first proposed that the West Indian writer should conceive of himself as addressing "society in general" in 1965, during the symposium at Mona that brought together several of the region's writers. "What concerns me as a writer," he began, "is the state of society. To me an artist has to speak *from* his society."[19] This was the lesson of his African experience that most strongly urged him to leave Africa for home: a writer should not only be physically present in his society, but should see himself as an integral part of it (an advantage the poets could then claim over the mostly expatriate novelists with their British publishers).

At the 1965 symposium Brathwaite went on to characterize three approaches to writing: the personal approach – poetry whether amateur or hermetic that is not primarily interested in addressing an audience; the humanist approach – in which the poet addresses the tradition and those familiar with it; and a third approach, which addresses "society in general." The heart of his formulation is this:

The humanist poet, of course, naturally takes his inspiration from his society, and his voice is often speaking away from that society rather than speaking in towards it ... A poet can either approach his subject in a humanist manner or he can attempt not only to take his inspiration from the broad base of society, but actually to try to communicate directly to this broad base of society.

While he calls his three approaches equally valid, Brathwaite thought it most urgent to cultivate the third. Brathwaite's position was not very clearly formulated and did not go over very well at the time. Walcott (who during Brathwaite's travels had been working hard at home as both poet and dramatist against substantial obstacles) responded by picturing "the earnest bard, his newest poem completed, rushing up to the hills and saying to a labourer: 'have you heard this one?'"[20] Their respective backgrounds are a factor here. Brathwaite came from Barbados, with a history of widespread literacy and education, Walcott from a bilingual island where barriers of class and status were marked by language. The Jamaican poet and critic Mervyn Morris was also present at the symposium. His own poetry is much more immediately accessible to a general reader than either Walcott's or Brathwaite's, and he was one of the first to insist on a place in the canon of literature for so-called folk poets like Louise Bennett and calypsonians like Sparrow; even so he found Brathwaite's suggestion "unhelpful." In fact he and Walcott were still carping about it in print three years later.[21] What seemed to Brathwaite a liberation seemed to his colleagues another externally motivated imposition on the working writer.

After ACLALS many equally sympathetic West Indians continued to be mystified by this ambitious conception of a general audience, which seemed alternately impossible, impracticable, or dangerously populist. However, it was proposed not merely as every poet's pipe-dream, but as an appropriate goal, suited to conditions in the West Indies. There is in fact no "general audience" in the West Indies, but argument on this point had led to considerable discussion of the nature of the local audience, and of the writer's possible relation to it. For that reason it is significant that the writers who urge this objective for the most part tend to be poets or dramatists rather than novelists, and tend to be residents rather than exiles. On both of these counts they are closer to the audience Brathwaite aspired to reach, and can be expected to argue in the light of direct experience of the obstacles encountered in addressing it.

It should not be surprising that a writer's favored genre will affect his conception of the society he writes for. The expectation of a middle-class audience goes hand in hand with an identification of literature with fiction, and especially with the novel, the preeminent form in the West, which requires, and often reflects, the culture of a leisured middle class. The novel is produced, and nowadays also read, in solitude; not surprisingly, serious novelists, like Raja Rao and Naipaul, think of "the writer" as self-absorbed, and would conceive of the poet as an even more extreme case than the novelist. But Brathwaite and others, when they consider a literature that addresses the whole of society, are thinking of poetry and drama more than of fiction. That drama can potentially make direct contact with all levels of society from any patch of open ground is obvious; to think of poetry as a literature of the masses is to have a conception of poetry which, though nobly pedigreed, is not at the moment common. Yet while the novel is almost literally consumed, only rarely reread and more rarely memorized, it is in the nature of both poetry and drama to be memorized and re-enacted. This softens the distinction between author and audience to the extent that these genres are participatory, and not bound to the physical book.

If the notion that poetry is closer to the people that fiction seems idealistic, it nevertheless reflects the actual situation of West Indian literature to a considerable extent. It is the poets as a rule who stay at home; partly because professional poet is a far more tenuous occupation than professional novelist, partly too because, while the poet can expect a different audience if he lives abroad, he can only rarely expect a larger one. For the poet, emigration is much more nakedly a matter of abandoning one's own place and people. For the novelist, exile is both more tangibly attractive and less emotionally costly, and successful exiles have regularly opened doors for those who stay at home in the Caribbean, making their work known in a larger sphere. The early apostolate of Lamming and Naipaul in England is not to be underestimated. But the price the novelist pays is to become in some degree a British or American or Canadian writer. Thus it is the novelists who are most conscious of the difference between their small audience at home and their anonymous, largely unprepared readership abroad. It is the community of writers at home in the region that can serve as the core of a recognizable literature, and that community is dominated by poets. Novels are now being written and even published in the region, but Ramchand's remark is still true: "the peasant in the city slum or in the country cannot be said to be conscious of these novels or affected by their significance."[22] The same can no longer be said with absolute assurance about poetry, however, and that development has as much to do with the changing nature of the "peasantry," particularly the development of the urban folk, as with the efforts of poets. Thus, while poets are increasingly being read abroad, they tend to think more about the two audiences they have at home: the popular and the "elite."

Resident poets toy with the idea of a general audience, not only because they find it attractive as an ideal, but because it seems attainable for poetry even on empirical grounds, considering the extent to which the practice of poetry, or at least its rudiments, is woven into the fabric of West Indian life. In the West Indies the composition of verse is remarkably widespread. Throughout the islands people from every level of society write and publish verse, not only in newspapers and in ephemeral little magazines like *Now* and *Scope*, but in small books, privately printed and distributed through local bookshops or by the authors themselves, who may be housewives, students, incarcerates. Derek Walcott may not have asked laborers, "have you heard this one?" but he did sell his first book of poems by buttonholing people on the streets of the tiny city of Castries, as young amateurs still do (and many regional critics, following Brathwaite's lead, would insist that the young Jamaican who tries to sell you his recording now has to be regarded as part of the same venture). Shabine, the poet-sailor of Walcott's later poem "The Schooner *Flight*" is an emblematic figure for widespread amateur poetic practice. And while Shabine has struck some North American readers as an incongruity, his like can be found alive and well throughout the Caribbean. Every society has its naive poets, but they are much more visible, more significant, and perhaps less naive in the Caribbean than in the mass societies of the West. The most extreme West Indian demonstration of this occurred in Grenada under the short-lived revolutionary government of Maurice Bishop (1979–83). During those years this small island produced a stream of poetry anthologies. The first of them, *Freedom Has No Price* (1980), is typical. The poems, with titles like "Beat Back Destabilization" and "Stand Firm Student," are rarely of abiding interest. As the book's "Forward" notes, this is not "the poetry of academics" but "the poetry of those who daily labour"; more than fifty authors are included in a book of fewer than one hundred pages.[23] There is plenty of rote bombast, but the enthusiasm is real, and occasional allusions to earlier Caribbean political poetry suggest that these writers are also readers – that a rudimentary tradition exists. Such promotion of poetry as a mode of expression accessible to all can only be productive; it cultivates both writers and an audience for them, and encourages the notion that poetry has a significant role to play in a contemporary society. Behind this phenomenon there is a habit of artful language that traces back to a variety of sources: to an Aesopian sense that verbal wit is the chief resource of the oppressed; to the premium placed on shrewd talk and rhetorical improvisation throughout the region; to African oral traditions; to the impact of the language of the King James Bible and the preaching style of Non-conformist missionaries.[24] These longstanding habits have been nourished by urbanization, and by the recent drives for literacy and general public education.

The local context is to this extent more hospitable for serious poets than for novelists, because poetic activity is actually more familiar to the audience at large. The whole spectrum of prose fiction, from high art to the pulp novel, has its origins in metropolitan tradition. In the West Indies even trash tends to be imported rather than locally produced; there is no real equivalent to such indigenous popular fiction as the Onitsha market literature of Nigeria. On the other hand, as is usually the case in a predominantly oral milieu, there is a wide range of models for verse in the indigenous tradition, so here as elsewhere verse is more significant than fiction as a vehicle for expressions of nationalism (and drama is close to verse in this). Poets on the spot have first of all an accurate sense of scale; that is one reason why they tend to insist that the Western conception of the writer in a mass society cannot apply here without some adjustment. In a small nation like St. Lucia, for example, the writer must function differently than his counterparts in Europe or the United States. The writer here can if he chooses gauge his precise audience almost on an individual basis. This very small scale accustoms resident poets to a blurring of the distinction between producers and consumers. They sense that the members of this audience will actively participate in the venture of a literature, and that their potential for active, individualized roles is grossly misrepresented by terminology that speaks of "proletariat" and "masses." In principle, poetry can address any part of society from a position in any part of society. Once poetry is not limited to what passes through the needle's eye of metropolitan publication, but embraces the whole intellectual commerce of the society, then the field is enriched by a range of poetry from the highest to the most naive.

Corollary to the vision of a wider audience is a broader definition of the term "poetry" so that it becomes descriptive rather than normative; not a touchstone for the evaluation of an exclusive high art but the name of a common human activity. In effect, this sort of definition increases the absolute number of poets in a society, and encourages them all, good and bad, by revealing the extent of a shared community of endeavor. Thus even the amateur is encouraged to think of himself as a poet, part of a cultural enterprise, and as a West Indian poet, with reciprocal ties to his society. An increase in the number and dignity of amateur writers increases the supply of good, skilled readers, while the recognition of more varied activity as "poetry" lets more people regard their experience of verbal art "seriously."

While Walcott has been most eloquent about the disasters

that can befall creativity in a small society – and they remain daunting – Brathwaite has led in insisting that artful language can be cultivated at large, that writers are no race apart, and that what identifies a writer is not his origin or psychology but the plain fact of literary production. From that insistence, he goes on to identify and single out for praise the kinds of art that proceed from the recognition that the writer is included in the society he addresses. The acceptance of such an inclusive vision among critics and readers must go hand in hand with an actual consolidation of society which the Conference audience only foreshadows, and ultimately it requires propitious conditions far beyond the reach of art. Vision cannot, for example, halt the alarming decline in the number and quality of bookstores throughout the Anglophone Caribbean. Most West Indian poets still feel isolated and unregarded, but this does not diminish the value of a visionary program as an alternative to the debilitating assumption that most of society is inaccessible in principle. On the other hand, to the extent that a preconception of audience affects the conception of a work, it disposes the writer to think of accessibility as a virtue, and demands of him a sense of wider responsibility that is equally salutary: it requires of him a commitment not only to his art, but to his readers and to their nascent sense of themselves as a community of interest.

Chapter 1 has depicted the situation of West Indian poetry, and the perception, the idealization, of that situation by some of its leading writers at the moment when West Indian literature sought to consolidate itself as a going concern with a distinctive function in the societies of the region. In their adjustments of the balance between the two touchstones "seriousness" and "society in general," we have seen poets redefining the audience for their work on the widest possible scale, redefining the term "poetry" so that it becomes less evaluative and more capacious, and considering what makes their work "West Indian." The development of a poetry appropriate to that static situation (the poet functioning in society) is complicated by rapid historical change, in the stream of which it is

occurring: the sequence of colonialism, nationalism and federation, black consciousness, micro-nationhood, and trans-nation-
alism through which Caribbean cultures have been passing in
the course of this century. For that reason the next two chapters
(2 and 3) detail the effects of that temporal passage on the
practice of poetry throughout the region. The chapters that
follow (4, 5, and 6) go on to investigate how poems themselves
address these issues. For example, how they wrestle with the
various traditions that are the region's heritage and play them
off against one another in characteristically creole fashion. Or
how the necessity of negotiating the constraints on publication
(scarcity of presses, and even of paper), leads poets to exploit
the resources of electronic media, and this in turn enhances the
appeal of an aesthetic of performance – already attractive
because it draws on both the oral folk tradition (enriched with
African associations), and the power of electronic media, and
further because it elevates the West Indian voice over literary
diction, asserting the force of presence in a post-colonial
culture of invisibility and erasure.

CHAPTER 2

The Caribbean neighborhood

A self-consciously West Indian poetry develops against the background of cultural awakenings occurring throughout the Caribbean during this century; like colonialism itself, this is one of the shared experiences of nations sharply isolated from one another as much by history as by geography. Literary self-consciousness unfolds at different times in different islands, but while even territories that spoke the same language (such as Haiti and Martinique) were often barely in communication with one another until quite recently, common external pressures induced sometimes strikingly parallel – though not simultaneous – patterns of cultural development across the board.

In 1912 the Panama Canal was completed; in 1914 war broke out in Europe. The first of these events strengthened political, military, and economic ties between the United States and the Caribbean as a whole; the second weakened ties with Europe. Both events had a profound impact directly on the people of the region, since many of them served as workers in the one venture or as troops in the other, and returned home transformed by the experience. Both contributed as well to the momentum of emerging nationalism, for which world events of the 1930s and 1940s would provide the final catalyst. Equally significant for the Caribbean, in the long run, was the transformation wrought by war on the metropolitan cultures themselves, on Europe and North America. When World War I was over, the "modern world" had begun, and an inspired generation survived the Jazz Age and the Depression until World War II ushered in the post-modern period. In those years between the wars, the West seemed to have two cultural capitals: Paris and New York. Paris attracted everyone, from expatriate Americans to Russian emigrés (even Latin American intellectuals looked to Paris rather than Madrid), while New York produced the Harlem Renaissance. The two capitals simultaneously developed a taste for the exotic. This interest in the arts and cultures of what would later be called the Third World was certainly a sort of sublimation of the West's old acquisitiveness. Unlike grosser imperialisms, however, it was substantially motivated by a thirst for self-discovery – the new fashions of anthropology and psychology were plainly complementary. It was local conditions that differed. Paris, seeking the exotic, rediscovered the rest of the world (or at least those parts of it that had resisted a century of French civilizing missions), and in doing so perceived the horizon that enclosed Western culture. It was in defiance of that perception that "blackness" became fashionable in Paris after World War I. But in New York Harlem *was* exotic, a revelation of difference even in its own eyes, worlds away from downtown Manhattan. In the Renaissance black America discovered its "African" self, and made the discovery available to blacks throughout the world. These two developments, and their interaction, were to affect the Caribbean deeply.

This chapter will outline the course traced through this field of forces by three episodes from Caribbean literary history which are especially pertinent to the development of West Indian poetry: Haitian poetry of the 1920s and 1930s, Negrista poetry in Cuba during the same period, and the origins of the Negritude movement out of a convergence of Martinican and African students in Paris during the 1930s and 1940s. Against this background the following chapter will take up in detail the evolution of literary self-consciousness in the Anglophone territories, the West Indies proper.

HAITI

The hemisphere's second revolutionary republic won independence in 1804. Perceived as a nation of rebellious black slaves,

Haiti throughout the nineteenth century was regarded as an active threat to the region, very much as was Castro's Cuba after 1960. As a result it stood in splendid but impoverished isolation among the neighboring island colonies. With only tenuous hemispheric ties, the highly developed culture of Haitian cities maintained strong contact with France. Out of this sophisticated milieu emerged some very precocious voices.[1] Hannibal Price can serve as representative. In 1900, he described Haiti as "the Mecca, the Judea of the black race" because "it was there that the Negro became a man," and went on to envision Haiti as the leader of a program of world-wide cultural renewal.[2] In the cultural needs it expressed, and in its proposals for dealing with them, Price's was one of several Haitian books which very early on called for what would eventually be provided by a coalition of Africa and the Caribbean in the Negritude movement of Césaire, Damas, and Senghor.[3] As in Negritude, this was a case of "Overseas France" turning the concept of a "civilizing mission" against the masters who devised it. Indeed the Haitians of that era might have generated a "black consciousness" movement, wholly indigenous to the Caribbean, with Port-au-Prince as its center rather than Paris, had they not been hampered by a real ignorance of Africa, an incomplete awareness of the nature and strengths of Haitian culture, and in the end the lack of both a clear impulse in that direction and the cohesive social group to serve as its vehicle. After the World War I these obstacles were gone, but by then a different sort of movement, more local in its goals, had preempted the attention of Haitian intellectuals.

The chief catalyst for the inward-turning of Haitian attention was military occupation by the United States. Motivated at first by the need to secure the newly completed canal in wartime, the occupation extended from 1915 until 1934. The insult was exacerbated by the preoccupation of France with war on its own soil. But the strain was greatest after the war, and the installation of a Haitian president in 1930 brought only limited relief. From a literary standpoint, 1925 is the significant year. With the war ended, both established intellectuals and students could once again leave for Paris. There the establishment spoke in Louis Morpeau's *Anthologie d'un siècle de poésie haitienne 1817–1925*, a formidable effort to consolidate a national heritage. From among the students came Emile Roumer's *Poèmes d'Haiti et de France*, which combined classical forms with distinctively Haitian subjects and even creole language. In his poem "Declaration paysanne," for example, a peasant compares his beloved to a series of such local dishes as crab in eggplant, but he speaks in unimpeachable alexandrines. By a nice irony, these alexandrines have themselves been set to the music of the Haitian *meringue*,[4] and the irony cautions us to avoid facile antitheses here; in fact Morpeau included an introductory essay about poetry written in creole ("La Muse haitienne d'expression creole"), and Roumer was a contributor to his anthology. Meanwhile it was at home in Haiti that a new periodical, *La Nouvelle Ronde*, presented itself as the official "organ of the younger generation," and in its second issue attacked the techniques and aims of such older poets as Morpeau had collected.[5]

These publications are symptomatic of cultural ferment, and the direction in which to channel this energy was pointed out two years later in the immensely influential lectures of Jean Price-Mars, published in 1928 as *Ainsi Parla l'Oncle*. Above all, Price-Mars urged renewed attention and respect for Haitian folklore, and especially for its African aspects. His first aim was to revitalize Haitian culture by bringing together both the French and the indigenous strata of the ancestral heritage. Like Hannibal Price before him he saw this as making possible a universal role for Haiti: "May it not be that we have something to offer to the world which is not something watered down or imitated? In the accelerated speed and dryness, we shall be still for the rest of the world one of the precious reservoirs of poetry, joy, and love." Coulthard quotes this passage as "a prefiguration of the very essence of Negritude," perhaps because it anticipates the later slogan "return to the sources" even in its implicit valuation of fresh water from the local ground.[6]

In 1927 conditions were perfect for response to Price-Mars's call. Five young Haitians who would be the leaders of a new movement known as Indigenism returned from Paris: Roumer, Normil Sylvain, Carl Brouard, Philippe Thoby-Marcelin, and Jacques Roumain. For Haitian students of those days, as for West Indians later in the century, metropolitan education was a paradoxical affair. Paris in the 1920s saw Europe rejecting many of its own cultural assumptions and challenging its traditions in the wake of a war that had reshaped society. For the Haitians then, it was part of becoming a good Frenchman to turn against French cultural assumptions, as the French themselves were doing. Having learned this lesson, the students returned ready to reject the assumptions of their parents' generation and particularly any acquiescence to French cultural leadership. They were thus in a frame of mind highly receptive to Price-Mars's insistence not only that Haitian culture was coherent and self-sufficient, but that it preserved precisely the kind of features that European culture now saw itself in need of. Some had already published poetry; Philippe Thoby-Marcelin's "Sainement" (written in Paris in 1926), had already struck a stance indistinguishable from the Negritude of a decade later:

> Jurant un éternel dédain aux raffinements européens,
> Je veux désormais vous chanter:
> révolutions, fusillades, tueries
> Bruit de coco-macaque sur des épaules noires,
> Mugissements du lambi, lubricité mystique de vaudou
>
> . . .
>
> Me dépouiller de tous oripeaux classiques
> et me dresser nu, très sauvage
> et très descendant d'esclaves.

[Swearing eternal scorn for European refinements, / from now on I want to sing you: / revolutions, executions, killings, / Noise of coco-macaque on black shoulders, / Groans of the conch shell, mystic voluptuousness of vodun . . . / I would strip myself of all classical trappings / and stand naked, very much the savage, / and very much the descendant of slaves.][7]

Joining Price-Mars and others who had remained at home, the group established *La Revue indigène* almost at once, in July

1927. Its last appearance, in February 1928, was capped by an *Anthologie de la poésie haitienne 'indigène'*, projecting the new voice, and in effect proposing to supersede the anthology of Morpeau. Here prosody itself provided an arena for the struggle between metropolitan and indigenous cultures, as it did for every similar struggle throughout the Caribbean and indeed throughout the Americas.[8] We have already seen the attempt in Roumer to commandeer the alexandrine for distinctively Haitian purposes. Such a poem is the correlative to the mixed heritage of the cultural (or the biological) mulatto, deriving a successful artifact from the compound identity that may be problematic in its author. The uncertainty whether mulatism is a burden or an accomplishment finds its most famous expression in the poems of the relatively conservative Léon Laleau, who was not an Indigenist. A familiar example is his "Trahison" (1931), often reprinted since its appearance in Senghor's anthology, where Laleau is the most heavily represented Haitian poet:

> Ce coeur obsédant, qui ne correspond
> Pas avec mon langage et mes costumes,
> Et sur lequel mordent, comme un crampon,
> Des sentiments d'emprunt et des coutumes
> D'Europe, sentez-vous cette souffrance
> Et ce désespoir à nul autre égal
> D'apprivoiser, avec des mots de France,
> Ce coeur qui m'est venu du Sénégal?

[This haunted heart that doesn't fit / My language or the clothes I wear / Chafes within the grip of / Borrowed feelings, European ways. / Do you feel my pain, / This anguish like none other / From taming with the words of France / This heart that came to me from Senegal?][9]

While the words of the poem assert an African heart ready to burst its bounds, its structure communicates something quite different: the absolute confinement of any African or Haitian kernel within the bounds of a traditional and even old-fashioned rhetoric at the hands of the poet himself. The poem is stirring, but not because of the single final word that calls up Africa, for that last gesture is riding an emotional wave

generated by purely rhetorical means, by the great curve of
syntax arching between the nearly parallel first and last lines.
Laleau's efforts suggest that indigenous material will always
be hard pressed by metropolitan forms (a phenomenon considered in greater detail in chapter 4). This handicap can be
overcome; the Jamaican poet Claude McKay, for example,
used the sonnet form for two very different treatments of the
same theme of mixed heritage, "Outcast" (1922) and
"Mulatto" (1925) – both of them subtler poems that successfully
communicate emotions Laleau merely asserts. A more dramatic
choice is the rejection of classical forms altogether, as in
Roumain's powerful poem on the same subject, "Quand bat le
tam-tam" (1931):

> Ton cœur tremble dans l'ombre, comme le reflet
>   d'un visage dans l'onde troublée
> L'ancien mirage se lève au creux de la nuit
> Tu connais le doux sortilège du souvenir
> Un fleuve t'emporte loin des berges,
> Entends-tu ces voix: elles chantent l'amoureuse douleur
> Et dans le morne, écoute ce tam-tam haleter telle la gorge
>   d'une noire jeune fille.
> Ton ame, c'est le reflet dans l'eau murmurante où
>   tes pères ont penché leurs obscurs visages
> Et le blanc qui te fit mulâtre, c'est ce peu
>   d'écume rejeté, comme un crachat, sur le rivage.

[Your heart trembles in the shadows, like a face / reflected in
troubled water. / The old mirage rises from the pit of the night / You
sense the sweet sorcery of the past: / A river carries you far away
from the banks, / Carries you toward the ancestral landscape. /
Listen to those voices singing the sadness of love / and in the
mountain, hear that tom-tom / panting like the breast of a young
black girl. // Your soul is this image in the whispering water where /
your fathers bent their dark faces. / Its hidden movements blend you
with the waves / And the white that made you a mulatto is this bit /
of foam cast up, like spit, upon the shore].[10]

This appeared in the same year as "Trahison," but it is
technically very much the master of its own fate. The proportions implied by the parallelism of "your heart (*ton cœur*)" and

"your soul (*ton ame*)" barely suggest something like the ghost of a Petrarchan sonnet, and while there is a turn to rhyme in the second part, it is initiated by a pointedly unorthodox enjambment after a relative pronoun "where (*où*)." Yet in such formal freedom, too, the young Haitians were enthusiastically joined, even preceded, by young Frenchmen. The modernist French poet turned to free verse as a rejection of Victor Hugo, of the bourgeoisie, and as a way of letting the deepest self speak. For the Haitian, free verse made possible the rejection of French cultural tyranny, and the expression of his African soul in opposition to the "collective bovarism" of the Haitian middle class.[11] In retrospect, the similarity between these positions is patent, but fifty years ago it was the differences that mattered: the French poet was a reformer, paring away accretions from an entity that he expected to recognize; but the Haitian was an explorer, seeking out a national identity whose whole evolution had taken place out of sight.

Just as the Indigenists were leading Haiti away from the oppressive model of the mother country, a more benign, fraternal literary model was being introduced from a very unlikely quarter. Throughout the Caribbean in the early part of this century, the United States was condemned by intellectuals as pragmatic and materialistic, a soulless monolith. In Latin America particularly it was regularly abused as the hemisphere's Caliban (only later did a semantic shift associated with Negritude transfer that term to the black population of the Caribbean).[12] But under often contemptuous occupation by US Marines – Caliban's Calibans – black Haiti discovered its affinity for the cultural nationalism (it was nothing less) of America's own indigenous black culture, oppressed by the same oppressor. Thus Haitian literature welcomed the influence of the Harlem Renaissance.[13] The harbinger was a short article on Countee Cullen, with translations of three of his poems, that appeared in *La Revue indigène* in October, 1927.[14] But what may be said to have provided Haitian writers at large with their first contact with black American literature was Franck Schoell's article "La 'Renaissance nègre' aux Etats-Unis," in *La Revue de Paris*, January, 1929. Interest in the Renaissance continued to grow; Marianne Pierard's anthology *Poètes nègres d'Amérique* (1930) was soon available in Haiti. There was little sense among Haitian writers that the Renaissance was to be imitated; it was taken rather as a source of confidence, a continuing reassurance that the goals of Indigenism were not only necessary, but also of more than local significance. The relationship between Port-au-Prince and Harlem was soon stabilized as one of reciprocity between equals. Several writers associated with the Renaissance visited Haiti during this period; most important for Haiti was a visit by Langston Hughes in 1931, since it helped establish his friendship with Roumain, one of the most active of the Indigenists. Their connection served throughout this period as an essential channel for communication between the two movements. In 1932 Price-Mars published a series of articles on black American literature in the first issues of Jacques Antoine's *La Relève*.[15] That journal, which carried on the work of the Indigenists from 1932 to 1938, continued to provide articles on American writing along with translations, many of these by Rene Piquion, who published the first book on Hughes in any language (*Langston Hughes: un chant nouveau*, 1940), and went on to champion the poets of Negritude as well.

As in North America, the Depression of the 1930s saw a noticeable shift of interest from idealizing folklore to social realism (and from rural to urban settings). This was reflected by a corresponding shift in the dominant medium: while the movement began in poetry, after 1930 its best work was in fiction. Researches into peasant life advocated by Indigenism were also a factor here; increasingly accurate accounts of folk culture made picturesque or idealizing poetry less acceptable, while at the same time they inspired more ethnographic novels. The year 1931 can stand as the symbolic date of Indigenism's maturity, since it marks the publication both of the movement's first great novel, Roumain's *Montagne ensorcelée*, and of Laleau's *Musique nègre*, which records that poet's belated acceptance of Indigenist principles.

Under the pressure of American aggression and European self-criticism, Indigenism strove to bring Haitian culture to a new self-consciousness. In the course of the 1930s, however, there was an increasing tendency to penetrate beyond Haitian roots to remote African origins. More and more in the literature, the counter-term to "Western" is not "Haitian," but "African" or simply "black." Insofar as this was a self-conscious program, it culminated in the group associated with the review *Les Griots* of 1938–39.[16] If Indigenism dispelled the mirage of European culture that had obscured Haitian reality, the "Griots" sought behind that reality a "cultural unconscious," an "African soul" that was largely another mirage.[17] This position too had its reflection in the arena of prosody. While free verse was still acceptable for its supposed transparency, as a virtually unmediated form of expression, there were among the "Griots" for the first time calls for a specifically black poetics. "Griot" is after all an African, not a Haitian, word for "poet," and Félix Morriseau-Leroy, for example, argued against free verse in 1938 because "the authentic Haitian poet will adopt an African prosody with parallelism and repetition, the means peculiar to our race."[18] These developments betray the influence of the Harlem Renaissance, and of concurrent events in Paris which Haitians of course never ceased to monitor. But soon the Negritude movement would internationalize at least one aspect of the Haitian vision, its glance to Africa, and soon World War II would bring about the realignment of countries like Haiti into a Third World of common interest. At the same time, wider attention was drawn to Haitian history and culture by two seminal works in English, Melville Herskovits's *Life in a Haitian Valley* (1937) and C. L. R. James's *The Black Jacobins* (1938). In a sense then Brouard's manifesto for the "Griots" is the last word of purely national self-discovery.

Surely because of the impact of Negritude throughout the French-speaking Caribbean, Indigenism in the end suffered critics rather than revisionists. Dantes Bellegarde voices the most common objection:

Some Haitians, who want a closed and self-sufficient Haiti, have taken offence because I observed that Haiti is an intellectual province of France . . . They don't want to hear about French or even Latin culture . . . [Haiti] should therefore set itself the ideal of becoming in the middle of America a small Dahomean island, with a Bantu culture and a Congolese religion to entertain Yankee tourists . . . This does not prevent our aesthetes from proclaiming themselves Baudelairians, Proustians, Futurists or Surrealists.[19]

To some extent historical conditions are speaking here. In 1941 nationalism was discredited and isolation dangerous. At least one writer had attacked the nationalism and race-consciousness of *Les Griots* in the same breath as those of Hitler and Mussolini,[20] and Bellegarde's honest affection for French culture is made more poignant by the fact that his book was published in Montreal, presumably because France had fallen to the Nazis in the preceding year. On the whole, however, Bellegarde's criticism arises naturally out of Caribbean conditions. Haiti is merely the strongest example of the widespread pattern: there is an educated elite oriented unavoidably toward Europe, and there is a peasantry with a coherent indigenous culture deriving primarily from Africa. The elite is not intellectual – often the opposite – but for obvious reasons it is almost without exception the class from which the intellectuals come. In these countries, the discovery of national identity has been largely the discovery of folk identity, but it is the intellectual from the scrambling middle class who most likely makes the discovery, and Caribbean intellectuals continue for the most part to discover their peasants initially in Paris, London, or the writings of ethnographers, rather than in the countryside. Hence the gnawing insecurity common among intellectuals throughout the Caribbean, and hence too the recurrent pattern of each generation's Oedipal rejection of its predecessors as "tracing-paper poets," "exoticists," or "mimic men." The intellectual cannot become a peasant; perhaps he can come to speak for the peasant, but his fear will be that he speaks only of the peasant, a tourist in his own country, writing socialist picture-postcards.

CUBA

Cuba, the center of Spanish-language culture in the Caribbean as Haiti was of the French, presents a very different setting.

Much larger and more populous, it remained a plantation colony until late in the nineteenth century. Slavery was abolished only in 1886. Independence from Spain was won in 1898 with the help of the United States, but the price of that help was intermittent military occupation (under the terms of the Platt Amendment) until the outbreak of World War I.

Cuba differs from many of the Caribbean islands in having a large white population, and the long struggle for independence was punctuated by a literature in which white Cuban authors projected black or Amerindian heroes. Opposition to slavery served as a transparent metaphor by which to protest political dependence, and nationalism in the face of European domination expressed itself by emphasizing the importance of non-European elements in Cuban society. Coulthard is among the first to demonstrate how this literature also displays considerable psychological acumen in the presentation of the complex relations of blacks, mulattos, and whites, thereby providing a ground on which later cultural self-awareness could build.[21] But it was only after the external pressures of slavery and colonialism had been removed that the strains woven into the fabric of Cuban society itself could be gauged accurately.

White Cuba's fascination with "its" blacks as a literary subject evolved along these lines until the interest took more definite shape after the war as "Afrocubanism" (also called the Negrista movement, though it was more a literary fashion than a true movement). Fostered overwhelmingly by whites, its thrust was not the exploration of the individual's suppressed black identity, as in Haiti, but the exploration of blacks as an element in Cuban identity – as the romantic or picturesque core that made the Cuban unique and distinguishable from his European ancestors, the "African heart" not of the individual but of the new nation. Since as in most of the Caribbean no truly native population survived, in Cuba the black peasantry was fancifully cast in the role of an indigenous people and in that guise was seen as the catalyst for crystallization of the national identity, for the integration of the Cuban personality. The course of Haitian history made the mulatto a problematic figure, and throughout the literary movements of this period there are echoes of a political tension between blacks and mulattos; in Cuba by contrast both demography and history seemed to argue that the identity of the culture was and should be mulatto.[22] Cuban Negrismo thus bore less resemblance to events in Harlem or Haiti than to the purely European cult of the primitive and the exotic. But this was not merely an empty imitation of the metropolis, for when these interests were transplanted to the Caribbean they turned out to be of much more immediate use than on their native ground. There was a difference between encountering "Africa" in the galleries of the Trocadero and encountering it in your blood.

Cubans were also unusual among Caribbean peoples in that their interest was in the Germanic rather than in the better-known Parisian aspect of this cult of the exotic.[23] In Havana the intellectuals were reading Spengler, his teacher Frobenius, and Freud, and in the process absorbing a world view that encompassed the decline of the West, the resurgence of the non-Western world, and the revelations of the unconscious. The combination of Freud and Frobenius encouraged the risky Cuban (and European) habit of conceiving the Negro as a sort of psychological entity, a dark secret self that (as Luis Palés Matos puts it) "lives physically and spiritually within us all."[24] Cuban enthusiasm for Spengler may seem odd, but in the wake of World War I his thesis promised that Europe would soon pass the torch of cultural superiority to the Americas. More specifically he was perceived as "the intellectual apostle of the appearance of the Negro in the artistic hemisphere of Europe." In effect, he contributed a metaphysical base for the superficial "negrification" of the arts in both Europe and the Americas: "The apogee of the Negro, *as an artistic novelty*, follows on the appearance of Spengler's theories."[25]

As in Haiti the work of one man served to focus these preoccupations. The Cuban counterpart of Price-Mars was Fernando Ortiz, whose studies of the culture of black Cubans had begun early with *Los negros brujos* (1906) and *Los negros esclavos* (1916), and continued into the 1950s. As those titles may suggest, Ortiz begins much further from his subject than Price-Mars; for him the black Cuban is not yet part of the family, not yet an "uncle," but still the indigenous exotic. As in Haiti, however, the work of the ethnographer was an inspiration to poets who were themselves generally even more remote from the life of the peasants. In particular Ortiz's *Glosario de afronegrismos* (1923) was much utilized as a sort of handbook or thesaurus of local color for poets.

The Negrista manner flourished in the late 1920s and early 1930s and its evolution follows a scenario strikingly parallel to that of Haitian Indigenism. The year 1926 saw the publication, in Madrid, of *La Poesía Moderna en Cuba*, a monumental anthology not unlike Morpeau's in its attempt to assemble the work of the period from 1882 to 1925. In the following year the established journal of the Cuban intellectual community, *Cuba Contemporanea* (1913–27) ceased publication and the journal of a new generation, *Revista de Avance* (1927–30) began to appear. Negrismo was essentially only an available style; it was never embodied in any particular group or journal. But this public changing of the guard was symptomatic. Apart from a few harbingers, the first Afro-Caribbean poems to appear in Spanish were "Pueblo negro" and "Danza negra" by Palés Matos, published in Puerto Rico in 1926, and reprinted in Havana in the following year.[26] The first Cuban poems squarely in the Negrista style appeared in 1928: Ramón Guirao's "Bailadora de rumba" and José Tallet's "La rumba."

Afrocubanism was precipitated by the Caribbean's dawning awareness of its uneasiness with things European, but also by the more disconcerting spectacle of Europe's revulsion at its own image. Recognition of the African element in Antillean cultures was the key to disengagement from the evident decline of the West. So white writers turned to the black element in their national identity – its least familiar element – in order to project an image of Cuba and of themselves as candid, passionate, strong, anything but European.[27] But because of the writers' distance from the actual experience of black Cubans, the poetry of Afrocubanism is for the most part a poetry of gorgeous surfaces: highly colored, gratuitously primitive, and full of "prancing niggers."[28] The emphasis of the Negrista poets is overwhelmingly on the *sound* of the poem.

Most of these poems are technical experiments in the use of argot, onomatopoeia, and imitative dance rhythms. The distinctive structure and sound of local creole language, so important to the poetic development of the French and later of the English Caribbean, is not a factor in the Spanish-speaking Caribbean; instead these poems are studded with a picturesque lexicon of Africanisms (often drawn from Ortiz's *Glosario*). Ortiz himself speaks of the effect intended here as "oral sonority," "the aesthetic effect . . . oral but not verbal . . . which modern poets try to produce by means of words whose phonic value is more predominant than the semantic."[29] Such an effect seems to have been thought of as vaguely "African" and at the same time as a defiance of European rationalism. But poetry composed along these lines can come out resembling, of all people, Wallace Stevens. One need only juxtapose the Stevens of lines like "Chieftain Iffucan of Azcan in caftan / Of tan with henna hackles, halt!" (from "Bantams in Pinewoods," 1922) with a typical passage from Palés Matos's "Danza negra":

> El Gran Cocoroco dice: tu-cu-tú.
> La Gran Cocoroca dice: to-co-tó.
> Es el sol de hierro que arde en Tombuctú,
> Es la danza negra de Fernando Pó.
> El cerdo en el fango gruñe: pru-pru-prú.
> El sapo en la charca sueña: cro-cro-cró . . .

[The great Cocoroco says: tu-cu-tu. / The great Cocoroca says: to-co-to. / The iron sun blazes in Timbuktoo. / The negroes dance in Fernando Po. / The pig grunts in the mud: pru-pru-pru. / The toad croaks in the pond: cro-cro-cro.][30]

In these poems, black Cubans are observed and overheard, but they rarely speak for themselves. In "Danza negra," or any of the endless series of rumba poems, we see, hear, even smell the dancers, but the considerable human distance separating poet and dancer is revealed at once by mere juxtaposition with a poem like McKay's "The Harlem Dancer" (1922). This poem too has its moments of opulent tropical color: "To me she seemed a proudly-swaying palm / Grown lovelier for passing through a storm."[31] Yet McKay exploits the form of the

Shakespearean sonnet to transform a poem of observation into one of empathy by means of the closing couplet: "But looking at her falsely-smiling face, / I knew her self was not in that strange place." In the change from looking to knowing, the poet makes contact across the human distance maintained by the fact of a performance, rather than by barriers of race or class. He thus ends the poem estranged not from the dancer but from the circumstances which he shares with her both literally and metaphorically.

Negrista poetry contributed valuable technical innovations; it also made the reading public aware of the folkloric investigations of Ortiz and others and thereby created an atmosphere of receptivity for more concrete social integration later on. But initially the drift of criticism was as in Haiti: after the effects of the Depression began to be felt, there was a call for more socially responsible writing. Regino Pedroso, for example, whose personal heritage was African and Chinese, ended his best-known poem "Hermano negro" (1939) by complaining to his fellow poets: "Da al mundo, con tu angustia rebelde, / tu humana voz . . . / ¡y apaga un poco tus maracas . . . ! [Give to the world your cry of rebellion / Your human voice . . . / and stop playing your maracas so much!][32]

The most enduring poet to emerge from the Negrista period did just that. Nicolás Guillén, significantly one of the few actual Afrocubans involved in Afrocubanism, has consistently endowed the gaudy tropics with a conscience. He is the preeminent poet of *America mestiza*, of *mulatez*, admirable for both the strength of his verse and his exemplary posture as a poet. For both reasons he is to West Indian eyes the most significant Latin American poet. His first Negrista collection, *Motivos de son* (1930), is said to have been inspired by a sudden obsession with the rhythm of the *negro bembon*.[33] But while he begins with the imitative rhythms and emphasis on sound which are characteristic of the style, he quickly rejects the circumstantiality of Afrocubanism.[34] Beginning with *Motivos de son*, his poems allow black Cubans to speak for themselves. The Prologue of his next volume (*Sóngoro cosongo*, 1931) announces, "I am not unaware of the fact that these verses will be repugnant to many persons, because they deal with issues concerning blacks, and the people, but that does not matter to me. Rather, I am happy."[35] The sentiment closely echoes Langston Hughes's manifesto of 1926:

We younger Negro artists who create now intend to express our individual dark-skinned selves without fear or shame. If white people are pleased, we are glad. If they are not, it doesn't matter . . . If colored people are pleased, we are glad. If they are not, their displeasure doesn't matter either.[36]

The echo may be coincidental, but Guillén had met Hughes in Cuba in 1929. With an ear tuned to the Negrista style, Guillén noted the importance of music in Hughes's poetry, and the two poets talked about the place of blacks in Cuban society.[37] In the same year Guillén had publicly taken what would be his characteristic position that Cuban identity was mulatto, that Afrocuban poetry should not be conceived as an activity set apart from some other kind of Cuban poetry, and that "a movement of integration of the factors which make up our social structure . . . ought to be the ideal of all Cubans."[38] Guillén's emergence as a formidable poet overshadows the evaporation of Afrocubanism. The ethnographic work that supported the fashion continued, dignified by the founding of a journal, *Revista de Estudios Afro-Cubanos* (1937–40), and in 1938 the achievement of the Negrista poets was brought together in an anthology which at the same time marked its demise as a force in Cuban literature: Guirao's *Orbita de la Poesía Afrocubana 1928–1937*.

Afrocubanism was a representative rather than a significant phase. It deserves attention here chiefly as a foil to Indigenism and Negritude, since the curve of development in all three cases can be seen as similar, and since the divergences within that similarity exemplify alternative responses to essentially the same external conditions: American writing, Paris fashions, German thought, economic depression, war. The histories of Europe and of America have always imposed themselves on the Caribbean. Contemporary criticism tends to dismiss Afrocubanism as too innocent and even too white, but the harshness of such criticism reflects more on current ideological needs in the region than on the quality of work that Afrocubanism produced. Caribbean writing is often self-conscious about its youth; there is a strong sense that every poem must carry its weight, and prodigals are not welcome. But even in the parable the errant son can only be welcomed by the combined security of age and wealth, not by the serious older brother. We can expect, I think, that a time will come when small doses of this rather repetitious body of poetry can again be enjoyed without remorse.

NEGRITUDE AND AFTER

Negritude is one of the great intellectual accomplishments to come out of the Caribbean, the elaboration of an extremely subtle ideology out of an essentially simple *prise de conscience*, most vividly exemplified by Césaire's lines: "Eia pour ceux qui n'ont jamais rien inventé / pour ceux qui n'ont jamais rien exploré / pour ceux qui n'ont jamais rien dompté / mais ils s'abandonnent, saisis, à l'essence de tout chose" ["Eia for those who invented nothing / for those who have never discovered / for those who have never conquered / but, struck, deliver themselves to the essence of all things"].[39] Negritude arose out of the work of a number of Martinicans, but, unlike Indigenism and Negrismo, it was an international movement, and again unlike them, the movement as such hardly established a foothold in the Caribbean. It was created in Europe, under the pressure of European influences, and while it provided a cultural reference point for writers in Africa and the Caribbean, it remained a phenomenon of the metropolis.

It is hardly an overstatement to say that these developments could not have happened without the unique city that Paris was in the early decades of this century. Paris, which shortly before had driven Gauguin away to Tahiti, now embraced promiscuously everything perceived to be exotic. Tradition already offers us a symbolic origin for all that was to follow: the day in 1906 when Picasso "discovered" African sculpture at the Trocadero Museum. From that moment Paris became a vortex of iconoclastic artistic activity. Beginning in 1907 Cubism was the rallying point, but in 1912 an exhibition of Italian Futurist work competed for attention; Tristan Tzara's Dadaism entered the field around 1916, to be followed by Surrealism in about 1924. Out of the resulting quarrels came epochal works. This was also the period of the Ballets Russes, of Diaghilev, Nijinsky, and Stravinsky, who first came to Paris in 1910 with *The Firebird*, and made theatrical history with *The Rite of Spring* in 1913 – "barbaric" music literally drowned out by a barbaric audience of Parisians. With the end of World War I the Americans arrived, writers like Fitzgerald, Hemingway, and Pound, who made contact with established European artistic circles through the salon of Gertrude Stein.

From the point of view of this book, however, the important event was the appearance of Africa in these surroundings. In 1921, Blaise Cendrars published *Anthologie nègre*, a collection of African myths and folktales, and the next year saw two ethnographic studies by Maurice Delafosse, *Les Noirs d'Afrique* and *L'Ame nègre*. More widely publicized was the appearance of the novel *Batouala* (1921) by Rene Maran, a Martinican who had long been a member of the French colonial service in West Africa. A realistic account of African life which was also, almost necessarily, a critique of colonialism, the book promptly received the prestigious Prix Goncourt in 1922 (the year before, the prize had gone to Proust). These early essays in ethnology and anthropology (even *Batouala* was largely ethnographic in intent) added momentum to the growing interest among French intellectuals and artists in a vigorous but imaginary Africa. What has been called the "negrification" of Paris reached its peak in the late 1920s when the writers and musicians of the Harlem Renaissance arrived to usher in the Jazz Age. Most of this of course was entirely superficial, more faddish than anything in Afrocubanism. But just as the white Cuban fad found its enduring voice in the Afrocuban Guillén, so too did the Parisian rage for Africa find its true inheritors. It would be wrong to discount the authenticity of impact on a sensibility like Picasso's, but there were, among the artists and intellectuals of every nation living in Paris, African colonials and blacks from the Americas for whom the discovery of even a mythical Africa was a profoundly personal revelation. It was among them that a movement founded on the concept of "*négritude,*" of "being black," took shape.

Césaire's account is disarming. "It was simply that in Paris at that time there were a few dozen Negroes of diverse origins," he said; but energy and institutions were required to forge those few dozen into an effective movement.[40] This group had its own Gertrude Stein in Paulette Nardal, another Martinican, who provided not only a salon but a journal, *Revue du monde noir* (1930–34). Its stated aim was "to give the intelligentsia of the black race and their partisans [*amis*] an official organ in which to publish their artistic, literary, and scientific works. To study and to popularize . . . all which concerns *Negro Civilization* and the natural riches of Africa."[41] The *Revue* has been dismissed, by no less a commentator than Lilyan Kesteloot, as "middle class and assimilationist,"[42] and in retrospect one can easily smile at the suggestion that "of all the European races, the French is the nearest akin to the genius of the black race," or the earnest demonstration that cannibalism is caused not by moral decay but by vitamin deficiency.[43] Yet the *Revue* counted among its contributors not only Nardal and Maran, but McKay and Hughes, Price-Mars, Brouard, and Thoby-Marcelin, as well as all of the writers later associated with the short-lived journal *Légitime défense*. It is indicative of Nardal's vision that the *Revue* was published in both French and English; her house too served as a center for American blacks in Paris, as did Maran's, and she herself translated Alain Locke's *The New Negro* (1925), the anthology through which the Harlem Renaissance first made itself felt.[44]

By general consensus the Negritude movement proper begins with the appearance in June 1932 of the single issue of *Légitime défense*. This was the work of several young Martinicans, chief among them Etienne Léro, Jules Monnerot, and René Ménil. The group was predominantly mulatto and middle class, and had been sent to Paris for the customary education. Their revolt begins predictably enough as a simple Oedipal rejection of everything associated with their parents – an event that was virtually part of the French university curriculum. But then more specifically they criticized their parents' class, "la bourgeoisie de couleur française," for suppressing its own nature under a "borrowed personality."[45] The students rejected that unhealthy psychology, which another Martinican, Frantz Fanon, would later articulate so fully in *Black Skin, White Masks* (1952). Since they were writers, they also rejected the imitative literature associated with it. It seems fair to suggest too that at least some of their aggravation came from the fact that once again the Caribbean proved to be out of touch with the times, absurdly suppressing its blackness to go French while the real French were busily going African. It must have been disorienting to discover that, however badly they were treated on the street, fashionable Paris welcomed them because they were born with African blood, and not because they had acquired French culture.

Thus, when the Antillean students turned to an idea of Africa they were still in a sense imitating the French. They certainly had no sense that a coherent African *heritage* was to be found in the Caribbean, and their notion of Africa came at first, like everyone else's, from Harlem, or from the popular ethnographers.[46] Under these circumstances the term "Africa" stood primarily for instinct, inner nature, the true primordial man beneath the veneer of civilization and rationalism, and at first it had that symbolic value entirely apart from matters of race: "Africa" was whatever was not "France." On this point the specific language in which the writers of *Légitime défense* couched their manifesto is revealing: what they declared was "we refuse to be ashamed of what we *feel*"[47] – yet if the paramount issue were racial or even ethnic they would more likely have written "we refuse to be ashamed of what we *are*." In such a context the assertion of Africa was often hardly distinguishable from the assertion of surrealism; both served as methods of "disalienation," as ways to reclaim authenticity.[48] The youthful revolt against parents and the intellectual revolt against immediate forebears may have been typical of Paris at the time, but when black and mulatto colonials struck these poses, in the process they found themselves exposing very deep problems of cultural identity. The discovery of these problems was the *prise de conscience* with which Negritude begins, and its first result was a fierce resistance to the politics of assimilation and to the programmatic alienation of indigenous cultures which that politics prescribed.

The journal *Légitime défense* was a gesture of frustration and discovery; it did not itself produce a literature, perhaps because it had no real alternatives to offer. But its message reached a more diverse (and so more resourceful) group, headed by Aimé Césaire, Léon Damas of French Guiana, and Léopold Senghor of Senegal, who together in 1934 produced *L'etudiant noir*.[49] With this group Negritude found its human base, and – thanks to the presence of Senghor, Birago Diop, and others – the group established the first dependable contact between the Caribbean and Africa as it actually was. Even though the number of people involved remained small, what in *Légitime défense* had been merely a Caribbean phenomenon transported to Paris now became a phenomenon representative of the black diaspora. Where *Légitime défense* had rejected the role of European culture in the Caribbean, *L'etudiant noir* rejected the West altogether as a cultural model.

The appearance of this short-lived student paper was not a world-historical event. But one of the founders, Damas, began publishing his poetry in the same year, and in 1937 produced the movement's first volume of verse, *Pigments*. The volume declares both its intellectual affinities and its level of rage through an epigraph from McKay's poem of 1919, "To the White Fiends": "Be not deceived, for every deed you do / I could match – outmatch: Am I not Afric's son, / Black of that black land where black deeds are done?" Soon selections from an early version of Césaire's masterpiece, *Cahiers d'un retour au pays natal* appeared in the journal *Volontés* (1939), though amid the events of that year they seem to have attracted no attention. Then war in Europe brought about an almost novelistic coincidence. André Breton, the father of Surrealism, lionized by both *Légitime défense* and *L'etudiant noir*, evidently knew nothing about these admirers. But he fled France in 1941 (travelling on the same ship as Claude Lévi-Strauss, who describes their experience).[50] En route Breton stopped in

Martinique, and while there idly picked up a magazine lying on a shop-counter. It was the first number of *Tropiques*, a joint effort of Césaire and Ménil, both returned from France; the shop belonged to Ménil's sister. Astonished, Breton read essays and poetry after his own heart. Next day he met Césaire, and soon he was reading a reprint of *Cahiers*.[51]

The end of the war brought recognition for the individual poets and so for the movement as a whole. Senghor's first volume (*Chants d'ombre*) came in 1945, Césaire's first (*Les armes miraculeuses*) in 1946. Under the new French Union all three leaders of *L'etudiant noir* were elected to the French National Assembly in 1946. With help and a preface from Breton, a complete edition of *Cahiers* was published simultaneously in Paris and New York in the following year (remarkably, a Spanish translation had already appeared in Havana in 1943).[52] From the perspective of the Anglophone Caribbean this is by far the most important French Antillean poem; both Césaire's message and his technique clearly made a powerful impression on Brathwaite and Walcott (who read it very early in his career). But most writers in the former British colonies would not have had access to the poem until its publication as a Penguin paperback in 1969, by which time the substance of the poem and along with it the characteristic dialectical maneuver of Negritude had already been communicated, by a roundabout path, through the rhetoric of North American Black Power.

In 1947 Damas assembled the movement's first anthology, *Poètes d'expression française d'outre mer*. The book is a kind of homage to Etienne Léro (who had died in 1939): more space is devoted to his poetry than even to Césaire's, and Damas reprints several pages from Léro's essays in *Légitime défense* as the substance of his own introduction. It is noteworthy that Haitian poetry is not represented in this anthology; as we have seen, issues pertinent to Negritude were being debated in Haiti and even among Haitians in Paris at this time, but in spite of intellectual, cultural, and racial affinities, the country's political independence seems to have set it apart. The following year, 1948, is the high water mark of Negritude as a literary movement. The main event was the appearance of Senghor's *Anthologie de la nouvelle poésie nègre et malagache*, including a more balanced selection and bearing a kind of seal of approval in the form of Sartre's now independently famous introduction, "Orphée Noir." The same year saw a second volume of Senghor's own poetry, *Hosties noires*, and the migration to Paris of Richard Wright, preceded by a considerable reputation. Equally important was the founding of the journal *Présence Africaine* (1947) which, besides providing a center for black writers from throughout the world, also served as the arbiter of the ideology of Negritude. Each of these three events – the anthology, the journal, the arrival of a black American master – in its own way confirmed the authority of Negritude as an international movement and assured the rapid dissemination of its principles. The *prise de conscience* which I take it that "Negritude" most properly names had taken place successfully on a vast scale, and the result was an undeniable trans-formation of the world. Beyond this point however the move-ment transcended the production of literature, and succeeding issues of *Présence Africaine* fostered an increasingly critical and philosophical discourse. In fact there are indications that this growing body of thought soon became as much a burden for writers as a source of inspiration.[53] But here our concern with the movement's ideological dimension is limited to how it impinges on the situation of Caribbean literatures.

When Negritude was brought home to the Caribbean, it was identified primarily with the initial act of recognition, with the ensuing revaluation of the European and African heritages (and of their interrelation), and with a concomitant "arche-ology" of Africa as it survived in the Americas. Later chapters will investigate these developments in their West Indian setting, where (as in North America) an impressive body of protest poetry and autobiographical fiction draws inspiration from Negritude, and where individual writers, most notably Césaire, have measurably influenced literatures in several languages. But for the most part Negritude as an ideology failed to take hold in the Caribbean. For the region as a whole the years during and after the Second World War saw a shift of attention from European to local developments, and that marks one crucial factor: from the relatively distant viewpoint of the Caribbean, the Negritude movement appeared as an intellectual revolt very much within the French tradition, a tradition which already had the means to account for the movement's ideology, as an antithetical position arrived at within a dialectical framework.

Negritude begins with the recognition of color as the sign not only of a common racial origin, but of an elided cultural heritage. It becomes an ideological program as soon as the possible consequences of this recognition come under consideration. In the process Negritude calls into being two metaphysical entities: one the mythically satisfying past known as "Africa" and the other a "new race," defined by the projection of this recovered heritage into the future.[54] But this "Africa" is still conceived as the world's heart of darkness, only now charged with a positive value, and its primary function is antithetical; it serves as a kind of universal alternative, to be set against France, Europe, the West, "civilization." Similarly, the "black soul" is defined by what it is not, by what it is different from. Yet this is to commandeer European ways of thinking about Africa and the black race, without appreciable change.[55] The condescending white view is transformed, virtually by an act of will, into a point of pride, but such transformations are always a little suspicious, and the analogy Sartre applies to the colonized may illuminate the area of doubt: "in certain psychoses the hallucinated person, tired of always being insulted by his demon, one fine day starts hearing the voice of an angel who pays him compliments."[56]

Thus Negritude as an ideology begins in negativity; it intentionally assumes the role of the Other, embodying all the values that the West does not predicate of itself. In effect it agrees to be precisely the erotic, irrational, instinctive antagonist that the West had been dreaming for itself. So George Lamming, writing under the influence of this ideology, can say that "the Negro is a man whom the Other regards as a Negro."[57] But as the theatrical metaphor of role-playing suggests, the formulation of Negritude along these lines very strongly invites its proponents to envision themselves as enacting an episode in the drama of the West. That is certainly the thrust of the dialectical account of Negritude best known from Sartre's introductions to Senghor's anthology and to Fanon's *Les damnés de la terre* (1961). This view of black self-consciousness as a phase, "the weak stage of a dialectical progression,"[58] has come to be widely accepted even among partisans of Negritude, in spite of the objections of such diverse and authoritative black commentators as Fanon, C. L. R. James, and Wole Soyinka.[59]

Here the perspective of Sylvia Wynter is valuable, since she is one of few West Indians (after Lamming) who make use of the term "Negritude," and since she is thoroughly at home with dialectical argument. Where Sartre among others sees Negritude as part of the solution of a European problem, as an "antiracist racism" by which the original (white) racism is transcended,[60] Wynter in the same context appropriates the term to name the achieved solution of a problem created *outside* Europe, but by European hands. In her terminology, "Negritude" is the synthesis, the acknowledgment and celebration of multi-cultural creole reality after both the long rule of "White Power" and its short-lived antithetical response, "Black Power."[61] The implicit objection here harmonizes with Wynter's position as we encountered it in chapter 1: there is no justification for treating black consciousness as marginal or as an incidental part of a process which, while "universal," is firmly centered in the metropolis. But her view also expresses the fundamental Caribbean critique of Negritude as an ideology. The movement is perceived as a new, but still *external*, focus, for which the region itself remains peripheral. Antithetically conceived as rival to the European Great Tradition, it nevertheless asserts an equally homogeneous culture grounded not on the conditions of life but on the mysterious authority of "the black soul," of "an identity of passions."[62] It is symptomatic that, given the international nature of the Negritude movement, its writers were virtually compelled to cultivate a sort of "black French" rather than any actual indigenous language.

As we will see in the following chapters, Caribbean writers

are inclined to exploit Great Traditions, but they no longer submit to them, and the ideology of Negritude is widely regarded as a foreign monolith, especially dangerous because it ignores or effaces colonial history, the diversity of colonial cultures, and the racial diversity of the colonized. To exaggerate only slightly, Negritude appears in the Caribbean as an alternative colonizer, motivated by a "civilizing mission" of its own. Essential to that mission is the repression of the colonial past, which is to be elided as a traumatic episode to make room for some link to an ancestral Africa. This makes sense for the Africans involved in the movement; there the colonial period was relatively short, and the substantial survival of traditional ways made the idealization of those ways easy and effectual. But in the Americas the colonial period was very long, and there was no physical continuity with Africa. Further, during the period of Negritude's ascendancy the Caribbean suffered widespread ignorance not only of Africa, but more importantly of the details of its own colonial past, including both the survival of a fragmented African heritage and the evolution of an indigenous creole culture. Indeed, one of the initial motives for the Martinican pioneers of Negritude was this sense of deracination from history; as O. R. Dathorne puts it, "It is no accident that the crucial glance backward, the creative attempt to invent a past (which is really what Negritude is) was the product of French West Indian colonials, those notably who found themselves in alien lands that had bred no indigenous culture, raised no gods, fathered no new consciousness."[63] Negritude begins, for example in *Légitime défense*, as a gesture of despair in the face of this apparent sterility. But in much of the region real cultures did exist, merely invisible to the colonized eye. This myopia came to be corrected by a steady diet of researches by men like Price-Mars, Ortiz, Herskovits, and C. L. R. James. By that time, though, Negritude had already left the actual Caribbean behind.

In the Americas then the call for a denial of the colonial past required a real leap of faith in the direction of a truly mythical Africa, and willful blindness to the formative effects of each territory's colonial history on its present and future. In practice such a leap can be accomplished, but it requires the support of religion, not Hegelian dialectic; thus we find it in Haitian vodun, in the teachings of Garvey and preachers like the Jamaican Alexander Bedward, and in Rastafarianism – but not, as a rule, among secular writers and thinkers. The critic Michael Dash puts the case very strongly: "The failure of the negritude movement can almost be explained by the single fact of its conception of historic circumstance as so potentially destructive that the inheritors of such a past of slavery and colonisation are frozen into a prison of protest. It is a notion of history inherited from those who conquered."[64] Contingent on this treatment of colonial history is Negritude's attitude toward the nations that have evolved from it. To quote Dash again, "The common denominator of those who opposed the myth of an all-embracing black culture was an acute awareness of the evolution of specific national communities – that is, a sensitivity to the fact that the past was not as empty and uncreative as it was made out to be."[65] This objection had been voiced by James Baldwin as early as 1956, but it is particularly common in Haiti, bound by its heritage to French intellectual discourse, but perhaps the most pointedly autonomous culture in the region.[66] Outside the Francophone territories of course Negritude did not seem so threatening on this score, though it is worth noting that in the early days of Jamaican Rastafarianism the leap to Africa is similarly accompanied by an imperviousness to national culture and its goals.[67]

The salient feature of Caribbean cultures in this regard is another of the consequences of colonial history: creolization. The brute fact is the region's large mulatto population, product and in several senses inheritor of the colonial heritage. But as biological blackness provides the foundation that supports Negritude, so too the biological creole can support a metaphysics and indeed an ethics of Creolization – we have already seen it in Haiti and Cuba, in Guillén's theme of *mulatez*, and even in the Anglophone Caribbean the term has begun to appear with its telltale initial capital.[68] Creolization has long been proposed as an ideal for the "post-racist" society. It lies behind the recurrent formulae for national identity throughout the Americas (North American melting-pot, Latin American *ajiaco*, "*e pluribus unum*," "out of many one people," "all ah we is one"), and like Negritude this idealization aims to make the best of the facts, turning stumbling-blocks of illegitimacy into cornerstones of harmonious society. Just as the literature of Negritude explored the experience of blackness from within and without, so there is a literature of creolization, though it is not always identified as such, which anatomizes the mulatto and variously regards him as everything from monstrous progeny of servitude to redeeming synthesis.

The mulatto was not excluded from Negritude's conception of itself; thus Alioune Diop in the first issue of *Présence Africaine* wrote of constituting "a new race, creole in consciousness (*mentalement metissée*)."[69] But this mulatto is metaphorical; his archetype the acculturated African, a black skin in a white mask, Laleau's Senegalese heart in the costume of Europe – it is a matter of overlay, not of true mixture. And the Antillean Laleau was himself mulatto. The image he created in the spirit of Negritude only poorly accounts for the riddle in his own blood. If the black man in a white world tends to think in antithetical terms, the mulatto cast away in the Caribbean is inclined to synthesis, led by the lesson of his flesh to judge Negritude superseded once it has led him to recognition of the options he embodies.

Creolization as ideology, asserting that Antilleans are not Africans, is one Caribbean response to Negritude. Its literary equivalent might be Marvellous Realism (sometimes called "Magical Realism"). The term was used by Carpentier as early as 1943 (in describing a visit to Haiti), and applied to the discussion of Latin American fiction generally by the critic Angel Flores in 1954.[70] The continuing currency of the term "Marvellous Realism" derives from its prominence in the novels of the Latin American "boom," and what we talk about when we talk about Marvellous Realism is plainly evident in West Indian fiction, from Harris's *The Palace of the Peacock* to Antoni's *Divina Trace*. Since what it names is a representational style, the term has rarely if ever been applied to Caribbean poetry (which unlike fiction need negotiate no contract with realism); even so, it seems to suit some of the most ambitious recent West Indian poetry: arguably Walcott's *Omeros* and certainly Brathwaite's second trilogy (*Mother Poem, Sun Poem,* and *X/Self*). In French, the term was first applied quite broadly to Haitian art and literature by J. Stephen Alexis, speaking at the First International Congress of Black Artists and Writers in Paris in 1956.[71] Alexis's formulation is a frank descendant of Indigenism, as is evident when he counterpoises the logic and formalism of Western art to Haitian practice: "our art tends towards the most exact sensual representation of reality . . . with its accompaniment of the strange and the fantastic, of dreams and half light, of the mysterious and the marvellous."[72] But this Marvellous Realism is just as clearly a reaffirmation of the principles of Indigenism *in opposition to* Negritude. Part of Alexis's point is that the origin of this art is Haiti and its historical experience, not "Africa." Hence the significance of the occasion: the First International Congress was at once the first forgathering of world-wide Negritude and the first public evidence of a schism over the issue of local indigenous culture. Similarly the Cuban Alejo Carpentier, whose first novel marked the climax of Afrocubanism, came to see Marvellous Realism as an improvement on the aesthetics not only of Negritude, but of Afrocubanism and of Surrealism as well.[73] Indeed Marvellous Realism has been perceived as the fulfillment of all the movements we have been reviewing, at least insofar as they apply to the Caribbean.[74] For the literature of Marvellous Realism comes to terms with place and with being in this place; it explores the landscape for the roots or wellsprings of regional experience, and in doing so stresses the region's survival, the contours of its emergence from colonial history.[75] In contrast to Negritude, it takes the imagination as the chief resource of the colonized and asserts the creative effulgence of the Caribbean imagination in the face of chronic mortal danger. Colonialism too is a mother of invention, and as a result the experience of the people, particularly the common people, is enriched by the real presence of accumulated marvels. Negritude is inclined to see the imaginative activity of the colonized as psychosis or opiate, as protective but alienating integument. Marvellous Realism on the other hand insists that experience itself is, so to speak, creolized, that what we call magical is of one flesh with what we call real, and that the experience of the Americas is for historical reasons significantly more "creolized" than that of any other area. "What is the history of America," asks Carpentier, "but a chronicle of marvellous reality?"[76] After absorbing generations of conquistadors, the Caribbean has become a landscape more hospitable to Quixote than to his condescending analyst Cervantes. In the eyes of its proponents, Marvellous Realism goes beyond Negritude, because while it "transcends territorial boundaries, narrow nationalism, and racism," it still "penetrates into the *nuances* of the regional experience."[77] By so doing it reclaims the *prise de conscience* as a local Antillean phenomenon, firmly set in the context of an achieved accommodation to place and history, an accommodation that amounts to possession.

Without attempting to propose an anatomy of cultural revolution, we can discern a common armature in all of these literary movements discussed here, which will be operative in the Anglophone Caribbean as well. There is first of all a matrix of historical factors: all the Caribbean territories share in the colonial history of Plantation America, which radically shapes not only their economy, society, and politics, but also the individual's relation to the land, and to history. The traffic patterns of Plantation America yielded after emancipation to those of what Paul Gilroy has called the "Black Atlantic" – thus the Jamaican McKay, acculturated and politicized in New York, then active in Paris and avidly read by the Negritude poets, was only belatedly influential at home in Jamaica, while the American Hughes maintained close contact with Haiti and with Paris, though they were not much in touch with one another.[78] Each island's particular experience of that history varied tremendously, but the effects of these important differences on the literary history of the region in this century have never obscured the common matrix. All the territories also share an inordinate insularity. This originates in differences of colonial culture and especially of language, and it is perpetuated by the fact that for a long time the systems of their political and economic relations hardly made contact with one another except in time of war. Isolation was reinforced by each island's marginality in the eyes of the metropolitan powers, and so in the eyes of other islands even under the same hegemony. Independence has hardly improved this state of affairs. From the scant attention that Haiti and Jamaica, for example, expend on one another it would be difficult to deduce that they are separated by fewer than two hundred miles of ocean.

Even now the islands as a group remain the unwilling victims of metropolitan events; a fall in sugar prices or a European war affects them all. The Caribbean has repeatedly provided a theatre for Europe's wars – even in the 1940s ships were torpedoed near the Allied coaling station at St. Lucia, only twenty miles from Vichy Martinique. But the events of this century have had the effect of turning the islands back on their own resources, thereby contributing to the movement toward nationalism and independence. To varying degrees, all of the islands became aware of their dependence on the fickle attentions of the metropoles, and realized too that while the islands were of strategic value to Europe, their people were not.

Within this matrix literary developments also offer considerable parallels. In the period we are reviewing, the young regularly returned from their education abroad with the advantage of an external perspective on their own country, but between the wars this objectivity was heightened into critique by exposure to European tendencies toward self-criticism and alienation. At the same time virtually all of the Caribbean saw an increasing nationalism in every sphere of activity, one aspect of which was an increasing interest in the recognition and cultivation of identifiable indigenous culture. In the name of this interest, established literatures that prided themselves on meeting metropolitan standards of excellence were rejected by the younger generation. As we have seen in several cases, it was while the polarity between metropolis and nation was evolving that the loose metaphysical notion of Africa became available as a sort of third force.

Ironically, access to the metropolis seems to be essential to this course of events, since it offers education, a base for expression, a long perspective on the homeland, and indeed models for revolt. In most Caribbean societies, literature depends on (though it is not limited to) an intelligentsia drawn from the social elite and often distinguishable by color or shade from the mass of the people, and for this reason their programs come to be challenged, especially after the fact, because of this suspect tincture of the metropolitan culture even in their revolt. But their writing is with few exceptions unquestionably part of a drive for distinctive national identity, and comes increasingly closer to its target both as the group is educated in the substance of its projected goals, and as individually competent writers emerge as conscientious and informed leaders. On the other hand, it appears that the longstanding *cultural* relationship to the metropolitan center is little changed by independence or rhetoric. The metropolis is still conceived as a convenient place for sojourn short or long, and more frequently as the site of valuable income or education. The metropolitan education of the children of the elite, and their return to the Caribbean, is an established custom. These habits of exile and education have the added virtue of maintaining a sort of fifth column in the metropolis, ready to protect the island's interests, and occasionally to face about and attack the island's leadership. On this customary cross-pollination depends the vitality of a small island's intellectual life, since it makes possible regular contact with the external cultural weather in a stimulating atmosphere.

With some variations, we will encounter all of these factors in the development of Anglophone Caribbean literature, and will find, as might be expected, that the same issues materialize as well. These can be reduced to three. First, those questions of identity that initiate cultural awakening and readily lead to questions of personal, cultural, and national independence. Second, the question what to make of the colonial experience, which entails exploration of the meaning and consequences of history, and of myths developed in response to it, and of the meanings of decolonization. Third, questions centering on the relation to Europe, Africa, and America, as human realities and as myths, as external traditions imposed or available, as sources and resources for the articulation of identity. The relevance of these factors and issues to the Anglophone Caribbean is already apparent in the proceedings of the ACLALS Conference, but we turn now to examine the roles they play in the formative period of West Indian poetry.

CHAPTER 3

Overview of West Indian literary histories

The territories of the Anglophone Caribbean share with the rest of the region approximately the same historical circumstances and experience the same intellectual trajectory, which can be described loosely as leading from a *prise de conscience* through assertion and subsequent exploration of national identity. But there are significant differences in the West Indian situation. Most important, West Indian literature begins in this century virtually from nothing. Writing in Haiti or Cuba builds upon an extensive history of literary activity in the island. However imitative it may be at certain periods, it remains a local phenomenon with a local audience. Literary activity is underwritten by a coherent tradition, and has earned acceptance from the society. Whether an individual writer chooses to embrace or resist this tradition, its mere existence legitimizes his work, and so relieves him of the task of legitimizing himself. In the Anglophone Caribbean, on the other hand, the only literary tradition was metropolitan, not local. This meant that an individual undertaking to write in the West Indies had recourse only to a tradition of *books*, not one of literary activity. The aspiring poet had to stand in relation to English literary history at its best, as it survived in monuments of accomplishment. Since very few West Indian writers or would-be writers had the experience of working in London (or for that matter in North America) until the 1950s, this intimidating circumstance was not relieved by familiarity with well-known living writers, the contemporary face of English literature as a social activity.

The habit of local writing, as distinct from a literature, is relatively easy to support, and we find its characteristics throughout the region: a certain self-effacement, concern about limited audience, and dependence on literary clubs and small magazines which, if they encourage production, also encourage self-congratulation and cliquishness. The array of discussion groups and debating clubs extant in the first half of this century testifies to the activity, and perhaps the desperation, of the cultured minority. But literary success depends on groups not only of readers but of writers, and in the West Indies a uniquely important role was played by individuals who could envision and maintain such groups. Some were themselves writers with an added gift for organization (A. J. Seymour in Guyana and Frank Collymore in Barbados), but others whose contributions were crucial were not themselves writers at all: for example, Edna Manley in Jamaica and Harold Simmons in St. Lucia. The formation of literary circles responded to an historically determined deficiency; for while it is possible to write anywhere, a literature very nearly requires a city. The issue here is something like critical mass, the need for a certain minimal number of writers who in some loose sense work together, are aware of one another's work, and as a group are able to sustain the interest of an audience. Throughout the Caribbean, literary awakening is closely tied to urbanization, which in turn is tied to colonial policy. While the British built sugar factories under absentee landlords, the Spanish and especially the French established colonies. Their people came in larger numbers, had a more favorable attitude to the islands (if not to their non-European inhabitants), and in the course of time bred up a large mulatto class. Thus from an early date the French and Spanish islands had established colonial cultures, creole societies perhaps inordinately attentive to metropolitan fashions, but offering considerable support for local practitioners of the arts. Until very recently, the Anglophone territories had nothing to match the intellectual atmosphere of Port-au-Prince or Havana; as we shall see, the recent rapid growth of Anglophone literature was nourished first by London and shortly by the explosive development of Kingston and Port of Spain.

Yet the role of the metropolis too has been different for the

Anglophone Caribbean. Until very recently West Indians did not study in Britain in anything like the numbers that Haitians studied in Paris. The migrations after World War II changed dramatically the number of West Indians in England, and established an exile community in London which then began to function very much like the black community in Paris a generation earlier. But until the results of that change could make themselves felt, the West Indian attitude was peculiar: metropolitan culture was felt and conceived only as it made itself felt *in the islands*. This attitude is preserved, for example, in the accounts of the Great Tradition we have already encountered, according to which the Great Tradition is represented as an impersonal institution, while the Little Tradition is embodied in human activity. By the same token the literary tradition was conceived, again, not as a habit of activity but as a heap of books – all of them published abroad.

There are some other divergences in the West Indies from the models sketched in the preceding chapter. For one thing, there is a much smaller ideological component. The development of these islands goes through the *prise de conscience* and the discovery of Africa, but the programmatic natures of Indigenism and Negritude have only oblique bearing; in this the long rejection of Marcus Garvey in the West Indies is symptomatic. Perhaps for the same reason there is surprisingly little generational conflict in the course of Anglophone literary history. Quarrels tend to occur within a generation. Cultural differences come into play in this regard, but the most fundamental cause has to do with the relative lateness of Anglophone literary beginnings. While modern literature in Haiti or Cuba can begin by rejecting its immediate past, West Indian literature had first to recover a past. Printing presses were operating in Jamaica and Barbados in the early eighteenth century, and in the much less developed territories of Trinidad and British Guiana in the nineteenth, and West Indian scholars are starting to unearth traces of earlier literary activity, but the first works that can plot any kind of continuity appear only in this century. This is finally what makes the West Indian situation unique: the fact that until very recently it was possible to question the very *existence* of a literature here.

Even a critic as committed to West Indian literature as Bruce King can be found to argue that "the concept of a West Indian literature is useful" because "no one country has yet had a sufficient number of major authors to be able to speak of a developed literature of its own."[1] We will return to the question at the end of this chapter; but to reach that point the first order of business is to trace individually the indigenous literary histories of the various West Indian territories.

JAMAICA

About the size of Connecticut, Jamaica is the largest of the English-speaking islands. Virtually all of its nearly three million inhabitants are of African descent. Its history has been, by Caribbean standards, extremely stable; seized from Spain in 1655, it remained a British colony until Independence in 1962. For that reason the island is predominantly Protestant in character. Jamaica's terrain varies dramatically; the high Blue Mountains in the East and the rugged karst topography of the aptly named Cockpit Country in the Northwest create small but virtually inaccessible interior areas. These have supported marronage (settlements of runaway slaves) since Spanish times, and have perhaps unobtrusively predisposed the Jamaican imagination for images of inward retreat and upward ascent. In any case Jamaica has a reputation as the most self-conscious and culturally the most advanced of West Indian nations – the "principle scene of West Indian self-awareness," as Henry Swanzy put it in 1956.[2]

The first poet of note, by current West Indian standards, is the Jamaican Claude McKay. In 1912 he published two volumes of dialect verse: *Songs of Jamaica* appeared in Kingston and *Constab Ballads* in London. In the same year he left his homeland and soon settled in New York. As a leader of the Harlem Renaissance he had tremendous influence in Haiti, in Paris, and among the poets of Negritude, who brought his work back to the Caribbean. At home his reputation has been rising steadily and he is now widely regarded as the first West Indian writer – though this acclaim is due chiefly to his novels and partly to local pride. McKay after all left Jamaica behind, and in his work its image is enhanced by a compelling nostalgia.

He also left behind, among the many literary and debating societies active at the time, a small circle of poets which would be institutionalized in 1923 as the Poetry League of Jamaica, under the leadership of J. E. Clare McFarlane. A subsidiary of the Empire Poetry League, as later the PEN Club was of International PEN, this group is the closest equivalent in the Anglophone Caribbean to the vilified colonial poets we have encountered elsewhere in the region. The League had no political orientation, and its output demonstrates more will than talent. Edward Baugh and Frank Collymore, two of the most humane West Indian critics, dismiss the group outright; more often it is treated with scarcely veiled contempt – the young Derek Walcott spoke of its "necrophilia."[3] But the character and role of the League, its will to produce distinctively Jamaican poetry, deserves some attention in a study like this, not least because the League rejected the moderns just as readily as it was rejected by them. McFarlane voiced the group's opinion in this regard in a series of newspaper articles written during 1929–31, then revised and finally published as a book in 1956 (one wonders about its reception in that very different era). Here as elsewhere in the region the year 1930 is recognized as a watershed, but though the book is entitled *A Literature in the Making*, it is more a commemoration of something lost than a prologue to a new literature. Noting the nationalism of the 1930s, the author observes that "the majority of the poets appraised here . . . grew to maturity in another kind of world; a world which had some appreciation of universal values."[4] The most important of these values seem to have been natural beauty and patriotism (one poet is praised as "an imperialist in the best sense of the word"). But all that is gone; McFarlane notes with evident regret that Jamaica is becoming "active and articulate,"[5] and points to the ill effect of this change on a new generation of poets. This is apparent for example in his guarded evaluation of McKay: "One may disagree with the philosophy expressed in most of his writings, but one cannot deny his outstanding gifts. His faults are very largely the faults of his age. His excellencies are his own."[6]

McFarlane particularly undervalues two poets of limited but genuine talent who spent long periods out of the island. Una Marson he finds disturbingly "modern," while W. A. Roberts is called "detached" as much for his Parnassian style as for his emigration. Yet while living abroad both of these poets worked for the wider recognition of Caribbean accomplishments, and after returning to Jamaica both played energetic roles in providing a future for Jamaican writing. Marson, the first considerable female poet in the region, worked as a publisher, journalist, and playwright both at home and abroad, and during the 1930s produced four books of verse. Based in New York for most of his life, Roberts presented the Caribbean in a dozen books of history, biography, and fiction, while he published three books of highly crafted verse, the last of them in Kingston. Wycliffe Bennett called him "the most un-English of Jamaican poets,"[7] but he is the first Anglophone poet to conceive the Caribbean position from a hemispheric perspective. Throughout the period of growing nationalism and race consciousness in the 1940s Roberts urged a vision of the Caribbean as an American Mediterranean, cultural successor to the Greek archipelago.[8] McFarlane had no such visions of the Jamaican or the Caribbean cultural future, and his final verdict seems truly to come from another kind of world: "Something of great value has been lost to the modern Jamaican. The faith of Tom Redcam and of Bunbury; the spiritual vision and certitude of Mrs. Hutton, the trustfulness of Nicholas, the calm and serenity of Lena Kent, the joy of Constance Hollar, the courage of Arabel Moulton-Barrett; these are positive qualities making for stability and direction in the life of the community."[9] That final clause merits respect; it is an early statement of the very Jamaican insistence that poetry have a social function. The rest of the passage, however, is a roll-call of the Poetry League, and with one exception the names mean nothing now, even in Jamaica.

The exception is Tom Redcam, the League's one great figure, if no great poet. Tom Redcam was the pen name of

Thomas MacDermot. Poet, novelist, and for twenty years the editor of the *Jamaica Times*, he was committed, though without much success, to the development of a national literature and a reading public. His projected series, "The All Jamaica Library," began publication in 1903, but failed after its fourth offering in 1909, and no similar effort was made for forty years. Redcam himself thought that the West Indian's chronic mistrust of local products was to blame.[10] Shortly after his death in 1933 Redcam was declared Poet Laureate of Jamaica by the League, and while the event may not have received much attention, McFarlane's explanation of the gesture sounds a sad note heard many times since: "In Jamaica we are afraid to ascribe greatness to any of our fellows. We seem to believe that greatness is the exclusive right of peoples other than ourselves, and we are inclined to discourage even the aspiration to it."[11] But though the All Jamaica Library failed, Redcam's efforts bore fruit in the younger writers he encouraged, especially McKay and Roberts. Recent critics dismiss Redcam as an uninspired purveyor of moral pastoral, but in his own time he was singled out as the first distinctively Jamaican poet, and the reason sounds thoroughly modern: he not only described his island's beauty, but was capable of conveying its character and especially the weight of its history.[12] More recent poetry is quite different from Redcam's, but this attention to history persists as an important criterion in its evaluation.

The poetry of the League was vapid, but not inconsequential. In what appears to be the very first published anthology to include West Indian poetry, a British anthology of colonial verse called *From Overseas* (1924), only Jamaican poets appear, and most of the nine included are recognizable as active members of the League. The group thus drew metropolitan attention, at least as a curiosity. McFarlane shortly presented the League's work in the first anthology of Jamaican poetry, *Voices From Summerland* (1929). As the title indicates, this book was intended for a metropolitan audience and at the same time, like Morpeau's Haitian anthology of 1925, marks the end of an era. Beyond this point the chief accomplishment of the

League was to serve as a reference point against which a succeeding generation of poets could define itself.

The Depression set off labor unrest throughout the Caribbean, and in 1938 disorders reached nearly revolutionary proportions in Kingston as in other cities on several islands. Out of this period emerged not only Jamaica's labor unions and political parties, but a group of writers with a new orientation, fully aware of social and political conditions, and closely associated with the new People's National Party. One link between literature and politics was the PNP journal *Public Opinion*, founded in 1937. Another was Jamaica's foremost political family, the Manleys. While Norman Manley set the British-socialist tone of the PNP and served as prime minister (an office later held by his son Michael), his wife Edna, a recognized sculptor and an indefatigable patron of the arts, was the force behind Jamaica's first entirely literary periodical. The first *Focus* (1943) introduced a new Jamaican poetry of protest and social consciousness, exemplified by the work of George Campbell, M. G. Smith, H. D. Carberry, and Basil McFarlane (son of Clare). Campbell is by far the most immediately compelling poet. His spare, powerful style still not only expresses but inspires anger at injustice and affection for the land and those who work it; Jamaican school-children continue to memorize some of his poems. After publishing his *First Poems* (1945), Campbell emigrated to New York and seemed silent until the publication of a second collection, *Earth Testament*, in 1982, which makes it clear that his best poems depend more on urgency of occasion than on natural talent. His corpus is very uneven, but at his best he demonstrates that poetry can be fully political without any aesthetic sacrifice, and that demonstration has proved crucial to nourishing the growth of West Indian poetry. M. G. Smith's more religious and rhetorical poetry had its influence on writers as different as Kamau Brathwaite and Anthony McNeill, but it never fully matured; he soon turned from poetry to what we have already seen as a related field of cultural awakening, anthropology. Yet as an anthropologist he continued to influence other poets; his formulations about the Caribbean's "plural society" provided a basis for Brathwaite's revisionary conception of the "creole" society.

After World War II, the tempo of events quickened. A second *Focus* appeared in 1948 with more from the PNP poets and several important new voices, among them Roger Mais (better known as a novelist), and A. L. Hendriks. During that year the British magazine *Life and Letters* published both a Jamaican issue and a West Indian issue. In 1949 Langston Hughes' influential anthology *The Poetry of the Negro* appeared in New York; it presented fifty-one West Indian poems, and all but seven were by Jamaicans (though most space was devoted to the "New Yorkers" Roberts and McKay). At the same time Clare McFarlane's second anthology, *A Treasury of Jamaican Poetry*, offered an unsettling marriage of the Poetry League and the *Focus* poets. In suggesting what distinguished this Jamaican poetry as a whole, McFarlane pointed squarely to what divided it: he saw it as based not only on images "drawn from exuberant tropical Nature, but also more subtly on a rhythm which proceeds from the very life of the people."[13] West Indian critics still praise in precisely those terms, but most of them would insist that the *absence* of such a rhythm is what condemns almost everything written before 1940. In 1948 the University College of the West Indies was established outside Kingston (the arts faculty began to function in 1950), extending its influence from the outset through extra-mural programs and the journal *Caribbean Quarterly*. But Kingston, growing rapidly and without plan into a modern city, soon came out to engulf the university. At about the same time the first free public libraries appeared, as did the first attempts to overcome widespread illiteracy, still affecting perhaps 80 percent of the population in the 1940s. One literary response to all this activity was the institution of the Pioneer Press to encourage local publication – Redcam's deferred dream. Publication began with four small books in 1950, but in spite of the editorial supervision of Marson and then Roberts, the project failed again, and its failure coincided with a large-scale migration to England that helped to make the 1950s the golden era of the West Indian novel.

This was the era too of Norman Manley's drive for a West Indian Federation, which he saw finally defeated by a popular referendum – by the very nationalism he had done so much to nourish. As a result, Jamaican Independence came in 1962 – the event was marked by a blandly representative *Independence Anthology* – but West Indian interdependence was a reality even if the Federation was not, and this was as true for literature as for economics or politics. Beginning in the 1960s poetry rises to a high level of ambition and accomplishment, but its frame of reference becomes decidedly West Indian rather than local. Anthologies of exclusively Jamaican work, for example, become rare after Independence. There were some collaborative efforts. Three poets published the texts of a reading as *Poems From 'On The Offbeat'* (1966), and with four others then published *Seven Jamaican Poets* (1971); four younger poets collaborated on *One Love* (1971). But there is no anthology in the strict sense until *New Poets From Jamaica*, assembled for the supranational journal *Savacou* in 1979. This was followed in 1980 by *Jamaica Woman*, and in 1987 by *From Our Yard: Jamaican Poetry Since Independence.* Together these three anthologies demonstrate the vitality of Jamaican poetry in the quarter-century since Independence, and draw particular attention to the accomplishment of more than a dozen women, poets of real stature, whose work did not begin to appear in book form until the 1980s.

The presence of a regional university in Jamaica has had considerable impact on local poetry. Walcott was a student there, and Brathwaite a professor; the work of these two giants, coming to prominence in the mid-1960s, galvanized the younger poets but had the effect of overshadowing their own near-contemporaries, the generation that falls between *Focus* and *New Poets From Jamaica*. This has been especially unfortunate in the case of several fine poets associated with the university – Edward Baugh, Pamela Mordecai, Mervyn Morris, Velma Pollard, and Dennis Scott – whose work deserves less distracted attention. The university has also played an important if unlikely role in legitimizing the Rastafarian movement, as a result of which a strong link has been forged between the country's intellectuals and what is probably the most important cultural force in Jamaica. The effect of this link has been extremely salutary for poetry, providing vital subjects for more academic poetry as it offers the encouragement of a receptive and informed audience to artists who earlier would have been dismissed as "folk poets" or cabaret artistes. The language, imagery, and fervor of Rastafarianism were the overwhelming influence on classic reggae and on the culture of Jamaican popular music generally, and the convergence has produced a generation of "cross-over" artists, who think of themselves as poets rather than lyricists, but draw upon the resources of musical performance. Most promising and most controversial has been the investigation of the oral rather than the print-oriented dimension of poetry, a project associated with the "dub poets" like Bongo Jerry, Michael Smith, Jean Breeze, and Valerie Bloom, but hardly limited to them. Indeed, the inspiration for all such work is Louise Bennett, who since the 1940s has built up an impressive body of poetry *written* in colloquial Jamaican for dramatic *oral* presentation. Pigeonholed as entertainment for twenty years, her work was not taken seriously until after Independence. This broadly based investment in the oral and performative aspects of poetry has generated new solutions to the chronic Jamaican difficulty of publication. While both the Institute of Jamaica and *Savacou* have begun to undertake traditional publishing ventures, the poets themselves have turned to broadsheets (Ras Dizzy), audio cassettes (Oku Onuora), and recorded performances with established musicians (Michael Smith with Light of Saba). The advertisement for a book of poems by Mutabaruka that appeared on Jamaican television in 1981 suggests that the accommodation of electronic media to the service of poetry is only just beginning.

TRINIDAD AND TOBAGO

In area and in population Trinidad is about half the size of Jamaica. Originally an unimportant Spanish outpost, Trinidad was only belatedly transformed into a sugar island in the 1780s, when it welcomed thousands of French planters unsettled by

the French and Haitian Revolutions and by capricious Napo-
leonic Caribbean policies. The British took over the island only
in 1797. The late development of the plantation system required
an extensive program of indenture, and as a result the island
has a very mixed population and culture. Loosely speaking, the
population is 40 percent African descent, 40 percent East
Indian. The official language is English, but it is distinguished
by a strong underpinning of French patois. The dominant
religious culture is Catholic, though religious practice is almost
equally divided among Catholic, Protestant, and Hindu. The
island has a fairly open topography, with low mountains in the
northern range but no interior in the Jamaican or Guyanese
sense. Oil reserves make Trinidad the most prosperous (and
sometimes prodigal) West Indian nation. The small island of
Tobago, Trinidad's partner in sovereignty, presents a sharp
contrast not only in size but in culture: it is uniformly black,
rural, and Protestant.

The earliest concentration of significant talent anywhere in
the West Indies materialized in the late 1920s in Trinidad as an
informal circle of intellectuals centered on Alfred Mendes and
C. L. R. James.[14] Their first activities were literary: Mendes
published a volume of poetry in 1925, James had a story
published in an English magazine in 1927, and Mendes followed suit two years later. In 1929–30 they together brought
out what they considered the first literary magazine in the
island's history, *Trinidad*.[15] Only two issues were printed, but
thanks perhaps to the uproar about its "obscenity," it sold
about a thousand copies – a hugh circulation by the standards
of the time and place. The torch of "defiant bohemianism" was
passed on, however, by one of those fortuitous encounters on
which the history of Caribbean literature seems to depend.[16] A
copy of *Trinidad* was sent to Albert Gomes, then an 18-year-old
studying in New York. Impressed, Gomes made contact with
the circle when he returned to Port of Spain in 1930, and the
result was a new magazine, *The Beacon*, which between 1931 and
1933 published twenty-eight issues of creative writing and
political commentary. James emigrated to England in 1932, and
Mendes to the United States in 1933. The young Gomes was

left to maintain the magazine almost singlehandedly, often using money his mother siphoned off from the household budget. There was a Marxist edge to *The Beacon* that sometimes brought the police – unlike the later Jamaican *Focus*, *The Beacon* routinely mixed poetry and politics. The foresight of its special "India Section," and the acuity of its editorials on black consciousness, federation, and church–state relations are still impressive, and the impression they made on their time is reflected in a circulation that reached 5,000. On its literary pages *The Beacon* introduced the poetry of Mendes and Gomes, along with forgettable work by a number of hands. But while most of this verse was in the Poetry League mold, with titles like "Moonlight" and "Exquisite Hour," the large number of contributors was a very good omen. On the whole too, the fiction published in *The Beacon* was far more mature than the poetry, anticipating an imbalance of quality that continues in Trinidad. The momentum of the group continued even after publication ceased, with Mendes's two novels *Pitch Lake* (1934) and *Black Fauns* (1935), James's *Minty Alley*, and what appears to be the island's very first anthology, *From Trinidad: Fiction and Verse* (1937), edited by Gomes.[17] Here again the poetry is disappointing; these are after all the same writers who contributed to *Trinidad* and *The Beacon*.

The end of the *Beacon* period coincided with Trinidad's political awakening in 1937–38, precipitated by Uriah Butler's oilfield strike. Parallel events in Jamaica at that time created the intellectual circle that spoke through *Focus* and *Public Opinion*, a circle that permanently transformed the face of Jamaican literature. Though the *Beacon* group seems at first a precocious version of the Jamaican circle, it was sufficiently different that it could not survive, as a group, the confrontation with raw politics. Perhaps the social base was too narrow, the habit of emigration too chronic, the time simply not ripe. Perhaps there was a failure of literary talent; the group's only lasting contribution was to fiction, and even that was left for others to pursue. But the unique strengths and weaknesses of the group derived from its special character; from the fact that it brought together not politicians and poets, but poet-politicians. In that time and place, as Mendes recalls, "we were contradictions in terms."[18] The *Beacon* writers conceived of themselves as a cosmopolitan enclave on a provincial island, and they made it their business to be aware of the tides that swept nationalism and social upheaval into the Caribbean. Reacting to the vices of their class much as their Haitian contemporaries did, they aimed to be not mimics but masters of assimilation; not to suffer assimilation but to forge it into a creative act. It was in that light that James could say, "the West Indian native, in order to establish his own identity, must seek ideas and develop conceptions about history and the fine arts that are way beyond what the British and the others are doing."[19] In this period they turned to American stylistic models for their literary leverage, and to a shadowy "Africa" for metaphysical leverage, but at the same time they partly received, partly contrived for themselves, the training of European intellectuals. This underlay their vision of the Caribbean's potential; so James (not unlike his Jamaican counterpart, W. A. Roberts) saw Trinidad and Barbados in particular as incipient Greek city-states, as Italian Renaissance towns just awakening to self-consciousness.[20] James saw this as equally the root of their politics: "In my youth we lived according to the tenets of Matthew Arnold; we spread sweetness and light, and we studied the best that there was in literature in order to transmit it to the people – as we thought, the poor, backward West Indian people."[21]

Like most of the *Beacon* group, C. L. R. James in the 1920s saw McKay as the region's literary trail-blazer, George Padmore and Marcus Garvey as his political counterparts; in the 1930s James became a Trotskyite, and when war in Europe was imminent, he published *The Black Jacobins* (1938), his cogent history of the Haitian revolution. It preceded Césaire's *Cahier* by a year and is no less significant for the history of Caribbean self-consciousness. Together they are the first assertions that the region deserved intimate and passionate attention, that it was a real place with a real history and a people of its own. Not the least remarkable was James's insistence that African emancipation was part of the coming social revolution, and that "the road to West Indian national identity lay through Africa."[22] In the decades after *The Black Jacobins*, James proved himself to be the one lasting contribution of the *Beacon* group, embodying in his own person the leading edge of West Indian consciousness as it made the passage from the old world of the 1920s to the present.

For Trinidad, World War II meant a virtual invasion by American troops and American dollars, ushering in a period of rapid growth for the society as a whole. But poetry lay fallow, and after the war the long ascendancy of the Trinidadian novel began in earnest – nowhere else in the West Indies had the success of the novel so constantly eclipsed poetry. The anthology *Papa Bois* (1947) included several writers whose work had appeared in Gomes's anthology of 1937 and even in *The Beacon*, but most of the poetry is still of the Poetry League variety.[23] C. A. Thomasos is represented by four poems while the other contributors have only one or two. Unless he was simply more prolific, this must indicate regard for his work, but what distinguishes it from the rest is only a characteristic petulance, perhaps at the time perceived as toughness, in imitation of the strengths of American Modernism. By far the most ambitious and rewarding poem in this small collection is "Island Tints," one of only a handful of poems written by the Guyanese Edgar Mittelholzer during a full career as a novelist. Long and cranky but playful, the poem meditates on color in its social, philosophical, and even painterly aspects, as this account of Grenada seen from the air illustrates:

> A body, as seen to-day from aloft,
> stacked with many eyes; carmine, terra-cotta,
> buff and brown; and in shape rectangular;
> results of the constructive manipulations –
> just habitations – of irrepressible,
> depressible, competitive humankind.[24]

Papa Bois marks the end of an era; decades passed without another anthology of Trinidadian poetry. The lack of local journals during this period was also damaging, though a few poets managed to publish volumes of their own work, and eventually some outlet was provided by the BBC and the regional magazines. The *Guardian* newspaper played a supporting role; among the poets who worked there at one time or another were Lamming, Mittelholzer, Roach, and Walcott. But poetic activity was circumscribed, and there was little recognition from the outside world where, for the most part, "West Indian poetry" still meant "Jamaican poetry." The *Life and Letters* anthology of 1948 included only three poems from Trinidad; Langston Hughes's *The Poetry of the Negro* (1949) just two. Of the collections that appeared a decade later to celebrate Federation only that of *Caribbean Quarterly* adequately represented Trinidadian efforts, including the work of nine poets. Even recent critical literature overlooks Trinidadian poetry of this period, though certainly figures like H. M. Telemaque, Eric Roach, and (somewhat later) Ian McDonald deserve attention as the island's first significant poets.

One kind of Trinidadian poetry did prosper during these years: the popular poetry of calypso. It too had experienced a golden age before World War II, but no decline followed; the events of the war provided new material for verse, while surplus oil drums led to the creation of the steelband as a powerful adjunct to calypso performance and to the culture from which it arises.[25] From being looked down upon and even outlawed, calypso became Trinidad's most democratic institution, and with the appearance of Sparrow, greatest of calypsonians, the lyrics reached a level of sophistication that justified treating calypso as poetry.[26] Indeed, it is arguable that calypso has served as an important source of energy for more literary poetry since Independence.

In any case, 1962 saw Independence and the good omen of a borrowed glory: Derek Walcott's first mature collection, *In a Green Night*. It was welcomed as bringing an end to "a simple mindless romanticism, a weak historicism, over-rhetorical protest and sterile abstraction"[27] – the quotation is a deft catalogue of the chronic vices of West Indian poetry as a whole. Two years later Clifford Sealy's *Voices* (1964–66) began publication. It was the first important literary magazine in Trinidad since *The Beacon*, and introduced the poets of a new generation, chief among them Roger McTair, Judy Miles, and Wayne Brown. But it is symptomatic of the island's long poetic drought that at least two significant poets of an older generation, Victor Questel and Anson Gonzalez, began to publish only after these younger poets. The primary factor here was the political atmosphere in those Black Power days, which brought together several groups of writers and intellectuals, finally mobilized by the February Revolution of 1970. Out of this political crisis came *The Beacon*'s true heir, *Tapia*. Now called *The Trinidad and Tobago Review*, it combines political initiative with consistently high standards for poetry and criticism. In the large group loosely associated with the journal Trinidad finally has the human base for a rich and varied poetry, appearing not only in *Tapia*, but in a number of small magazines spawned by the same events, of which the most important have been *Kairi* and *New Voices*. At the same time Trinidad has become a center for literary criticism, through the combined resources of *Tapia*, the *Trinidad Guardian*, and the University of the West Indies campus at St. Augustine supporting and making available the work of Rohlehr, Ramchand, Questel, Gonzalez, Wayne Brown, and Walcott.

Since the 1970s, Trinidadian poetry has developed a character of its own, distinguishable by its concerns and style as a nucleus within the extended family of West Indian poetry. Yet despite the vitality of social life that Port of Spain would seem to provide, Trinidadian poets often seem as isolated from one another as writers from a much smaller island. Anson Gonzalez continues to function as the indefatigable heart of the enterprise; he is still active as poet, editor of *The New Voices* (since 1973) and general facilitator. If Gonzalez is the Trinidadian Collymore, the veteran performance poet Paul Keens-Douglas has played a role analogous to that of Louise Bennett in Jamaica (though the exploration of local language as a medium for poetry is much less prominent in Trinidad than in Jamaica). But among the mainstream poets Wayne Brown, whose work was first perceived as too imitative of Walcott, has produced only a small body of poetry, and many of the best writers from several generations live abroad, prominent among them Ian

McDonald (Guyana), Faustin Charles (Britain), Amryl Johnson (Britain), Dionne Brand (Canada), and Claire Harris (Canada). Young writers in particular depend on anthologies for exposure, and the astonishing fact is that there has been no general anthology since *Papa Bois* in 1947. One attempt to compile one in the mid-1970s was abandoned, though not before it had inspired an encyclopedic essay on the history and context of recent Trinidadian poetry by Rohlehr, which was to have served as its introduction.[28] In 1990 an anthology of poems by women of Trinidad and Tobago brought together an impressive array of two dozen poets – it constitutes in effect half of the comprehensive collection Trinidad still lacks.[29]

GUYANA

A South American country with twice the area of Cuba, twenty times that of Jamaica, Guyana has been described as a West Indian island inadvertently attached to a continent.[30] Most of the population of less than a million lives on the narrow coastal strip running eastward from Georgetown; this is the "island." Behind it is the vast hinterland responsible for the unique character of the country and incidentally of its literature. The landscape of jungle, savannah, and high plateau that stretches for 400 miles to the Brazilian border challenges the imagination. This is not an interior such as Jamaica has, but a frontier, the Wild West of the West Indies, a land of pioneers, gold rushes, and hostile Indians. The rivers that flow through it are broader at their mouths than several West Indian islands are long, and have had a substantial impact on the country's writers. Guyana suffered a turbulent colonial history at the hands of the Dutch, English, and French; the epic of that history already exists in Edgar Mittelholzer's melodramatic *Kaywana* novels. Various settlements were finally united as British Guiana only in 1831, and the country achieved a difficult Independence in 1966. Officially Guyana boasts six races; just over half the population is East Indian, about a third African, and in the interior there is a significant minority, perhaps 5 percent, of Amerindians.

As elsewhere, 1930 approximately marks a turning-point for the country's literary history. While a student at Cambridge, Norman Cameron realized that he knew more about England than about his own country; it was the typical *prise de conscience* of the intellectual sent to the metropolis.[31] He compiled the colony's first anthology, *Guianese Poetry 1831–1931*, after returning home to find that the hundred-year period had produced only eight publications by local poets. The scope of their work is limited to bland nature poetry, imperial patriotism, and religious verse. Egbert Martin (known as "Leo") is considered the most important nineteenth-century poet, but too many of his poems follow an identical pattern, beginning with generalized observation of nature ("Moonrise," "The Sea") and ending with God. His ethnographic poems, such as "The Negro Village" or "The Hammock Maker, an Indian Eclogue," are striking in their time and context, but while compassionate they hold their subjects at a great distance. They can hardly bear comparison with, for example, the anti-slavery poems of a relatively minor poet like William Cowper, writing in England a full century earlier. Henry Dalton's poem "The Carib's Complaint" fares much better in the same comparison. It is a dramatic account of an Amerindian who chooses suicide because "He cannot bend low like his white brother slave."[32] Dalton's reputation as "the first poet to describe local life and nature"[33] is justified in the poem's closely observed details, as in the precisely differentiated physical movements mentioned in these lines from the same poem:

> I see the red curlews in columns fly by,
>> And parrots in pairs flying tardily home;
> I hear the wild ducks screeching shrill as they fly,
>> While plover and pigeon in flocks round me roam.

Among the anthology's younger poets can be found an increasing interest in local weather and climate (Harold Moore, "The Dry Season" and "The North Wind" [both 1907]), in dialect (S. E. Wills, "Before and After," 1910) and in folklore (Cameron's own "All is Fair in Love" is a version of a folktale). Even if the collection as a whole supports rather than contradicts A. J. Seymour's reference to "the silence and desert of those years between 1840 and 1930," it remains true that no other West Indian territory can boast a heritage of so much early poetry.[34]

The prolific work of Walter Lawrence in the 1930s marks the end of the pre-modern period. He is now regarded as a dedicated but colonized poet: "His language was too coloured by Wordsworth and Swinburne . . . his themes – even his Guianese themes – were too impressed by memories of how men had written of the old temperate lands."[35] An anthology of verse in English from the East Indian community appeared surprisingly early (C. E. J. Ramcharitar-Lalla's *Anthology of Indian Verse*, 1934), and Seymour published his own first volume in 1937, but the first effectual step toward the steady cultivation of Guyanese literature came only with the founding of a magazine in 1945. *Kyk-Over-Al* emerged from the British Guiana Writers' Association, but it was more than a literary magazine. Under the purposeful editorial guidance of Seymour it set itself broad cultural goals: "*Kyk-Over-Al* we hope will be an instrument to help forge a Guianese people, to make them conscious of their intellectual and spiritual possibilities."[36] As in other early periodicals like *The Beacon* and *Bim* there is much editorial carping in *Kyk-Over-Al* about the inadequacy of contributed material, but *Kyk* is remarkable for the high quality of its poetry from the very beginning. Thanks largely to the work of Wilson Harris, Martin Carter, and Seymour himself, the magazine's poetry was consistently better and more forward-looking than its fiction – a reversal of the usual West Indian pattern. *Kyk-Over-Al* made pioneering efforts in literary criticism, and opened its pages to writers of the whole region, even publishing translations of works from the French Antilles. As that initiative suggests, its liberal outlook was closely tied to the dream of West Indian Federation; when that dream failed *Kyk-Over-Al* ceased publication in 1961 after twenty-eight issues.[37]

A. J. Seymour was for half a century the patron and chief mover of Guyanese literature, and *Kyk-Over-Al* was very much the embodiment of his own thinking. In its pages Seymour subscribed to a Spenglerian view of the Westering of culture:

"the accident of forced immigration into the Caribbean has isolated us to the impact of a dying civilization so that we can pass on some flaming torch higher up the line."[38] He saw that the era of easy identification with the metropolis was ceasing, and he even saw that the process of revolt from it could bring on, as in Negritude, an unproductively negative phase.[39] In the face of that threat Seymour insisted that the impulse to revolt against the old order must be transmuted into attachment to one's immediate surroundings: "we must make an act of possession somehow of our environment and the faster the better."[40] The conflicting intellectual alternatives that presented themselves in those days were apparent even to an outside observer, Michael Swan:

There is some attempt among the Creole intelligentsia to be conscious of the country beyond the coast . . . But in the main the intellectuals are more properly concerned with hammering out the question of the form their Guianese or West Indian culture should take, with producing a civilization based on that of Europe, yet not a sycophantic copy. Thus, unlike the English [in Guyana], they cannot yet afford the luxury of inquiries into Indian folklore or a passionate feeling about the beauties of the Guiana forests.[41]

Yet "the country beyond the coast" was the foundation of Guyana's individuality, and for many of the country's writers the investigation of its imaginative resources was no "luxury" but an essential part of the process of forging a distinct national culture. The literature of Guyana more than any other in the West Indies reflects Seymour's insistence in its characteristic engagement with the land, its people, and its history.

The early years of the decade fired the crucible of Guyanese national consciousness, in which the active if narrow intellectual life of Georgetown, crystallized by *Kyk-Over-Al*, combined with extraordinary political events: the victory of a Jagan–Burnham coalition in 1953 followed by the arrival of British troops and the suspension of the brand-new Constitution. One activist, Martin Carter, was detained in 1953, and his *Poems of Resistance* (1954) established him as a poet of political conscience more accomplished and probing than Jamaica's George Campbell. At the same time the not-yet-novelist Wilson Harris published

Eternity to Season, and *Kyk-Over-Al* brought out an *Anthology of Guianese Poetry*. Except for *Fourteen Guianese Poems for Children* in 1953, this was the first anthology since Cameron's, and A. J. Seymour provided a worthy successor to that inaugural collection, assembling more than a hundred poems by forty-six poets, chief among them Jan Carew, Martin Carter, Harris, Seymour, and Ivan Van Sertima. Another of Seymour's projects, the Miniature Poets Series, ushered in the 1950s with small collections by poets from throughout the region.

Succeeding years brought a disintegrating political situation. The split of the ruling party (the PPP) into Jagan and Burnham factions along racial lines led to virtual race war between blacks and East Indians in the early 1960s, while the failure of the Federation eliminated the alternative to bitter self-determination. Riots and fires throughout Georgetown in 1962 were followed by another British occupation, and by an incongruous independence.

Until this time Guyanese literature was hardly known outside the country, and it was predictably in London during the 1960s that other West Indians began to encounter Guyanese writers on a regular basis. But at home the steady translation of the nation's experience into words continued with, of course, the constant encouragement of Seymour. A new journal, *Kaie*, carried on the work of *Kyk-Over-Al* from 1965 to 1973. There were Guyanese anthologies in 1968 and 1971.[42] When Georgetown hosted the international Caribbean Arts Festival (Carifesta) in 1972, Seymour produced the commemorative anthology, *New Writing in the Caribbean*, and managed to include thirteen Guyanese poets, many of them from the younger generation. Yet another anthology, *Independence 10; Guyanese Writing 1966–76*, presented the work of sixty poets, many of them for the first time, and appended an impressive bibliography of creative work for the first decade of independence. This bibliography is a reminder that Guyana has made a significant contribution to Caribbean critical literature as well, from the early efforts of Cameron and Seymour to the recent work of scholars and thinkers like Harris, Rohlehr, Gilkes, Dathorne, and Carew.

The country's commitment to critical thought has been institutionalized in the annual Mittelholzer Memorial Lectures which since 1968 have consistently inspired major theoretical statements from such invited speakers as Seymour, Denis Williams, Martin Carter, Harris, and Michael Gilkes. Through the National History and Arts Council the government has played an important part in sponsoring and publishing literary work. It must be added, however, that most of these critics have left the country, and that the Mittelholzer lectures are more highly regarded at the UWI than in Georgetown. Wilson Harris, for example, returned in 1970 as the internationally recognized author of nine novels to address an audience of about twenty.[43] This is certainly one of the reasons why Harris lives in London; Guyanese landscape and history inspire a literature that Guyanese society cannot yet fully support. The country's literature first became known in the work of a prodigious generation, but while Seymour and Carter continued to write substantial poetry, for a time the inheritors seem few and scattered. Guyana has produced, by West Indian standards, a surfeit of anthologies. Among the many poets represented, however, there are only a few clearly individuated voices besides Carter and Seymour: to my ear Wordsworth McAndrew, Milton Williams (living in England), and Ian McDonald (born Trinidadian). Happily, in recent years many new poets, not all of them young, have begun to be published.

The conditions of life in Guyana have been difficult for decades, and a staggering number of the country's poets live abroad, but most of them continue to write about – and very much *for* – Guyana. This is certainly true of John Agard (UK), Cyril Dabydeen (Canada), Mark McWatt (Barbados), Grace Nichols (UK), and Fred D'Aguiar (USA), to mention only the most familiar names. Similarly, though Sasenarine Persaud lives in Canada and David Dabydeen in England, their poetry joins that of Guyanese residents like Mahadai Das and Rooplall Monar in carrying forward something unique in the Anglophone Caribbean, an almost independent tradition of work (dating back to before the 1930s) that draws explicitly on the East Indian cultural heritage.

BARBADOS

Unlike most Caribbean islands, Barbados was formed by coral, not by volcanic action. As a result it is relatively flat and dry, its open topography densely planted with sugar. Barbados has had a remarkably quiet history: uncontestedly British since the seventeenth century, resolutely Protestant, and now one of the most densely populated and most literate nations in the world. Its 300,000 inhabitants are, like Jamaica's, almost entirely of African descent, but nationalism in Barbados has until very recently been expressed as pride in the country's role in the Empire. Barbados is still "little England" in many respects, though there are those who, rephrasing the epithet, call it "a Victorian outpost."[44]

The country's literary history is similarly placid. The first known native-born poet was Nathaniel Weekes, who published in the mid-eighteenth century. Better known is Matthew Chapman, whose *Barbadoes, and Other Poems* was published in 1833. The first books of poetry printed on the island by Barbadian authors appear around 1900 (it is worth noting that the first book of dialect poetry, Edward Cordle's *Overheard*, appeared as early as 1903),[45] but the habit of local publication and indeed of local writing can hardly be said to begin before the 1930s. The Depression brought labor unrest to Barbados as to the rest of the region, and this was followed by the island's first concerted literary activity.[46] But this activity was not associated with trade unionism or a political party, as in Jamaica, nor with a political philosophy, as in Trinidad. In the spirit of "little England" it grew instead out of men's clubs that were civic rather than political in outlook, clubs dedicated to presenting Barbadians as worthy of self-government, rather than acting for it.[47]

From 1931 to 1934 the Forum Club published *The Forum Quarterly*, edited by Gordon Bell and later resurrected as *The Forum Magazine* in 1943–45. The *Quarterly*'s literary horizon was impressive; in its first issues it published articles by Bell on Langston Hughes and Claude McKay which included some of their poems. Of unforeseeably greater consequence was the formation in 1935 of the Young Men's Progressive Club, which three years later turned out a small magazine, *YMPC Journal*, that offered light creative writing, topical comment, and club news.[48] This journal continued to appear until 1942, when several members began to conceive of a more ambitious publication. Two of these, E. L. Cozier and W. Therold Barnes, enlisted the aid of their friend Frank Collymore, a schoolmaster neither young (he was already 50) nor a member of the Club. From this collaboration *Bim* was born, its first issue appearing in December of that year, perhaps because Christmas was already the traditional time for literary supplements. In the early days, *Bim* was buoyant and frivolous, full of quizzes, nonsense verse, and anecdotal fillers; in 1944 a prize of 10 dollars was offered for the best ghost story, and in 1946 *Bim* was still trying to avoid undue seriousness; a small sampler of poems by a dozen West Indian writers was introduced like this: "We've put all the poems together, so that they may be the more easily skipped."[49] The "Editors' Notebook" in several early numbers repeats delicately phrased advice about how to write an acceptable story or poem (the same kind of advice was appearing, at about the same time, in *The Beacon* and *Kyk-Over-Al*). After the war, attractive and promising collections came from Collymore (*Flotsam*, 1948), H. A. Vaughan (*Sandy Lane and Other Poems*, 1945) and A. N. Forde, whose lyric poetry in *Canes by the Roadside* (1951) has a particularly sharp political edge. Collymore continued to publish, building up a significant if sometimes self-deprecating body of work, but neither Vaughan nor Forde produced another volume.

Bim went on to become a regional magazine almost by accident. A story by Edgar Mittelholzer was submitted from a Bridgetown address for *Bim* no. 5, and the editors only later learned that Mittelholzer was a Guyanese living in Trinidad, and the author of a published novel (*Corentyne Thunder*). Mittelholzer proved to be a staunch supporter; his work appeared in nearly every issue for ten years. The link to Trinidad was reinforced after the war, largely through the efforts of George Lamming, a former student of Collymore's. *Bim* no. 9 (1948) includes contributions by several Trinidadians: E. A. Carr,

Cecil Herbert, H. M. Telemaque, and Ruby Waithe. With the next issue in 1949 *Bim* comes of age as a journal for the region. Its cover is unique in listing contributors by country, and the representation is impressive: Lamming and five others from Trinidad, Gloria Escoffery and A. L. Hendriks from Jamaica, Derek Walcott and Harry Simmons from St. Lucia, A. J. Seymour from British Guiana, as well as a dozen Barbadians. *Bim* no. 11 included the work of seventeen poets from seven West Indian territories, and no. 12 includes several pieces on the art and literature of the French Caribbean. The scope of the magazine broadened beyond stories and poems to include critical essays and features such as Collymore's "Glossary of Words and Phrases of Barbadian Dialect," ongoing from 1952. During the late 1950s *Bim* almost died, in the midst of its success, of a financial condition that has since become chronic. *Bim* has never projected a political or even an aesthetic party line. As Collymore wrote in 1964, "If *Bim* has any policy other than that of fostering creative writing, it has been one of encouragement."[50] This hospitality has been rewarded for half a century by the presence in its pages of nearly every West Indian with literary ambitions. Until its publication became intermittent it was, in effect, the journal of record for the region; the best of local publication, particularly in criticism, was eventually reprinted in *Bim*. Collymore, in maintaining *Bim* as an open rostrum, earned himself a name as the greatest enabler of West Indian literature. He has literally been the teacher of some writers, figuratively the teacher of many others, and his lesson has never been an ideology or a philosophy, but the simple injunction to write, to hector one another into writing, and to provide one another with occasions. His antecedents were men like Redcam, de Lisser, and Gomes. Only A. J. Seymour and Anson Gonzalez come close to being his equals, and his likeliest successor is Edward Brathwaite, who demonstrates his aptitude for the role in his extensive work as publisher and bibliographer – and of course in his editing of *Savacou*'s 1973 "Tribute to Frank Collymore."

Like Collymore himself, and perhaps because of him, literary Barbados seems to have sacrificed itself to the larger interest of the West Indies. It has given to the region Lamming and Brathwaite, but both have for the most part lived elsewhere. In fulfilling its broader mission *Bim* itself has ceased to be the organ of Barbadian literary activity, but no other journal has yet arisen to take on that role. Even more surprising, there has never been an anthology devoted exclusively to Barbadian writing. Brathwaite's annotated bibliography, *Barbados Poetry: A Check List*, is the closest thing to a survey of the island's writing, though it is hardly that; in the other islands such reflective essays have been produced with some regularity since the 1930s. But Barbadian poets do continue to write, and to write well. Though publication is uncertain, the presence of the university at Cave Hill since the early 1960s and of organizations like the Barbados Writers Workshop have offered special support to younger writers, among them Michael Foster, Dennis Foster, Anthony Hinkson, and Tony Kellman. Since the late 1960s Brathwaite has played a crucial role in the emergence of performance poetry throughout the West Indies, so it is curious that the first significant performer of poetry in Barbados, Bruce St. John, seems to owe a greater stylistic debt to Louise Bennett of Jamaica, and to the calypsonians of Trinidad, than to his countryman.

ST. LUCIA AND THE SMALLER ISLANDS

The situation of writers in the smaller islands (and in mainland Belize) is rather different. For poetry as for other arts there is an analogue to critical mass; the *number* of poets, regardless of quality, seems to increase the number of significant poems produced, by providing both the goad of competition and the reassurance that great poems do not come solely or even dependably from some remote race of great poets, but from working writers. With short-lived magazines and the likelihood of only private publication in short runs, the smaller islands can support writers to a limited extent, but they cannot be expected to sustain a literature. As a result, most writers migrate to seek nourishment elsewhere. That "elsewhere" is often another country, but the anecdotal evidence suggests that for poets more than for other writers the world of books itself becomes such an elsewhere, "another life" to which the budding author resorts. In several autobiographical essays, Derek Walcott has left a particularly well-documented picture of that response to the harsh climate and thin soil in which his own career began, and this can stand as typical of small island experience during the crucial formative years of West Indian literature.[51] There were no local models Walcott could turn to, and indeed he seems not to have sought out any. Instead, in describing the roots of his vocation he speaks of his parents and their circle, certain mentors, and his voracious reading, but he mentions only one West Indian author as a motivating factor: the Jamaican George Campbell. Walcott's father Warwick, a civil servant who died shortly after the poet's birth, was the "moving spirit" of a middle-class cultural circle. He wrote some verse, was an accomplished watercolorist (as is Derek), and encouraged others, including Harry Simmons, to paint. The circle of talk, music, and amateur theatricals was carried on after his death by his wife. Looking back, the poet admires the spiritual strength of "this circle of self-civilizing, courteous people in a poverty-ridden, cruelly ignored colony living by their own certainties."[52] From this circle, Simmons emerged as the most important influence in Walcott's development, and while his earliest writing drew an immediate and repressive response from the hierarchy of the Catholic Church, the role of the particular Irish brothers who were his teachers and later his co-workers at St. Mary's College was much more supportive – they seem to have responded to Walcott's vision of his colonized situation more as Irishmen than as clerics.

Thanks to Derek Walcott (and his playwright brother Roderick), St. Lucia has achieved great literary visibility. But they are not solitary phenomena. There is also a "third wave" after Walcott: Kendel Hippolyte and Robert Lee have published between them several highly distinctive and original volumes, while other poets, such as McDonald Dixon and Jane King, have produced rewarding if less visible work. The *Confluence* anthology collects the work of nine poets all approximately of the generation born in the 1950s (the title seems an implicit rejection of the term "influence" – these poets pointedly do not present themselves as descendants of Walcott).[53] There are St. Lucian poets and St. Lucian poems (and the periodicals *Link* and *Konte*, and a hospitable newspaper *The Voice*); is there a self-sustaining literature? A literature that depends on a handful of individuals is necessarily precarious, but if the younger writers can stay, and if their promise is fulfilled, then in the wake of Walcott's accomplishments, and with his continuing investment in the culture of his homeland, there might be created a setting for writing acknowledged by the society as its own. Certainly St. Lucia is better situated than most nations of its size for such an outcome.[54]

At the other end of the Caribbean Basin is Belize, like Guyana (though on a much smaller scale) a *continental* West Indian nation with an island-sized population approaching 200,000. Its cultural situation is potentially very complex, and there is a local anthology (*Belizean Poets*, 1965), but so far only two poets are at all familiar to readers elsewhere in the region: George Price (for decades the prime minister of the country) and Raymond Barrow.[55] The Windward Islands, such as St. Vincent and Grenada, with populations of the order of 100,000, have indeed produced noteworthy poets, but those known outside the island have left it, often permanently (from St. Vincent especially Shake Keane and Daniel Williams; from Grenada Syl Lowhar, now in Trinidad, and Paul Layne, who died prematurely in Barbados). There is a comprehensive poetry anthology from St. Vincent, but many of the almost twenty poets, including the anthology's editor, live abroad, and the book itself is published in Canada.[56] The much smaller Leeward Islands have correspondingly smaller populations, ranging down from about 70,000 in Dominica to only a few thousand in Montserrat. There is often no local center to support poetry, quite literally no place for it to appear, in print or otherwise, except perhaps in newspapers. As a rule when writers from these islands emerge it is in London. E. A. Markham from Montserrat and Paul St. Vincent from Antigua are typical – both have lived in England since youth. Writers who stay on in the small islands tend to be very active on the local scene in a variety of roles, therefore writing less poetry, and less likely to be known away from home. Howard Fergus of Montserrat is representative of the breed: though he seems to have only one collection of poems, published locally, he has pursued a busy career in politics and education while writing frequently on local history and culture, and has edited his island's first anthology, *Flowers Blooming Late: Poems from Montserrat* (Montserrat, 1984). St. Martin presents a characteristically Caribbean anomaly: one side of this small island belongs to the Netherlands Antilles, the other is part of France, yet the one publishing local poet, Lasana Sekou, writes in English. Another anomaly that reflects the established traffic patterns of the colonial period: the Bahamas have produced some poetry, primarily under sponsorship of the college there, but this work is usually regarded as Caribbean literature only by Bahamians. Paul Gilroy's concept of a "Black Atlantic" – a model based on somewhat different traffic patterns – draws attention to the fact that Anglophone writings (like Anglophone persons) circulate in that space, defined fundamentally by shared language, rather than in a strictly Caribbean space, defined by contiguity and shared history. As a result of the post-war migrations, a period of intensive circulation that consolidated the domain of the Black Atlantic, West Indians have now established "colonies" of their own in London, Toronto, Brooklyn, Miami, and elsewhere, some of which are now beginning to develop cultural autonomy. There is certainly already a distinct "Black British" literature. This colonization has been carried out, however, by people who think of themselves as West Indian, rather than specifically Jamaican, Trinidadian, or Guyanese. That fact, taken together with the need of the inhabitants of the smaller islands to make contact with something larger, something more capable of sustaining his or her work, underscores the need to return now to the question of the *West Indies* as cultural unit.

THE WEST INDIES

The British often and early spoke of their West Indian colonies as a whole, but the Anglophone Caribbean's first projection of itself as a cultural unit was perhaps Jacob J. Thomas's *Froudacity*,

West Indian Fables Explained (Trinidad, 1889), a response to James Anthony Froude's notorious *The English in the West Indies* (1887). To Froude's condemnations – "There are no people there in the true sense of the word, with a character and purpose of their own" – Thomas opposed the potential of the "extra-Africans": "ten millions in the Western hemisphere, dispersed so widely over the surface of the globe, apt apprentices in every conceivable department of civilized culture."[57] Thomas, who was secretary and chief contributor to the *Trinidad Monthly* and a leader in the formation of the Trinidad Athenaeum in 1872, also produced *The Theory and Practice of Creole Grammar* (1869), still an important text on the subject. His work provides the germ of every positive, forward-looking analysis of the inherited West Indian situation, just as Froude is standard-bearer for such pessimists as Naipaul.

The late nineteenth century saw the British Empire in its prime, and saw the Anglophone Caribbean genuinely proud to be a part of the enterprise. Even British expansion in Africa was seen at the time through British eyes; Kitchener, Gordon, and Rhodes were the heroes of the story, and the West India Regiment fought beside the British in the Ashanti War. The empire reached its fullest extent as a result of World War I, and in the Caribbean the war was the occasion for fervid Imperial patriotism, reflected in much of the poetry of the period. We have already noted factors arising in the aftermath of the war that encouraged increasingly local loyalties; but perhaps the most striking sign of change was the revolt of the West India Regiment in Italy in 1918 and related disturbances led by demobilized soldiers in Trinidad and British Honduras during 1919.[58]

The earliest discussion known to me in which the term "West Indian literature" is taken for granted is in the pages of *The Beacon* in 1933, though the point of the article is that such a thing does not yet exist, and cannot be wished into existence:

The leaders of the literary club movements hope by their childish pranks to bring about a "West Indian literature." The fallacy of this vain hope is evident. When the West Indies attains a literature it will not be through the efforts of any one body of persons but through the appearance of one or maybe two persons who will produce art of a high literary standard . . . The day will come when we, like America, will produce our Walt Whitman; then, and only then will the movement towards an art and language indigenous to our spirit and environment commence.[59]

The sentiment itself is characteristic of the West Indies; it reflects a facet of the old Anglophone distaste for overt ideology and becomes itself almost ideological in the *laissez faire* editorial policy of *Bim*. But if the sentiment seems to go against the grain of literary development in the rest of the Caribbean, it should not obscure the fact that, while literary groups cannot create a literature, they seem an essential condition for its emergence – a fact corroborated by nothing so much as the role of *Bim* in West Indian literary history. Among other things, the early literary clubs began the consolidation of an audience for indigenous literature.

A less prickly editorial stance was adopted by *The Beacon*'s coeval, the *West Indian Review* begun in 1934 by Esther Chapman, an Englishwoman resident in Jamaica. The *Review* bears a striking resemblance to another of its contemporaries, Paulette Nardal's *Revue du monde noir*: accepting material in English, French, and Spanish, the *Review* published fiction and poetry as well as historical and ethnographic essays, and its stated objectives were, first, to break down barriers between the Anglophone territories in preparation for a future West Indian Federation, and secondly to establish "bonds of closer intellectual union" linking "all the territories of the Caribbean and Central America."[60] As already remarked, Chapman was English; Gomes came to *The Beacon* from study in America; most of the pioneers of a West Indian perspective, like C. L. R. James and W. A. Roberts, spent long periods abroad, and of the early visionaries only A. J. Seymour and Collymore resided permanently in the region. Broader experience seems to have been important for the formulation of a broader perspective. It was metropolitan education that made it possible to envision the Caribbean in terms of Greek city-states, the Italian Renaissance, the Westward progress of poetry or civilization. But it would be a mistake to dismiss these as borrowed ideas, early instances of cultural mimicry, for they function not as impositions but as projections; they are convenient means of articulating and communicating a prior, and quite original, vision of Caribbean potential. All of these writers shared a sense that something was about to happen in the Caribbean, a sense of enormous accumulated energy. Men like James, Roberts, Seymour, and others later, independently conceived it their own duty to communicate their sense of imminent growth both in the region and outside it.

It is in the 1940s and particularly after World War II that the West Indies emerges as both a political and a cultural unit. When independence comes peacefully, its shape is substantially engineered by the metropolitan power, and this holds true for literature as for politics. So several factors encouraged envisioning literature on a regional rather than an island scale. Most important of these was probably the BBC "Caribbean Voices" program, begun in 1945 and discontinued in 1958 in conjunction with the transfer of political power from London to the Federation. Under the direction of Una Marson and later of Henry Swanzy the program broadcast to the Caribbean readings of fiction and poetry by West Indians. Many of the region's leading writers first became known in this way, and it is particularly important in the light of later developments that their voices were literally *heard*. The existence of the program implied not only the respectability of writing by West Indians, but the respectability of their spoken language as well. Also significant, though not so immediately, was the institution in 1948 of the University College of the West Indies as a branch of London University. The UCWI began publication of *Caribbean Quarterly* in 1949, a journal that from the start embodied a regional perspective. Its early issues included a series of articles by Roberts on Toussaint, Martí, and Bolivar, and another by Eric Williams on the poetry of Guillén, Brierre, Roumain, and Palés Matos. After Independence the college was reorganized as a self-sufficient university of the West Indies, its supranational identity manifested in its three campuses in Jamaica, Barbados, and Trinidad.

Only in the late 1940s does a critical literature begin to grow up around the concept of a West Indian literature. Bryan King first raised the question of definition in 1946:

Now what was I looking for, in poetry, which I thought of as being West Indian? Firstly, I think, verse which was already familiar to me at home – that is folk song . . . Secondly, I was looking for West Indian imagery . . . I don't think it occurred to me to look for new forms, new ideas, or even new rhythms. It occurs to me now, however, that . . . I must first and foremost seek out, not so much West Indian subjects or imagery as West Indian poets.[61]

Two years later Peter Blackman had to admit that there was not yet a distinctive West Indian literature, because with the possible exception of Jamaica there was "no definite tradition rooted in West Indian soil." He felt too that West Indian literature needed writers before it could afford the luxury of defining categories, but he expected these writers to be born out of the struggle for nationhood then beginning, and introduced the expression "West Indian aesthetic" for the self-definition their future work would make possible.[62] In 1949 Henry Swanzy took up the same question and gave the same answer: there was not yet any clear sign of a definite West Indian literature. But from his work with the "Caribbean Voices" program he could vouch for the presence of genuine poets, especially Derek Walcott, still in his teens, whose work was only beginning to appear. What concerned Swanzy was the impediments to poetry: the lack of readers in the region, the treacherous dependence on local literary clubs and on the support of a social elite. Now that there were poets, Swanzy proposed a new touchstone for the emergence of a West Indian literature: the presence of a distinctive *language*, in which term he included not only idiom and rhythm, but also the climate of ideas and values that finds expression in a literature.[63] Two years later the poet Ellsworth ("Shake") Keane responded directly to Swanzy's article: "Within the last two decades there has grown up here in the West Indies a body of literature that is definitely West Indian, if not so much in 'language,' in spirit and purpose."[64] Like Swanzy, Keane complained of the obstacles, even wishing that local radio stations would follow the example of the "Caribbean Voices" program. But for Keane, unusually conscious of the folk influences on literature, West Indian writing was already clearly distinguishable from "European literary nihilism" on the basis of its "underlying optimism"[65] – the position recalls the opinions of Price-Mars and Palés Matos cited in chapter 2.

Keane's rejoinder is especially significant because he wrote as a resident in close touch with grassroots literary activity. Swanzy was British; Blackman and King had both been living in England when they wrote. Keane is an early witness to the atmosphere on the spot, and what he registers, like Roberts and James, is a sense of incipient renaissance. A more florid account of the same charged atmosphere comes from another resident artist, Geoffrey Holder. The BBC had been broadcasting Walcott's early play, *Henri Christophe*, and in a review of the play Holder describes his experience of the broadcast:

I was listening at a wayside loudspeaker when the rain began to drizzle and three or four people took shelter. Two men, barefooted, were talking when Christophe momentarily flared up; then his voice grew quieter. . . . The two men stopped talking and even when the rain had ceased, they remained listening to the end of the play. At that late stage they could not have followed the events; they were held by the poetry, striking in its vividness and beauty and spoken with sympathy and sincerity. I thought of the Elizabethans.[66]

However accurately this reports the behavior of the little crowd, it is a fine portrait of what a sensitive young West Indian thought he saw, or wanted to see, going on around him. The West Indies was to be a world in which peasants listened to blank verse, where literature was a shout in the street, and where, incidentally, writers knew the value of electronic media for reaching their audience. How many young writers, as they sent their work off to the BBC, imagined something like this as the scene of its transmission?

At about the same time the now traditional account of the outline of West Indian literary history took shape, according to which there had been three phases of development. In this scheme, the work of the 1930s, expressing local pride in the context of Imperial patriotism, was the first worthy of serious regard. Then West Indian writing was transformed during the

1940s as new factors came into play. These "new factors" are variously identified; the mystique of Africa, American influence, nationalism, indigenism, and socialism are all invoked. But the overall effect is that local pride sharpens into self-assertion, and so the drive to political independence supports a flourishing literary activity. By 1950, West Indian writers are finding their models and challenges in the region's own earlier work as well as in external sources, and this emergence of a local literary *tradition* marks the beginning of a real literature. Thus Swanzy in 1952: "Caribbean writers are beginning to copy their own most successful authors . . . That is the beginning of a culture."[67]

As independence from England approached during the decade of the 1950s, the Anglophone colonies became increasingly aware of two alternative contexts: their shared identity as the West Indies, and their place in the polyglot Caribbean. Despite the pioneering efforts of de Lisser, Roberts, and James, there was little cultural contact across language barriers until surprisingly late, and when it came it depended for the most part on a few writers who by overseas education or employment had gone beyond the narrow horizon of their islands. Thus between 1950 and 1953 *Bim* published French Caribbean poetry along with articles on Haiti and the French novels of the region, but the force behind all of that was one man, John Harrison, an Englishman who served as art officer for the British Council in the West Indies for about four years. Lacking such an advocate, Spanish Caribbean writing left almost no trace in the first thirty years of *Bim*'s publication. We have already noted the early interest of *Caribbean Quarterly* in the region as a whole: an aspect of its commitment to Federation. But for a long time the channel between English and Spanish Caribbean writing was also the responsibility of a single individual, UWI professor R. G. Coulthard. Since his death the critics Michael Dash and George Irish have played a similar role for both the French and Spanish literatures. But it was only the Cuban Revolution, coinciding with the failure of the Federation, that finally turned West Indian attention once and for all to the Caribbean Basin.

As for political federation, we have seen how closely it was tied to literary development in the minds of West Indian intellectuals and especially in the literary establishment as embodied in the various journals; the political experiment brought celebratory anthologies from *Kyk-Over-Al*, *Caribbean Quarterly*, and *New World Quarterly*, while it set off a flurry of anthologies from Britain and America during the 1960s. The appeal was obvious. Federation meant a way out of the parochialism of the individual islands, meant larger audiences and better communication among writers. But it also required acceptance of a continuing sense of dual citizenship, of concurrent local and West Indian loyalties. In fact such a sense was preconditioned by the long habit of maintaining both local and Imperial, or local and Commonwealth, loyalties. But in the political sphere, increasing nationalism on the local level, though it contributed initially to the momentum toward a Federation, eventually made such dual citizenship more awkward and indeed less popular. The failure of the West Indian Federation had to do with what ordinary people chose to recognize as the proper object of their nationalistic fervor, and the choice of the most immediate object in preference to something larger must have reflected a wish to turn sharply from the chronically divided allegiances of the past, and to be at last simply one's own.

Even after 1962, however, West Indian literary and intellectual circles continued to move toward a kind of federation, in spite of logistical difficulties. Critical mass is again certainly a factor here: the need to have a sufficiently varied body of literature available to a sufficiently large potential audience. Further, local differences paled in the face of the discovery of shared experience and its expression, even though those local differences remained among the chief subjects that concerned a unified West Indian literature. Fuel for the movement toward a cultural federation came from the increasingly international perspective of the local journals, from the Caribbean arts festivals that have been occurring at intervals since 1952, and by the steady circulation of ideas and personnel animated by the mere existence of a regional university; but most important is the continued functioning of what is still the shadow capital of the West Indies: London. Certainly from 1950 until the mid-1960s London was the center for the most visible West Indian accomplishment, the body of fiction produced by Harris, Mittelholzer, Selvon, Lamming, and V. S. Naipaul, among others. It was this work that made West Indian literature known to a general (that is to say, a metropolitan) audience, and the presence of that audience encouraged an homogenized view of these writers as West Indian rather than Barbadian, Trinidadian, or Guyanese. Though in Britain all West Indians tend to be thought of as "Jamaicans" even now, it was actually the Jamaican novelists like Victor Reid, Roger Mais, and John Hearne who managed to work for the most part in the Caribbean, a tribute to that island's relative success in supporting a literature at this time. But even they published abroad as a matter of course. The success of novels from the West Indian community in London was accompanied by several important essays on the experience of exile, notably Brathwaite's "Sir Galahad and the Islands" (1957), Lamming's *The Pleasures of Exile* (1960), and Naipaul's *The Middle Passage* (1962).

In the shadow of all this achievement, poetry seemed virtually in decline. The fact that it remained a home-grown product may have had something to do with this evaluation; while West Indian novels were selling in England, anthologies that could make the region's poetry known there would not begin to appear until after Independence.[68] Another factor was variable quality. From the very beginning, the growth of a West Indian poet was impeded by the fact that he wrote for an uncritical audience that neither challenged him nor particularly respected him.[69] Until the filtering judgments of experienced editors (at home or abroad) could be brought to bear, the reader seeking poetry in the region found a great deal that was hardly worth the finding. Two authoritative opinions from about 1960 are representative. In *Focus* the Jamaican novelist John Hearne mourned the apparent death of West Indian poetry:

A detached observer in 1938 would have been justified in predicting the emergence of a passionate and beautiful West Indian poetry. . . . A great deal of [the poetry of the 1930s and 1940s] is derivative, clumsy, too loud, above all too *hasty*, but it is charged with a burning, veracious energy and a sense of individual resolution . . . The poet had a sense of participation in something greater than himself and yet in which he, as communicator, was indispensable.[70]

What became of all that promise? Hearne acknowledges the effect of a natural drift in any movement from lyric to larger forms, and especially to prose, but that accounts only for the dearth of poetry, not for its weakness. For him, the central failure of poetry in the 1950s is this: "the inability of the poet to complete a withdrawal from himself . . . Unlike the novelist, he still ejaculates incidents from his life instead of using those incidents as constituent arcs in a circle of new experience."[71] This is (rightly) to ask of poetry not only perspectives but visions, and while the 1960s did indeed go on to produce more than their share of thin confessional and raw protest, they also saw the long maturing promise of the 1930s bear fruit not only in the work of the acknowledged masters, but in the confident and consistent voices of many other poets.

R. J. Owens in an extensive review of two West Indian anthologies echoes Hearne: "West Indian verse is already given too much to 'describing experiences' instead of realising them through words."[72] Among the older poets he finds a cultural colonialism, "an attempt to react to their own experience in terms of someone else's sensibility."[73] But if these older poets, having little of their own to say, think of poems as stylistic exercises in imitation, the younger poets with a great deal to say on pressing subjects are often content with rhetorical assertion and rarely stop to shape their words into a poem. Like Clare McFarlane, Owens notes the shift in taste regarding nature poetry, according to which poets must go beyond description "to declare their consciousness of a 'spirit of place' and their community with it."[74] Owens's review may be the harshest detailed critique of West Indian poetry ever. He ends by writing off West Indian poetry altogether and putting his small hope in fiction: "Until the West Indian equivalent of

Mark Twain arises in the Caribbean, literature here will remain minor and bastard."[75] But the belligerence of his attack may be calculated, in part, to precipitate more of what he tries to exemplify: detailed literary criticism. Like Hearne he sees the continuing presence of such criticism as important not only for the improvement of writing, but for the cultivation of an audience, and for all its bluster his essay seems to have these two aims at heart.

In retrospect we know that these scoldings came in the dark before the dawn; the most impressive period of West Indian poetry thus far can be said to begin with the appearance of Walcott's *In a Green Night* in 1962. The book is most important, of course, for the quality and promise of its poetry. But Walcott is also the first poet produced in some sense by the West Indies: an islander from St. Lucia, educated not abroad but at UWI in Jamaica, and subsequently resident in Trinidad, who published three volumes locally in three different colonies before this London publication introduced him to the English-speaking world at large. Walcott's appearance on the scene was complemented by that of Brathwaite, who had been contributing poetry to *Bim* since before he went up to Cambridge in 1950. After university he worked in Ghana for eight years before returning to the Caribbean in 1962, but his return was heralded by the first of a staggering series of articles on and about West Indian literature, and even this only an aspect of the work of perhaps the most energetic figure on the contemporary literary scene. The years 1960–61 saw an essay on the poetry of Wilson Harris, a double article surveying "the new West Indian novelists," reviews of novels by Selvon and Hearne, and notices of two literary publications from Ghana. Where Walcott was the archetypal regional poet, Brathwaite returned to a position at UWI as the first poet with extensive experience in both of the Anglophone Caribbean's two metropolitan cultures: Britain and West Africa.

In 1965 Brathwaite returned to England to earn his doctorate, but took advantage of the occasion to found the Caribbean Artists Movement (CAM) in 1966. Its first objective was to bring exiled West Indian artists, writers, critics, and even publishers together for the first time, in effect transforming the exiles into their own audience, with very productive results. CAM had regular meetings and a newsletter (from 1966–1968), and mounted annual conferences in 1967, 1968, and 1969.[76] The first conference, at the university of Kent, attracted ninety participants. According to one of them, the overriding sentiment was of Caribbean awareness, of the need to seek West Indian destinies in contact with all the language groups of the region and their common history. Much of the discussion was about improving communication with the West Indian population, and about "the right use of the right language;"[77] much of the debate worried the question of the artists' mixed commitment to their art and to their society.

The success of this conference substantiated the paradox that "in Britain more than anywhere is the West Indies a reality,"[78] and the obvious next step was to carry that reality back to the Caribbean. But before that happened a new dimension was added to CAM, for the participants at the second conference had in the meantime been exposed to both Stokely Carmichael and Enoch Powell. Black Power was a divisive factor at this conference, heightening questions of social involvement and cultural commitment. For Brathwaite in particular, "Carmichael produced images of shared communal values. A black International was possible."[79] When Brathwaite returned to Jamaica in 1968 he brought with him CAM's message, and indeed for all practical purposes the organization itself. In 1969 it sponsored weekly symposia in conjunction with the local New World Group, and in 1970 CAM formalized its new venue by publishing the first issue of *Savacou*, "A Journal of the Caribbean Artists Movement," in Kingston. The London exiles never had the ideological clout of their French counterparts in the Negritude movement, and the literary establishments in the West Indies at this time, though small, were hardly reactionary (though some individual voices certainly were). Thus, when young writers came home, rather than rejecting the activity they found, they moved to build on it; the activities and concerns of CAM led directly to the debates at ACLALS a few years later.

Concurrent with CAM in the late 1960s was a self-conscious attempt to cultivate a body of literary criticism. Lamming's *The Pleasures of Exile* was the first "metaphysical" essay, the first exploration (it could even be called an archaeology) of the Caribbean imagination. Important theoretical work in the same vein came from Brathwaite, Walcott, and several Guyanese writers, most notably Wilson Harris, Denis Williams, and Gordon Rohlehr. Such groundbreaking thought comes only after a degree of confidence has been achieved, and it is closely associated with the emergence of individual critical voices, reliable judgments. Studies of linguistics and of West Indian literary history begin in earnest in this same period. The body of West Indian literature was by this time large enough to support and require whole books devoted to individual writers, and there is a kind of quantum leap in the number of local journals. In 1968 alone three collections of critical articles appeared, and the special West Indian number of *The Literary Half-Yearly* (1970) was described by its editor as a "testimony": "At a time when the region is engaged in a serious, necessarily revolutionary questioning of West Indian values and their political, social and economic implications, it is very heartening to find that the imaginative literature of the region . . . reflects this crisis and indeed is often pragmatically involved in the debate."[80] Like the beginning of poetic imitation, the emergence of a reliable criticism is a sign of a literature's maturity. Its importance was underscored by the institution of a West Indian literature course at UWI in 1969. This academic expression of local confidence melded with the urgency generated by CAM. At the same moment, political events with a peculiarly intellectual dimension occurred: in Jamaica the expulsion of UWI lecturer Walter Rodney by the government in 1968 and the student takeover of the new Creative Arts Centre at UWI in 1970, against the background of Trinidad's February Revolution. Into these circumstances ACLALS fortuitously inserted the open microphones and captive audience of its triennial conference. A more timely occasion could not have been contrived.

Until about 1950 literary criticism had tended to speak (for example) of Guianese or Jamaican literature, rather than of a comprehensive West Indian literature; this is apparent not only in essays, but in the organization of a number of the early anthologies. Bruce King's account of the factors that subsequently nourished the more comprehensive conception is unimpeachable: "a sense of community between writers of the various parts of the region was established through publication in the new journals, the 'Caribbean Voices' broadcasts, travel between the islands, the shared experience of those who emigrated to London, the rise of independence movements and self-government, and plans for a federation."[81] But it is striking how those conditions have changed in the generation since ACLALS. London no longer plays its paradoxical role as the capital of the West Indies. While regional anthologies have metropolitan publishers in England and now in America, initial publication, especially of poetry, is increasingly local – a matter of small, poorly circulated editions. School texts, anthologies, and critical studies preserve the notion of a West Indian literature, and bring together the work of writers from various nations; but the writers themselves are rarely in the same place at the same time. The network of communications maintained by the UWI is crucial, but even augmented by events like Carifesta and occasional conferences it has not replaced the central clearinghouse that London was. Meanwhile many of the journals are gone, and some of those that remain appear irregularly and face very uncertain futures.

In this changed context the issues have changed. The era of the struggle for independence was marked by a corresponding eagerness to distinguish West Indian literature from English literature, to establish the former's identity as a going concern. It was rare to find poets in the region exerting any influence on one another, outside a few sharply defined coteries like the *Beacon* group in Trinidad or the Jamaica Poetry League. But today, as we saw in the first part of this chapter, it is possible to trace national literary *traditions*. Increasing interest in the local ethnography, religion, folklore, and language of individual nations contributes to an increasing diversity among West Indian writers. It is also fair to say that local literatures now begin to have distinctive characteristics of their own, apparent in both style and choice of subject. To cite only a single substantial example, nature poetry remains an important genre for young poets throughout the smaller islands of the Eastern Caribbean, but is almost entirely absent (or radically politicized) in recent poetry from Jamaica and Trinidad. Though the various literatures have long been artificially isolated, there have been remarkable parallels in their developments, not least in their strategies for emerging from under the shadow of their respective metropolitan cultures. Today there is considerably more interest in the relation of West Indian literature to the body of polyglot Caribbean literature as a whole. Yet some poems are intentionally West Indian, and so obviously need to be read as such. Usually this is a matter of theme. The poems of Eric Roach, among others, frequently urge cultural if not overtly political federation (for example his "Love Overgrows a Rock," or "I am the Archipelago"). Brathwaite's trilogy *The Arrivants* is the paramount example of a poem which must be considered West Indian because of its central concern with the islands' common history and common problems. Less frequently, a poem demands to be considered West Indian on the basis of its language. While most poems concerned with linguistic variety are interested in the poetic potential of a particular dialect, or with the problems of reducing one to legible print, others participate in the project of developing a common West Indian grapholect, a written form of the *regional* standard language. In much the same way that the Federation would have shifted the political reference point from London into the Caribbean, this project aims to shift the linguistic reference point closer to home.

Whether poetry can usefully be regarded as "West Indian" or not must depend on the level of its engagement with myths or assumptions about the place and the past which it inhabits. The characteristically West Indian metaphysics of place embraces (among other things) the topography of volcano and coral, climate of trade winds and hurricane, myths of paradise or jungle, of an Eden lost, found, or brutalized. The characteristic history or meta-history is equally mythic, a matter not of historical fact but of significant pattern, and it takes in all the charged imagery to be found in the details of a tumultuous past. Each feature may be linked to some other realm: to Africa or Europe, to various histories of diaspora or colonization, to Plantation America as a whole. But taken together they stake out an imaginative field, the contours and fertility of which are accessible to study (just as an analogous field of myths, metaphors, and patterns of understanding that seem to characterize the "American" in a work or an imagination constitutes the subject-matter of what is called "American Studies"). It would be erroneous to deduce, from the richness of the field, the conclusion that poets will necessarily continue to work it. Even so, no matter how extensively subject-matter, language, or even form are "nationalized" in the poetry of the coming years, it is likely that a considerable number of poems will continue to include elements which reveal themselves fully only in a West Indian light, and further that those elements will often prove to play a crucial role in generating the emotional resonance of the poem by providing the points of most intimate contact with readers in the Caribbean.

CHAPTER 4

The relation to "Europe"

This chapter traces the separation of West Indian poetry from English poetry, a process which gets under way in the nationalist period. The process is not strictly sequential, though there is an apparent logical succession to the array of strategies by which poets work out their relation to "Europe": successful imitation or assimilation, uneasy divergence, asserted difference. While this separation is analogous to the earlier rejection of "tracing-paper poets" by nationalists elsewhere in the Caribbean, the best-articulated conceptual model is probably that provided by Houston Baker's analysis of the corresponding phase in African-American literature. Acknowledging that the Harlem Renaissance movement (like earlier West Indian poetry) has been severely criticized for its advocacy of "the standard," by which he means the norms of received literary practice, Baker argues that such formal mastery entails an element of "masking." "Such masking carries subtle resonances and effects that cannot even be perceived (much less evaluated) by the person who begins with the notion that recognizably standard form automatically disqualifies a work as an authentic and valuable Afro-American national production."[1] The model here is close to that of apprenticeship, the assimilation of traditional craft demonstrated in a culminating masterpiece which earns entry into the guild. But there is more to it than that. For Baker, "the mastery of form" makes possible – and legitimizes – what he calls "the deformation of mastery." So he writes

Gone in the work of a poet like Sterling Brown is the felt necessity to produce only *recognizably* standard forms. What replaces this drive is an unashamed and bold dedication . . . to rendering the actual folk voice in its simple, performative eloquence . . . The indisputably modern moment in Afro-American discourse arrives, I believe, when the *intellectual* poet Brown . . . gives forth the deformative sounds of Ma Rainey. . . The blending, I want to suggest, of class and mass – *poetic* mastery discovered as a function of deformative *folk* sound – constitutes the essence of black discursive modernism.'[2]

In the eighteenth and nineteenth centuries, poetry from or about the West Indies exemplifies mastery of an inherited medium, an almost automatic troping of Caribbean experience with British figurations. The models for form and diction derive from pastoral, epic, and satire, from odes, heroic couplets, and blank verse. This is true even of the most knowledgeable native authors, even of those poems which incorporate criticism of slavery and other colonial policies. The writers (many of them visitors rather than permanent residents) place their work unself-consciously in the British tradition, and seem unaware of one another. The most spectacular early case of "mastery of form" in the West Indies is that of Francis Williams, a Jamaican free black who was sent by the Duke of Montagu to study at Cambridge early in the eighteenth century. This was more a sociological experiment for Montagu than an opportunity for Williams; after Cambridge he returned to Jamaica, where there was of course little use for his training. He opened a school in Spanish Town and evidently addressed to each new governor an ode not merely classical but in Latin. His only extant poem, written for the arrival of Governor Haldane in about 1759, has been approved for its ironies and rather anachronistically praised for its West Indian consciousness.[3] But for my purposes it is worth considering the poem's function rather than its content.

The act of writing Latin elegiacs in Spanish Town was perhaps the sole outlet for Williams's hard-earned Cambridge skills; to the man himself an exercise in nostalgia for the days of his celebrity, and a periodic reminder that the skills were real. For black Jamaicans who knew of it, Williams's Latin poetry may have been intimidating – Williams is said to have been haughty and condescending to his fellow blacks, and though the testimony is that of the hostile Edward Long, it makes psychological sense in the light of Williams's frustrated ambitions.[4] But at the same time blacks could take this poetry in a positive sense, as a sign of what was possible. For Jamaican whites, on the other hand, it was a goad, an act of defiance, an embarrassment. For like his American contemporary Phyllis Wheatley, Williams makes a graceful but insistent point of his color. Though he advises his Muse not to be ashamed that her white body has a black skin, he insistently reminds his reader of that skin in the course of the poem. It was part of Williams's running (and losing) battle not just for prominence but for something like political power. For any of its possible audiences, the content of Williams's ode was virtually beside the point. What was important was the gesture: a black man writing Latin verse. Williams wrote for Governor Haldane a poem more to be admired than read, in the hope of bringing himself to official attention as a presence in the island, as a prospective candidate for patronage. The poem is written in Latin elegiacs because an ode in that form was traditionally the appropriate offering in such circumstances. Williams's goal was not to contribute to the generation of an acceptable culture in Jamaica, but to be personally acceptable. The use of Latin only emphasized his poem's functional opacity; it is not especially meant to speak. The content – the meaning of the words – is not the issue in this poem, any more than is the meaning of the text of a diploma (as opposed to the significance of the physical document as certification). Its primary effect on any reader of any race is as a social gesture.

In that his poem is imitative, and problematic as to both language and audience, Williams is emblematic of any pioneer West Indian poet. Poetry readily serves as a demonstration of capability and promise to one's self and to one's people, an assertion that "we can do what they can do." At the same time, it was until recently most often directed toward a British audience, and from that perspective asserted something slightly different: "we can do what you can do." On both counts imitation is an almost essential technique. Only a rare poet can innovate without first proving to himself and others his ability to copy judiciously; without the preliminary demonstration of competence, the masterpiece that assures entry into the guild, poets seldom feel secure about innovation. The attempt to write poetry begins with the writing of what others will recognize as poetry. In a sense, only the imitative poem is securely a poem; anything else risks the question: what is that supposed to be? and only a very confident poet will be ready to make – or to refuse to make – the necessary explanations. A colonial setting aggravates those anxieties of influence. Thus, insofar as West Indian work is directed to European eyes, to the eyes of authoritative "elders," it must imitate so it will be recognized as "Poetry." As the challenger must fight on the champion's ground before he has his own, so cultural equality (as distinct from viability or even excellence) can only be achieved on the terms of the more established culture. A small culture's claim to be excellent *in its own way* at first satisfies no one.

Around the beginning of the twentieth century, the seed-bed for serious writing within the West Indies is the new middle-class poetry clubs. Their goal remains "mastery of form," though that phrase is too grandiose for the goals of most of these poets, who merely want to write and be read by one another. But it is poems from these clubs that begin to show signs of the dawning recognition of incongruities between West Indian experience and the metropolitan tradition. In the very act of writing, poets encounter inklings that the received medium, though serviceable, is not quite right. As they work to represent their actual surroundings they discover that their medium predisposes them to describe their place as if it were an unusually warm county of England. Things do not always go smoothly when they employ the poetic forms and conventions developed in Europe as a medium for putting Caribbean experience into words. The need for some adjustment is felt most immediately as a technical problem, a matter of craft, even though that need of course reflects much larger social and political problems. The resulting stress is often apparent even in poems that do not address it at all; in effect, poets are beset by separation anxieties in addition to anxieties of influence.

To speak, with Houston Baker, of a "mask" is to emphasize the performative self of the poet, the projected voice, the authenticity of his chosen language of expression, and therefore of the "representativeness" of the poet, the inherent claim to embody not just a self but a people. The writer has occasion to regard his mastery as a mask when something, some discomfort, draws his attention to it; when the mask seems to be slipping a little. This is at first a source of embarrassment, but it leads to a sense that the mask is what is wrong, that one's self is misrepresented by it. Chapter 5 will consider how voice and social class, so important to Baker's account of "deformation of mastery," are also factors in the West Indies, despite the great differences between the African-American and the West Indian situations. The shifting of the mask, this discomfort about expressing oneself through a borrowed medium, is, however, not the only interposition; West Indian writers also discovered a sort of Foucauldian epistemic misfit, a new consciousness that their perception of their surroundings was mediated by "the filter of English eyes."

Awareness of this filter is what chiefly motivates "deformation of mastery" in the West Indies, as the writers' response to the intuition that they need to handle the medium differently if they are to succeed in capturing Caribbean realities. This chapter brings to light signs of the effort to *mark* poems as different, to show signs of private resourcefulness, of personal or cultural accent. Writing in 1962 about the Caribbean as a whole, Coulthard noted the centrality of this "search for a differential element, something characteristic on which to base cultural independence and national personality."[5] The perceptions of poets are sharper; as early as 1950, A. N. Forde put it this way: "fondly we search for regionalia in our poetry to fool a world that we are sprung from foam."[6] Paradoxically the search was facilitated by resources that were not West Indian at all. This chapter illustrates how second-hand American Modernism was invoked in the 1930s as an instrument of deformation, as a compensatory filter that might counteract the effects of the "filter of England." Chapter 5 will illustrate how another compensatory filter, the idea of "Africa," helps to make visible the folk cultures of the West Indies.

I began this chapter with a sequence: imitation, uneasy

divergence, asserted difference. Difference will emerge as an explicit issue in pre-Independence texts, and it subsequently ripens into themes (and gestures) of outright opposition. West Indian poets are concerned not only with social protest, but especially with the poetics of protest, and with protest against "Poetry" itself, as the metropolitan tradition seemed to define it. In the late 1960s and 1970s some took the logic of the sequence further and urged outright rejection of the relationship with "Europe." It was thanks to the developments already recounted in chapter 1 that the ensuing crisis was productive rather than disabling for poets.

FRAMING CARIBBEAN NATURE

Up until the 1920s, the principle subjects of West Indian poetry were religion, patriotism, and nature – all matters of harmonious connection to something larger. Norman Cameron was only the first of many West Indian critics to complain that religious poems tend to be the most trite and uninspired in the corpus.[7] This is not for the lack of sincerity, and in many cases not for the lack of poetic talent, but because these poems are conceived as exercises in cultivation, and because, more often than not, what is being cultivated is not literary craft but a kind of genteel highmindedness. As for the patriotic poetry of the early years, it is more Imperial than colonial in conception. While there are a few fawning poems to Mother England, it is more usual to invoke the empire as a whole, since this can be parleyed into an assertion of the individual island's active role in a common enterprise. West Indian "nationalism" was defined within an Imperial context by West Indians themselves, and this perception, whether consciously or not, took some of the sting out of Crown Colony status. When the Guyanese poet Egbert Martin ("Leo") won a prize for two additional stanzas of "God Save the Queen" written for Victoria's Jubilee in 1887, the award was more important in Georgetown than in London. This is presumably the first piece of Guyanese verse ever heard in England, and for that reason it is still anthologized.[8] But it was visible only because it was shaped in the mold of the

National Anthem; in any other form this undistinguished piece would have been invisible, as was other, better, Guyanese poetry of that era, such as Henry Dalton's. As with the ode of Francis Williams, in this case the gesture is more important than the substance.

With neither army nor political power, however, the West Indians' attention tended to drift from "king and country" to a more immediate objective: "place and people." Thanks to this circumstance, and to the habits of nineteenth-century English poetry, pride in one's surroundings more often found expression in poetry about nature than in patriotic verse. The high proportion of such writing in the relatively small total of poetry before about 1950 should thus not be surprising. It is as a rule highly imitative of British verse, and stylistically rather out of date in its own time. But again the impulse, the gesture, is significant. It is here in nature poetry, rather than in religious and patriotic verse, that we find distinctly local experience brought together with metropolitan language and forms. To speak of the local in a poem which by its very imitativeness belongs to English literature first of all elevated the status of local experience. Such a poem also asserted, however, that this language could be domesticated to tropical realities, and that second assertion was not always demonstrated successfully. Language and subject-matter seem frequently at odds, and post-Independence criticism of this earlier poetry most often emphasizes its stylistic incongruity. Since the main business of nature poetry is physical description and the articulation of sensibility, it is particularly in this genre that the first signs of strain are apparent even before they are explicit – the first suggestions that the English language and its poetic tradition are not absolutely compatible with Caribbean actuality.

An incongruity between experience and poetic tradition can seem to originate with either term. A reading of, for example, H. G. Clerk's "Ode to the Jamaican Mocking Bird" (1929) may begin with the feeling that a pseudo-Keatsian ode is not entirely appropriate for this subject, if only because so serious a form seems at odds with the connotations of "mocking":

> Hail Seraph of Jamaica! Hail, seer bird!
>   Sweet when throughout the day,
>   The joyful roundelay,
> Pouring through all the lattice-leaved trees is heard;
> Or where pimento branches glist'ning play
> Fragrant accompaniments to thy wondrous song.[9]

But after that pimento, the orange groves of the second strophe, and a single *lignum vitae* branch later, Jamaica simply disappears, obscured by a "poetic" landscape of thoroughly British leas, glens, dells, and wildwood. After one extended foray into Greek mythology, and another into Italianate musical terminology, the reader is left with the perverse impression that the inappropriate element here is not the manner of the poem, but its erstwhile subject; that somehow everything could be improved by replacing that mocking bird. We must sympathize with Clerk's conviction that the Jamaican bird deserves its Keats, but here the attempt to enshrine the bird in a proven style makes it appear as the incongruous element in what should be its own poem. A later poet might be equipped to do more with the disruptive implications of "mocking" – allowing the bird to break the frame and assert his loud self. Constance Hollar's "Flaming June" (1929) suffers from a similar discrepancy.[10] Hollar personifies the month's arrival in a loose ode, beginning, "June has come to Kingston . . ." But there is little of Kingston in this poem, which seems intent on invoking comparisons as remote as possible. Thus in the course of a short poem June and her accoutrements are likened to Venetian glass, a gypsy, Gobelin tapestry, a Persian bride, and red wine in a jasper bowl. It is difficult to imagine what these comparisons are meant to achieve beyond a certain gorgeousness – does a Persian bride call up any reliable associations? Even assuming a Jamaican audience, the poem does nothing to make that audience see or appreciate the phenomenon it seems to celebrate. By leaping so far, it *enlarges* the gap between the poem's subject and its language, though Hollar seems to have intended to elevate her subject by the maneuver.

In a context of increasing personal and national self-consciousness, the challenge for West Indian poetry in the period between the 1920s and the end of World War II was to produce verse that was both "West Indian" and "Poetry" – that was, in other words, both successfully expressive of uniquely local experience and at the same time recognizable as a development linked to the tradition of poetry written in English. On the basis of differing responses to that challenge four kinds of poem can be distinguished: (1) poems that attempt to accommodate West Indian experience to highly virtuosic (and therefore prestigious) traditional forms – Clerk's ode is an example; (2) poems which by various strategies attempt to shape poems directly from the contours of represented local experience; (3) poems that speak explicitly about the incompatibilities between received form and immediate experience, sometimes to the extent of making that incompatibility their primary subject; and (4) poems in which nature, or poetry, is politicized.

The array of maneuvers described here is typical of the means by which various literatures emerge to stand on their own, in the clear. The same maneuvers are apparent in the evolution of Latin literature from Greek, vernacular literature from Latin, and post-colonial literature from colonial, but they can be traced with nearly paradigmatic clarity through the examination of a comparatively small literature like this one in the Anglophone Caribbean. Scholars of poetic influence have delineated the ways in which productive major poets take on the burden of the past, and by doing battle with the tradition earn their own names as independent poetic voices. For West Indian poets of this period, the issue was not only individual independence, but the cultural independence of the literature to which they saw themselves contributing: a West Indian, not a British, literature. Minor poets, even self-confessed amateurs with no explicit poetic agenda, also addressed this issue. But while a professional poet can make the process of defining himself into a career, the less productive writer can address it effectively only on the scale of the individual poem. Indeed, the nature of the West Indian case makes it particularly clear that the emergence of any literature from its cultural setting requires more than the accumulation of a certain critical mass of good writing. It is accomplished only as individual poets idiosyncratically win their own independence; that is, through the techniques by which individual poems are successfully realized. Literary independence tends to be associated with extraordinary writers or energetic movements, but it must ultimately be achieved in individual poems, and in the solution of extremely specific problems – problems encountered in the process of composition and addressed (successfully or not) with resources of craft.

It was paradoxically the poets who were most self-conscious about establishing a distinctively West Indian poetry who labored to acclimatize highly articulated traditional forms to local use. Their effort is understandable enough. While acknowledging the prestige of certain traditional forms, the West Indian poet could demonstrate his ability to exploit them for his own ends. And while the composition of a significant poem might actually contribute to the maturing of a newly literary language, the poem itself stands as an instance of achieved maturity. Finally, a poem in a prestigious form can confidently be measured against the array of prior achievements in that particular form, with the result that success can be recognized not only in the metropolitan center but even by the often hyper-critical local audience. This mixture of motives came into play when Claude McKay and W. A. Roberts wrote sonnets, or when (following the example of Roberts) Jamaican poets during the 1930s produced a flurry of villanelles. The task of canvassing the tradition for forms appropriate to West Indian expression had a high priority in the region's literary enterprise until about 1950. Widespread formal exploration was a matter of selection and adaptation within the British poetic tradition. West Indian poets sought a repertoire of forms that would not overpower their material with the burden of the form's own heritage, and would not skew the expressive intentions of the poem by ingrained habits of rhetoric, decorum, and subject-matter. It is the problem exemplified in the poems just discussed: to find or to adapt a style answerable to their experience. Caribbean nature may well deserve its Keats, but it became apparent that a West Indian Keats had somehow to resemble his English counterpart only in quality – any other resemblance courted either incongruity or irrelevance. On such matters poets were getting advice from every quarter. Roy Fuller, for example, in what was originally a "Caribbean Voices" broadcast, insists that Caribbean poets have to stop writing like Keats (among others he names); they have to learn to write like themselves. But what he means by "like themselves" is actually "like something else": "It is on the background of Eliot and Auden (and of the best American modern poets) . . . that I think Caribbean poets ought to be drawing the features of their own tradition."[11]

Later the drive toward independence would reject writing a villanelle or sonnet of any kind for any reason as ineluctable cultural imperialism, or as craven mimicry. But there is eloquent defense of what is seen as the West Indian writer's right of access to the European tradition. Walcott is probably the most prominent spokesman for this position, though it has had a particularly insistent supporter in John Figueroa. The turn to traditional forms for a new, not-yet-literary language has powerful precedents: Horace mimicking and so appropriating Greek verse, Tudor poets using Italian and French forms to the same end, and the consolidation of a "minor" local language in the process of translating the Bible – these are analogous instances of making a renaissance in the rough language of a marginal country. Other considerations apart, the mere discipline involved in working with long-refined traditional forms contributes to the resourcefulness not only of the language but of the poet. Further, there is the implication that if the new writer in a new language can work only by ignoring the received tradition, he is still in its thrall; what is required of the creole, the "American" poet, is confidence and strength to embrace, or subjugate even, the metropolitan culture as one among his resources. West Indian appropriation of the European archive has produced texts of powerful originality, from Wilson Harris's *Eternity to Season* (1954) to Walcott's *Omeros* (1990).

ENUMERATION

The effort to find a place for local experience in traditional forms was only part of the process of establishing a distinctly West Indian poetry. Converging on that objective was a complementary effort to derive poetry from local experience, an effort that eventually matured into a quest for indigenous formal models and even indigenous language. Where the first impulse sought to adapt English forms and diction by introducing West Indian elements as a kind of leavening, the other was at bottom an impulse to enumerate or list, grounded (consciously or not) in an insistent faith that the elements of West Indian life were poetic in themselves. At its most sterile, this impulse produced poems like the luggage of returning tourists: bundles of local place-names, totemic objects, or bits of colorful dialect. One symptom of this impulse is the appearance of poems with glossaries, characteristic of moments when the development of a poetry is closely linked to ethnography and national self-discovery. We have encountered glossaries already in Afro-Cubanism; the Belizean poet George Price wisely provides one for his poem on the "Limestone Pillars of Belikan" (1965), which "towered over milpas of Fri-jol-Buul and Ixim-Maiz. / Side by side they stood with ceiba, corozo and caoba trees."[12] The peculiar cultural history of the region is partly responsible for such textures: often in such cases the writer is making a poem of things he has himself just discovered, pressing his readers to share the excitement of his own sometimes very recent *prise de conscience*. Like Clerk, Price is enshrining the unique icons that define the nation, but there is a new effort to rely on local materials, so that the style of the shrine will be more compatible with its contents. Colonial education made the West Indian's immediate surroundings appear paradoxically exotic even to him. But correcting this perceptual distortion, first in himself and then in his audience, is perhaps the poet's chief contribution to genuine national feeling. The surrounding local culture – what people actually do and how they do it – becomes a tradition as such when a participant becomes self-conscious about it, comes to consider it as a heritage *for use.*

Several West Indian writers attest to the shock they felt on first discovering that local places and things and people could be set down in print, and that they became literary thereby.[13] The act transfigured everyday life, made it magical. But the very exercise of that magic, making the local into poetry, sometimes hypnotized the magician and resulted in shapeless, unjustified poems. The mere title of Alfred Mendes's "Tropical Lines" (1929) should prepare us for the kind of flaccid, mechanically "tropical" verse that appeared throughout the region during this period. The poem begins like this:

> All day long I heard the keskidees
> Lullilooing in the sun-stroked trees.
> And termagant corn-birds, with their raucous cries,
> Held in my guava-tree their high assize.[14]

It might go on this way, one bird to a couplet, for ever. In spite of the glance at Shakespeare's sonnet 73, this is a poem with no reason for being; a pure exercise in tropical decor. It is the sort of poem that eventually suggested to West Indian poets the importance of generating some frame to control poems impelled by enumeration.

A. J. Seymour's "Name Poem" (1946) is one of many that aim to put on paper, and so (paradoxically) to bring to life, the names of local places. Its success depends in part on the maneuver of framing the poem, justifying it, by an explicit premise. So Seymour begins like this:

> Beauty about us in the breathe of names
> Known to us all, but murmured over softly
> Woven to breath of peace.
> If but a wind blows, all their beauty wakes.[15]

Some forty lines later, the first and last lines of that quatrain combine to form a concluding couplet. By this gesture Seymour confirms the connection between the wind that animates a scene and the breath that, by the act of naming, also brings it to life. That frame established, the body of the poem is generated almost entirely from Seymour's inspired handling of the sound of Guyana's polyglot place-names. Consider for example the interweaving of "t," "k," and "r" in the following stanza:

> Through all the years before the Indians came
> Rocks at Tumatumari kept their grace,
> And Tukeit, Amatuk and Waratuk
> Trained ear and eye for thundering Kaieteur.

Unlike Price's poem, this offers alien readers some immediate rewards even without a glossary, and may draw them into learning more about the country, while for Guyanese readers it counterpoints verbal music with the interplay of emotions associated with these places. Though this poem may have begun in enumeration, a kind of "virtual" origin projected behind the compulsive listing gives it its emotional force and coherence. This particular method of framing-by-repetition is quite common in West Indian poetry of the period, and especially in Guyanese poetry. What such poems communicate is primarily the listed objects' impact on a persona, and in fact many of them are the work of exiles from or visitors to the Caribbean. Indeed, that stance of recollection or of anticipated recollection seems to make a dependable contribution to the success of these poems.

There are excellent examples of this effect in the work of the exile Claude McKay. "Flame Heart" (1920) is probably the best known, but "The Tropics in New York" (1920) is the most economical instance of such emotional framing of the enumerative impulse. The poem's opening stanza may seem very risky:

> Bananas ripe and green, and ginger-root,
> Cocoa in pods and alligator pears,
> And tangerines and mangoes and grape fruit,
> Fit for the highest prize at parish fairs.[16]

This has the potential to be as bad as Mendes's "Tropical Lines." We enjoy the immediate sensual pleasures of these lines with some anxiety that no poem may materialize (as in many enumerative poems, a nervous excitement builds steadily while we wait for a genuine verb). But the second stanza transforms its predecessor entirely, by revealing that the tropical fruits are displayed in a shop window in New York, "bringing memories / Of fruit-trees laden by low-singing rills." The first stanza taken alone offered a series of fully sensual experiences. Here in the second they are reduced to merely visual objects, literally framed and set at a distance by the window. Those experiences we thought we were being invited to share are now divided between objects on one side of the window and memories on the other. The immediacy of the opening lines is thus undercut: the objects are foods, brought together because they are (in New York) exotic and therefore desirable, while the memories are of a home place, a scene of original nurture.

The third and final stanza deepens the framing, and so too the distance:

> My eyes grew dim, and I could no more gaze;
>   A wave of longing through my body swept,
> And, hungry for the old, familiar ways,
>   I turned aside and bowed my head and wept.

Memory puts even the visual out of reach, and at the same time the vividly articulated memory of particular experiences is replaced by inarticulate present emotion. Both the fruits in the window and the remembered fruits of home are gone. The speaker, overtaken by a sensation as visceral as hunger, finds himself psychologically cut off from his immediate surroundings because cut off from his past. As for the reader, the literal hunger with which he responds to those first fruits turns out in the center of the poem to be inappropriate to what the speaker feels. The reader is implicated in the poem by being caught in a guilty pleasure, and so is set up for the unexpected outcome: his hunger has been stimulated to make possible an almost somatic participation in the speaker's emotion, an entirely metaphorical hunger, in the final lines. When the speaker turns aside at the end, he forces the reader to turn aside as well, thereby completing the reader's progressive and frustrating estrangement from the vivid stimuli of the opening (via the window, the eye, the eye dimmed, the eye finally turned away). In the end the reader too is left with memory, and hunger.

If anything, "The Tropics in New York" improves under examination, so a more ramshackle example of visitor's verse might better illustrate the potency of framing for poems committed to enumeration. The expatriate Alastair Scott's "Lines on Leaving Trinidad" (1932) begins "I wonder what I shall miss," and goes on to list some two dozen items in about as many lines of unmetrical verse rhyming in couplets.[17] The piece disintegrates under any close scrutiny, but unlike Mendes's "Tropical Lines" quoted earlier, it is pleasant, even engaging, to read once. What makes the difference? For one thing the bare framework of imminent departure, an accessible emotional situation which we can share even if we do not share a knowledge of Trinidad. For another, Scott is careful to select suitably poetic (or suitably anti-poetic) memories as potential souvenirs. He presents for consideration, among other things:

> Lime trees and
> the clean scent of their leaves? The dark sand
> With gasping, purple jellyfish? Bird-eaten mangoes lying,
> Like torn soldiers, among the dead leaves?

What most draws us in, however, is his framing all but the last section of the poem as a series of questions, in an effort to anticipate future memory by formulating experiences memorably and then reviewing them. In this way, the reader's judgment of the poetic aptness of each aperçu is deflected; instead of judging the poem, he finds himself participating with its persona, who is also in the act of evaluating each of its elements as they appear, but on entirely different grounds. Our critical instinct is thus appropriated to the mildly melancholy business of the poet. The use of these devices is very blunt, possibly accidental, but as soon as they shift our attention from facets of Trinidad to the more universal predicament of the departing visitor, the poem lays claim to considerable sympathy.

ACKNOWLEDGMENT AND APOLOGY

Under examination, the foregoing poems in their various ways betray the strain of accommodating experience to the expressive tradition, but they do not actually acknowledge it. Full recognition of that strain as a technical problem comes at the time of emerging nationalism on a larger scale, and gives rise to a body of poems that refer explicitly to the incompatibilities. At first, such reference was often apologetic and self-effacing. West Indian poets continued to worry whether either their own skills or their subject-matter rose to the standards of the tradition to which they sought entry. It was only around the time of the World War II that confidence developed on these two points, encouraged in part by the atmosphere of self-sufficiency that the war imposed on England's more remote colonies. During the same period, an alternative view of the situation gained currency: the possibility that what was inadequate was the tradition itself. Increasingly, dissonances were brought to the surface in West Indian poems as a way of insisting that a new kind of poetry in English had to be devised to express the realities of language, nature, and human experience in a new field of reference governed by new rules of decorum, by new values. Thereafter, West Indian poets aimed more often to adjust the tradition to this experience, where earlier the opposite tendency had prevailed.

Mendes can redeem himself from the embarrassment of "Tropical Lines" by providing an example of the moment just before the quarrel with the tradition becomes explicit for a poet. In his "Tropic Night" (1932) the challenge is all but spoken. This is the first of four quatrains:

> Over this city from the outside
> crawls the tarantula of night:
> long hairy legs and two bright eyes,
> and no light, no light.[18]

The striking image of night as a tarantula crawling over the city could come out of early T. S. Eliot, and there are other belligerently anti-poetic elements in the poem's imagery ("the moon has her backside to earth"), as well as in its diction and rhythm ("All the lights in this place have been switched off / by accident, or I know not what"). Yet in addition to these Modernist elements, there is a traceable West Indian dimension to the poem. Even for a Trinidadian reader the image of the tarantula may not be quite so domestic as "The yellow fog that rubs its back upon the window-panes," but the images of cat and spider are tonally much closer for him than for a cold-weather Anglo-Saxon who encounters tarantulas only in horror movies. Mendes makes the point that what is commonplace in the Caribbean may not be commonplace in the tradition, in the world of poetry, and the chief business of his poem is to assert the West Indian poet's right to the imagery his place affords him. Tropical decor implies a tropical decorum. The poem first appeared in *The Beacon*, which, besides being rather scandalous, was strongly influenced by North American literary and journalistic trends. *The Beacon* seemed to conceive of its audience as a middle class which, while in fact familiar with various creeping things, cultivated (with some pride) a drawing-room squeamishness; readers who had, in effect, trained themselves to react to such a poem like Englishmen. Some pleasure in assaulting those readers lies behind Mendes' insistence on his tarantula – the word is repeated in every stanza of the poem. One option for early poetry was a lushly tropical mode which domesticated the Caribbean to the Edenic sector of the poetic tradition. Mendes simply pushes that option to the edge: in this imaginary Eden there are real arachnids. On its much smaller scale, this is the gruff mischief of the Irishman Swift's poems about London.

Exposure to Modernism provided Mendes with effective leverage, or perhaps a sort of cudgel. But fully explicit recognition of the gap between tradition and experience begins for many poets in apology. Since we have already seen Constance Hollar straining to cope with June in Kingston, we can consider examples from a range of poems in which West Indians come to terms with their climate. The American novelist John Barth voices an extreme view of the problem: "No one who makes up stories can be much perplexed by the relative paucity of equatorial and polar literature, for example: Aside from the fact that there aren't many readers and writers at the poles and the equator, where on earth will you find your basic metaphors for life and death if the seasons don't change?"[19] Recognition that neither the facts nor the associations of those seasons have any real bearing on Caribbean climates first becomes explicit in poems oddly apologetic about the region's failure to have traditional weather. One of the earliest is S. E. Wills's "Christmas in the Tropics" (Guyana, 1907), of which these lines are representative: "We may not have the Yule log or the hanging mistletoe, / But then we have the sunshine and the hearts that with it go."[20] By such means Wills makes his argument that "Yes, 'tis Christmas in the tropics when 'tis Christmas in the world." Here, as so often, the West Indian sees his homeland as outlandish, not part of "the world." Lacking the "normal" seasonal drama of winter, the writer seems forced to propose plainness as a virtue, the sunny candor of the tropics. Snowblinded, he loses sight of such compensations as the high drama of Caribbean vegetation, here buried under the alien drift of the word "groves." The need to eliminate the filter interposed between poet and landscape by European traditions is often voiced quite explicitly, as in Slade Hopkinson's illustrative little poem, "Rain Over St. Augustine" (1970):

> The soiled sheet of the plain
> lay stretched in half-light.
> The rain walked over it on a lot of feet,
> Like a *congoree* . . . [= centipede]
> I thought of Turner, for I am educated.
> It is difficult
> To find your idiom
> Unclouded by the rain, which nourishes.[21]

Where earlier poets were impeded by the habit of seeing their weather in terms derived from temperate climates, Hopkinson is nettled to find himself seeing (and therefore trying to express) his weather through imported modes of representation. Chances are the poet first thought of Turner, and then, dutifully trying to see West Indian rain with West Indian eyes, came up with the passage about the centipede. The resulting grotesque diction recalls Mendes's "Tropic Night." There the entry of a Trinidadian tarantula causes a very similar problem, but Mendes' pugnacious Modernist tone makes a kind of virtue out of it. Here the emphasis is elsewhere, in the delineation through the final lines of the new *obligation* the poet feels (in the atmosphere of the late 1960s) to deny himself Turner and to make something of the congoree. The battle is still under way in Keith Warner's "Paradoxes" (1973), whose opening neatly inverts "Christmas in the Tropics":

> Have you ever dreamt of a white Christmas?
> I did, and it turned out bad
> Because visions of green palm-trees
> Kept blocking out the snow.[22]

A glance at any anthology makes it apparent that a remarkable number of early poems about Caribbean nature are marked by a defensive rhetoric, frequently signaled by the appearance of expressions like "but," "yet," or "even so" in the opening lines.[23] West Indian poets were conditioned by their colonial situation to doubt whether either their own skills or their subject-matter rose to the standards of the tradition to which they sought entry. In those circumstances, apologetic protestation had considerable appeal as a straightforward technique by which the poet could clear a space for his own poem in the gap between the expectation of his art and the realities of his experience. H. D. Carberry's poem "Nature" (1943) conveniently exemplifies this rhetoric, but does so in the very act of leaving it behind:

> We have neither Summer nor Winter
> Neither Autumn nor Spring.
> We have instead the days
> When gold sun shines on the lush green canefields –
> Magnificently.
> The days when the rain beats like bullets on the roofs.[24]

Even the title is symptomatic. An earlier poet with a strong sense of empire, or with the colonial habit of seeing himself only as others see him, might more modestly have called it "Nature Out Here" – and indeed a contemporary of Carberry (Daniel Williams) entitled a poem "Over Here" in just that spirit.[25] But it is illuminating to consider rewriting the poem by dropping the first sentence, so that it would begin like this: "We

have the days / When gold sun shines . . ." Carberry's opening
concession, while it provides a helpful frame for the catalogue
of local particulars that will follow, is more overtly a preliminary gesture (a backswing or running start) calculated to
make room for the poem in a tradition conceived as metropolitan. It is even tempting to read the explanatory opening
lines as if they established the poem as a nostalgic traveller's
tale, recounted in exile; as if they began "*In my country*, / We
have the days . . ." Yet "Nature" was written in Jamaica and
first published there in *Focus*. In that setting it appears as an
assertion of difference and independence, but as an assertion
made very consciously in the face of brave and longstanding
colonial attempts to have these canonical four seasons, or
something as like them as possible. So the opening lines hover
between aggressive assertion of the local facts and a kind of
chagrin; in doing so they illustrate the vexed relation of the
early West Indian poet to his work and to his audience.
Carberry takes things a step further, however. The motion from
traditional expectation to local reality is by way of "instead,"
measurably stronger than the "but" or "yet" of earlier poetry.
It sets one alternative literally in the place of the other, and the
balance finally comes down on the side of local pride even if
the external rhetorical frame is still all that holds the poem
together as a poem. Local material is still not readily shaping
itself into poetry here, but Carberry keeps the imposed frame
as spare as possible. The curt abstractions of "Summer nor
Winter . . . Autumn nor Spring" pale before the immediacy of
the rest of the poem, and they appear in the form of polarities
rather than in the normal dramatic sequence, so that by the
end those seasons have been reduced in the reader's eyes to
mere categories, appropriate only to another world. It is, after
all, to another world that the nationalistic West Indian writer
wishes to consign them.

If Carberry's "Nature" is representative of the moment
when a sense of inferiority is overcome, other poems of the
same period go further. We have seen that West Indian poets
read their own surroundings through European eyes, out of
ingrained habit and to some extent in anticipation of a

particular sort of audience, jealous of its metropolitan outlook. A. N. Forde's poem, "On Scanning Millet's Angelus" (1950), offers a refreshing reading of a European picture with West Indian eyes. The initial point of reference is again outside the region, a European cultural artifact, familiar as "great art" thanks to its presence in collections of reproductions available in the Caribbean. In this poem, however, West Indian land-scape and weather provide the norm, while Europe is genuinely seen as alien, a strangely tamed or exhausted world, and the movement of the poem is to find Caribbean correlatives for what Millet depicts. First Forde scans the painting:

> Stiff starched prayer
> As statuesque as stone
> And deep immensity of backdrop sky.
> Cold clods biting the
> Hoe's teeth and vomiting
> Birth of weeds.[26]

This picks out the three dominant features: the figures of praying peasants, back-lit and nearly black even among the generally subdued colors; the mild crepuscular sky; and the earth. This soil fills two-thirds of the picture plane with an almost malevolent presence, thrusting up small hillocks (in this light, even the distant church seems one of these), and accented with angular low vegetation, perhaps the shrivelled potato plants now being harvested. Forde preserves Millet's strong contrast between earth and sky, but makes some adjustments for his own purposes in the figures. There is really no impres-sion of starched coifs in the painting, but the detail is not incongruous, and Forde pursues it later in "ironed," "wing," and "apron." In the opening passage itself, the image of stiffened cloth helps to coordinate the conception of the peasants as sculpted representations of their own prayer (and of their humble virtues) with the very different implication later that the suffering heart stiffens into stone ("marbling") in order to endure. The absence of verbs in this passage reinforces the impression of immobility. This group of ideas will be picked up in the final lines, but first the poem reveals itself as West Indian in both its situation and its concerns. Departing from what seems the painting's least promising feature, the bland sky, Forde employs the familiar apologetic rhetoric of "not . . . but" to achieve an unexpected and original effect:

> A sky not swift impetuous
> Like ours screaming hell and drowning heaven
> In sadist freakishness;
> But ironed into selflessness
> Watchful with suave wing.

The Caribbean sky is still "freakish," *ec*centric, something marginal that departs from the norm. But for the poet who scans the picture *in* the Caribbean the implied question is clear: What sort of sky is this depicted here, what has been *done* to it to make it so different? It has been "ironed," has been made different from the sky the poet experiences directly (and here we are forced to bring to bear the inherent brutality of "iron"; even ironing cloth is in its small way a violent subjugation). This implication is pursued in the great central turn of the poem:

> But that earth is ours
> Cozened for a million weaving flags
> Of cane, slicing the air with wanton pennies [= pennions]
> And covering red blood in joints of brittle bars.

The "but" that usually signals apologetic difference here on the contrary, marks the point of contact, of recognition. Foreign as the painted sky is, foreign as the ethos of the picture seems, the Barbadian cane-cutter knows intimately that brutal, devouring earth. It is through this recognition, rather than directly, that he sees his relation to the peasants in the painting, an identity of condition. Yet the poem makes it clear that the European and the Caribbean peasants come to terms with their common condition in different ways, and that the difference reflects the difference in their skies. The peasants of Millet, at least for the duration of evening prayer, seem removed from the earth at their feet, absorbed into the selflessness of the sky, and Forde's description of them emphasizes this abstraction from insistent nature through the images of starched prayer and marbled heart. But there is no heaven in Forde's canefield. These peasants do not direct their prayers upward. They are "soil-suppliant"; in the very act of bending at their work they worship and nourish their "dark mother." In the tropics, the violence of the earth ascends to assert itself even in the air. Millet's cold clods bite only what intrudes into their realm, the hoes digging for tubers. But in the Caribbean the cane stalks, taller than a man, slice the air itself. There is no refreshing contrast between earth and sky here; the wanton life waving in the canes reaches up into the sadist sky. There is no alternative immensity for the West Indian peasant to turn to. The cane, like the earth itself, is a life that feeds on life. While the heart's-blood of Millet's peasant is wilfully stiffened into the devout posture of a statue, and reaches toward heaven in the form of prayer, the blood of Forde's peasant is pumped into the cane itself, figuratively producing the red sap that fuels the stalks' profane, almost obscene, surge into the air. In the end, this is a poem about Barbados, not about "The Angelus," and if anything it suggests that the special perspective of Barbadian peasant life may reveal important features of Millet's painting, and even of the life of European peasants.

Harold Telemaque of Trinidad and Tobago progresses even further in the direction of a self-sufficient West Indian poetry. His verse in the 1940s is consistently marked by a consciousness of what the Caribbean lacks. Several of these poems are enumerative lists, which tend to be framed by figures of having and wanting, as even his titles can indicate. Thus the poem "Riches" is constructed of three parallel stanzas following this model: "These are my gold; / *Only* the mellow mango leaves / Shrunk in a heap . . ."[27] Similarly, "Dowry" begins "I have nothing in my hands, / Nothing; / But I give to you . . ." and goes on to list tropical birds, trees, fruits, and so on.[28] As the "but" of "Dowry" makes obvious, both poems resort to the familiar rhetoric of self-effacement. But Telemaque's first collection in 1947 is dedicated "To the New West Indian," and in an important expression of self-consciousness about the issues we are considering here, the poet hopes that this new reader "will seek within these poems for what is intense and virile and

individualistic, rather than for the familiar theme, the old jingle
. . ."[29] Here Telemaque echoes Coulthard's emphasis on the
"differential element." The book's best-known poem, "In Our
Land," is a fine example of how Telemaque appropriates to his
own striking purposes the "old jingle" that he cannot entirely
escape; and in so doing he moves beyond Carberry's "Nature."

This poem too opens on an apparently negative note with
the admission of a lack, in what sounds like a variant of the
apologetic gambit. We are led (deceptively, it will turn out) to
expect the nostalgic, even cowed, tone of the traveller or exile:
"In our land / Poppies do not spring . . ."[30] But the rest of the
stanza deflects the poem toward another very different West
Indian topos, the contrast between the innocence of the tropics
and the inhumanity of the "world" – a topos which by 1947
had taken on a political edge:

> In our land
> Poppies do not spring
> From atoms of young blood,
> So gaudily where men have died:

This vision of Flanders' fields leads us to anticipate an anti-
strophe contrasting the lush peace of tropical paradise, far from
Europe's wars and perhaps (we might guess) adorned with
poinsettias, in fitting balance to the image of the poppies. But
instead the poem takes another unexpected turn:

> In our land
> Stiletto cane blades
> Sink into our hearts,
> And drink our blood.

The bitterness of these lines is compounded by the feints that
prepare them. "Our land" is even worse than Europe, because
the cane drinks the blood of the living, while the poppy only
memorializes a death in which it plays no part. Yet it was
Europe that first brought the cane; if the cane blade is a mortal
weapon, it is wielded by the same hand that sowed the crop of
Flanders. Thus for the second distinct time in eight lines the
poem turns against European dreams of empire that reached
a zenith in World War I. Sugar is a European import; the

most characteristic feature of island landscape is not indigenous, but, as the poem reveals, a kind of invading army, occupying with time all the best of "our land." The poem engages its reader by the changes it rings on a familiar argument: the Caribbean has no poppies, alas. But they are flowers of stupor and death; we are better off without them. Instead we have sweet and useful cane. But that kills more surely than any poppy.

Telemaque's subtle probing of the West Indian's sense of difference continues throughout the poem, to conclude by declining the invitation – or temptation – to challenge Europe on its own ground:

> We do not breed
> That taloned king, the eagle,
> Nor make emblazonry of lions;
>
> In our land,
> The black birds
> And the chickens of our mountains
> Speak our dreams.

There is some critical debate about the force of these final lines. Neville Dawes in particular cites the poem as an example of the kind of apologetic West Indian statement which, I have been arguing, only provides its point of departure. Taking the whole poem in the spirit of its deceptive opening, Dawes finds the conclusion "banal . . . a shining compliment to the colonial master's traditions."[31] But this is to miss the advance Telemaque makes here beyond such poems as "Nature," an advance apparent in the maneuvers of the opening stanza and reinforced by the complex ironies of the central stanzas. The first half of the third stanza, for example, seems about to boast, rather smugly, that unlike Europe the Caribbean has no wars, only the hurricane; but with the turn of the line the word "hurricane" is revealed as figurative, standing for the West Indies' even less justified "Clashes . . . for tint of eye." An expectation of apologetic contrast is built into the form ("In our land . . . not . . ."). But that is "the old jingle," and the originality of this poem is in the counterpoint.[32] Thus at the end the agility of the poem prepares us to see eagle and lion as glorious, but also as a little monstrous, and perhaps most pointedly as outlandish. In their place the closing lines offer, first, the apologetic proposition that humble local nature must serve as the only firm foundation for pride (though this nature is not quite so humble as it may sound to non-West Indian ears: "chickens" probably means not fowl but chicken-hawks). But the lines invite another reading: West Indian dreams are not of kingship, because they must first be of freedom, a value naturally associated in the islands not with escape but with rising – and uprising. The association has a topographical basis: in many West Indian nations movement inward is move- ment upward into mountains, into marronage. It finds its most common poetic expression in figures of birds of freedom, a common fixture of the West Indian imagination in the era before Independence. This symptomatic upward turn arises out of the earlier apologetic tropes, but replaces them with a gesture of resolution and independence that reflects the poli- tical atmosphere of the time as much as the literary.

Telemaque's own later paraphrase of his final lines is rele- vant here, not only for the light it sheds on this poem, but for its acknowledgment that the effort to achieve control over poetic forms was a manifestation of nationalism, of the effort to say "we." Thus Telemaque:

We are different. We did not fight wars; we did not have need for banners parading before an army or anything like this. This is what we were saying . . . We were special people, equal to anybody else; but special in that we were seeking to live a life of our own . . . Our poetry started as a poetry of identity . . . It became a poetry of protest, because they were not letting us live the life . . . we wanted.[33]

The emphasis on "us" and "them" reflects not only shifting attitudes but also the peculiar realities of West Indian writing. Like the trope of apology itself, it draws attention to the problem of audience. As long as one is writing poems meant to be "universal," one can write anywhere and assume a general reader, in effect any reader of English. But as soon as poetry becomes consciously West Indian, it encounters the problem of address, of intended or assumed audience. If West Indians wrote in Arawak there would be no problem. But because his language joins him to disparate cultures, the West Indian poet is in the position of any minority writer. Since the avowedly political, national, ethnic, or in any way partisan poet is in special need of the complicity of his audience, the problem becomes particularly pressing. Does he choose to address primarily only insiders, that is, West Indians? Except for its youngest stratum, the West Indian reading public, such as it is, has been educated (like the older writers themselves) to be British. What was British was their own; what was West Indian, and so truly their own, was seen through British eyes as exotic. Thus Carberry, a Jamaican writing for Jamaicans, could say: "I shall remember / . . . women from the hills / Bringing down *strange* fruits / To Saturday's markets" (1948).[34] Similarly C. L. Herbert's "Gardens in March" (1947) begins, "This is our dry season – / *Strange* admixture of Indian summer and spring . . ."[35] This is in effect to address the local audience *through* an illusory "standard audience" of which it is a peculiar subdivision. But addressing a standard audience, in principle all speakers of the language, raises its own questions. Does one assume a knowledgeable reader and present oneself directly? A metropolitan publisher will ask for footnotes, glossaries, and the excision of incomprehensible dialect. But to anticipate addressing readers who need this kind of help will soon have the poet thinking of his naseberries, his star-apples, his weather, and even his neighbors as "strange." In the face of diverse audiences even that group-defining "we" can invite ambiguity.

Telemaque's "In Our Land" once again provides an example. The non-West Indian ear will be disposed to hear in that repeating "our" the tone of a boastful jingoist, smugly going on about how things are done "back home." But a West Indian ear is more likely to hear the alert integrity of the poem's discriminations filtered through a homely and even humble voice (Dawes's dissatisfaction with the poem, for example, seems to depend on hearing the voice in this way). Telemaque, publishing in Trinidad, could estimate his audience reasonably well (indeed he may have known most of its members by name). But as long as West Indian writers may live almost anywhere and publish almost anywhere, the problem of audience will remain open, a hurdle for improving the muscle-tone of West Indian writing.

By about 1950 West Indian poetry came to stand on its own, through the gradual refinement of craft outlined here and the identification of characteristic issues, such as the problems of decorum and of audience. Thereafter poets generally have confidence in Caribbean material, feel ready to adapt traditional forms and diction to the expression of local experience, and have available to them as poets a position beyond apology, beyond defensive assertion. The most telling evidence that these objectives had been achieved is the inclination of the region's younger poets to seek their professional models at home, rather than abroad. The first such model was the Jamaican George Campbell. No earlier poet who remained in the Caribbean had any influence outside his immediate coterie, but the publication of Campbell's *First Poems* in 1945 soon affected the work of poets throughout the region. The post-war years encouraged an atmosphere of mutual influence, thanks to the new literary magazines and to the BBC's regular "Caribbean Voices" program. These developments laid the foundations for an indigenous tradition, based on a conviction that West Indian poetry could be self-sufficient.

FROM APOLOGY TO POLITICIZED POETRY

As Telemaque observes, the assertion of West Indian difference develops in the late 1940s from a textural feature of some poems to an explicit theme; the perception of difference solidifies into a stance of opposition. Poetry of protest, with its recognizable diction and forms, in effect projects the problematic rhetoric of "but" – of begging to differ – onto a larger plane. The maneuver reappears on an even greater scale when West Indian poets like Telemaque and Forde, beginning to be conscious of themselves as a group, programmatically treat the turn from the tradition as a defining feature of their literature.

Overt protest poetry can be traced as far back as the worksongs of slavery days, which voice objections to colonialism and its consequences in every area: economic, political, social, and cultural. If not so much protest, there is at least demurral even in very early poems that conceive of themselves as "literary." To the casual observer, poetry of social critique can seem to burst out in the late 1960s, in part because the technicolor vividness of a new kind of language could catch eyes previously fixed on fiction. Yet social observation veering toward protest is already present in the dialect poetry McKay published in 1912, before his migration to racist North America further intensified this dimension of his work. Protest is an increasingly important feature in the poetry of Una Marson in the 1930s, of the Modernist/socialist poets of Trinidad around the same time, and of George Campbell and the Jamaican poets of the 1940s who were associated with the Peoples National Party of Norman Manley. In the 1950s, when more poetry began circulating within the region (though not yet much abroad), Martin Carter and Eric Roach, among others, rose to prominence with politically conscientious poetry grounded in acute observation of Caribbean experience. If we are to judge from the choices made by subsequent West Indian editors and critics, this body of work has survived better than much of the more clamorous poetry of the 1960s. An exception proves the rule. The Jamaican poet and novelist Andrew Salkey published an anthology, *Breaklight* (1971), with the expressed purpose of demonstrating West Indians' turning away from the "banality of the forced nationalistic poetry" of the late 1930s and 1940s.[36] Salkey combines leftist leanings and Latin American connections with a real poet's eye, so the protest poetry of the 1960s is expertly represented in this collection. Sadly, of the forty-odd poets included, it is particularly that group – including such promising talents as Michael Als, Sebastian Clarke, Emmanuel Jean-Baptiste, Claude Lushington, and Basil Smith – which has faded from sight, and their poems have generally not been reprinted elsewhere. More often than not, these poems are passionate about abstractions rather than specific events or conditions. They attack colonialism, materialism, modernization, racism – the panoply of metropolitan impositions. This poetry can be especially strident on the subject of the West, and a posture of subjugated superiority is struck at every level of poetic practice, as poets good and bad distance themselves from the pathologies of the Western imagination: "mammon," "money," "science," "armageddon." For our purposes, however, since this book is about the poetry *as* poetry, protest as subject is less interesting in the long run than the impact of such concerns on poetry itself, on its forms and uses. Here and in the following chapters I will be concentrating on poems about poetic difference, or about West Indian poetry's cultural work.

Many of the poems that we have been examining in this chapter would qualify as nature poems, and what happens in that genre as West Indian poetry asserts itself against "Europe" is revealing. Even amid the bland verse of an early collection like *Voices from Summerland* (1929) there are individual poems that present very specific observation of nature. Poems dedicated to describing and naming the features of the landscape came to be valued for undertaking an inventory which provided an essential tool for overcoming the colonial filtration of perception. In the late 1940s and the 1950s, poetry throughout the West Indies turns away from such themes as beauty and truth and nature to take up a quest for the meaning of a people's life in its social and historical context. The shift reflects a change in the underlying political agenda. J. E. C. McFarlane (not at all the likeliest suspect) can provide an early instance of the peculiar effect of this new nationalism on the West Indian response to nature poetry. At one point he complains that Tropica (Mary Wolcott) "writes a bit like a northerner" (she was born in Jamaica of long-established American missionaries). That blot on what a later generation would call her "authenticity" provokes him to attack her poem "To the Scarlet Hibiscus" (*Island of Sunshine*, 1905) from an unexpected angle:

no native poet would think of identifying his country with the hibiscus, or even with the more popular poinciana, or poinsettia, because such tags, when self-consciously applied, are never the result of objective appraisal, but arise from hidden spiritual need or sentimental association. For some deep intuitive reason Jamaican poets have by common consent . . . adopted the lignum vitae as their national emblem.[37]

The poem in question, on the power of hibiscus to evoke "the South" when abroad, is actually much like McKay's later "Flame-Heart," a text from a "native poet" which annuls even more this legislative criticism in its refrain: "I have forgotten much, but still remember / the poinsettia's red, blood-red in warm December."[38] The poets' disregard for the critic's narrow rule is a harbinger of things to come: McFarlane's argument from national mystique and poetic intuition functions precisely like ideologically motivated proscriptions in a later period (for example, about what forms of language are "truly" West Indian).

As nature poetry becomes problematic, it tends to be avoided by writers, who are hesitant to offer observations filtered through metropolitan habits of perception and expression on the one hand, while on the other they are wary of producing exotic postcards for metropolitan consumption. In the larger islands, urbanization is surely an additional factor; with the passage of time fewer poets know the landscape. The sort of poem that takes off from an encounter with objects of nature remains fairly common in the smaller, less developed islands, like St. Vincent, though even in St. Lucia poets of the generation after Walcott's tend to depict an urban scene. Generally speaking, "mere" description and naming, no longer justified as essential inventory, now need to be motivated, to speak to or to illuminate human concerns. To meet this felt need, nature poetry after about 1950 tends to be politicized by one of two strategies: social realism (in effect, peopling the landscape as a way of assuring its value) or moralizing (causing the landscape to sermonize about human concerns). Social realism was cultivated particularly in Jamaica, following the lead of George Campbell, while the technique of moralizing is characteristic of Guyanese poetry, and is prominent also in the work of poets as diverse as Forde and Roach. Of course, both of these techniques, in their different ways, depend upon identifying the people with the landscape or its features. Certainly by

1970, however, the atmosphere in the literary centers was such that anyone caught writing about nature in Kingston and Port of Spain could be made to feel embarrassingly retrograde. Rohlehr has exhaustively documented how sharply the alienated urban vision of younger Trinidadian poets diverged from the work of Walcott, Roach, Cecil Herbert, or Wayne Brown with respect to nature.[39] Rather than repeat his analysis here, I will draw my own examples from Jamaica, where even a small sample demonstrates that the writers are engaged in just the kind of conversation that the spirit of ACLALS envisioned. The disinclination to take up nature as a subject is shared by "radical" and "conservative" poets about equally. Instead they share a common interest in the social world and in the exploration of voices, though this is pursued very differently by those who portray the middle registers of Jamaican speech and society (Mervyn Morris, Edward Baugh, Dennis Scott, Anthony McNeill), than by those who speak from – or for – the marginalized and the oppressed. Yet even politically radical poets regard the avoidance of nature poetry as temporary, as part of a dialectical phase. It is not the poetry for this particular time. Such an argument is apparent in this extract from Mutabaruka's "Two Poems on: What I Can Write" (1972): "can i write . . . of rainbow colored birds singin their nature songs in tall lush trees? all of this i can write. but now, i write . . . of negroes and coloureds shoutin their freedom songs in tall anti-freedom buildins."[40] At about the same time, Orlando Wong (now known as Oku Onuora) similarly answered the question, why don't you write about trees, flowers, and birds?, with these lines: "I write about flowers – / flowers on graves / I write about birds – / caged birds struggling."[41]

As those quotations imply, at the height of the 1970s the attack on "Europe" becomes in some hands an attack on "Poetry" itself as an alien conception. Rejection of the European tradition as archive of forms, diction, and decorum is accompanied by rejection also of the print medium, and of the elite audience. A redefinition of what the word "poetry" should mean in the West Indies, such as we saw in chapter 1, is pushed to the limits in these same poets. Thus Orlando Wong insists "I am no poet . . . I am just a voice I echo the people's thought, laughter, cry, sigh."[42] Mutabaruka takes up a profoundly dissociated position, publicly performing poems like "Call me no poet or nothin like that" (1970–71), which ends:

> no recitals
> no recitin
> no poems
> no poems
>   p
>   l
>   e
>   a
>   s
>   e[43]

So sharply antithetical a poetics can reach such a pitch of irony as to be either incapacitating or absurd: when Mutabaruka, the revolutionary poet, performs his own "Revolutionary Poets," the refrain, "revolutionary poets 'ave become entertainers," gets a big round of applause.

This impasse elicits conscientious responses from several Jamaican poets of a different stripe. Perhaps the most direct response is "More poem" (1982) by Dennis Scott, whose incandescent social conscience flares in such poems as "Squatter's Rites" and "No sufferer" (both 1973). "More poem" begins by quoting a voice which could be Wong's or Muta's:

> "No more poem!" he raged, eye red;
> "A solitary voice is wrong,
> Jericho shall fall, shall fall
> at the People's song!"[44]

Scott's sympathy with the view he quotes is strong, though he seems to feel, finally, that it leaves no room for the poet he himself is. On the one hand his poem is provocatively couched in rhyming quatrains, with conspicuous formal symmetries; on the other, the progress of the argument hinges on a feature of the subversive language of Rastafarianism – language intimately associated with the performance poets of that era. Crucial here is the Rastafarian antithesis between "I," the pronoun of the believer, and "Man," which always refers to profane outsider, the secular reprobate. The initial capital of "Man" is semantic; this fact makes possible the compression with which Scott restates his interlocutor's position: "Man must keep silent now, except / man without bread." Scott's response is sympathetic, even conflicted, but categorical:

> No. See the flesh? It is cave, it is
> stone. Seals every I away from light.
> Alone. Man must chant as Man can
> gainst night.

The final stanza begins with a "no" which has been stripped (as it were) from the poem's first line, "No more poem," to generate Scott's title. This outcome reveals the title to have had the force of an order, countermanding the poem's first line. For Scott, poetry is not a luxury, is not the exclusive property of either the elite or the subaltern. It is a human imperative.

Edward Baugh's poem "Cold Comfort" (1983) approaches the problem from the opposite direction; not in confrontation with a radical West Indian position, but in confrontation with "Europe." Reading a new poem of Larkin's ("Aubade"), Baugh feels the "authentic shivers" (the gooseflesh which was A. E. Houseman's touchstone for true poetry), and at once begins to worry that poems about love and death are "luxuries we in the third world cannot afford."[45] Can the shivers, the innocent language of the body itself, be politically incorrect? Baugh sets aside the question with a bit of vernacular body language. After sucking his teeth in the characteristic West Indian *cheupse*, he reads again – and feels those shivers again – for the brothers in all the worlds "first, second, third, and otherwise, not to mention myself." This is the opposite of an appeal to the "universality" of a poetry transcending politics; as Baugh writes most famously in "Truth and Consequences": "There's no such thing as '*only* literature.' Every line commits you."

It is Mervyn Morris who most vividly stages the confrontation for us, in "Literary Evening, Jamaica" (1961). The evening begins with readings of the work of two English poets (Larkin again, and Enright) who "speak their quiet honesties without pretence."[46] This part of the program is followed by "poems by the locals, undergraduates, / Some coarse, some wild, and many violent, / All bloody with the strains of rape and childbirth." Morris's poem is a reflection on this two-headed event, and it particularly picks up the strands of "honesty" and "quiet." At first, "Literary Evening" combines respect for the poetic tradition with an engaging solicitude about its vulnerability at rough West Indian hands. But that is only at first. Soon Morris complains of the inappropriateness of these British poets, whatever their virtues, to the young poets of a new beginning: "For to us standing here, a naked nation / Bracing ourselves for blows, what use / Is fearfulness and bland negation?" Behind that question is another, never stated directly: when will it be possible for us to hear British poets as interesting voices from another world, and not as normative models? This poem is really about an overbearing tradition that doesn't even have the decency to act overbearing:

> So many bulging poets must have blushed
> . . .
> And feared that maybe they were born too crude.
> Maybe they were; but it was bloody rude
> Seeming to ask for things that don't belong out here.

It is not, in the end, the "wild" West Indians who are misbehaving here; Morris saves his strongest language for the rudeness of "quiet honesties." If the received notion – and practice – of poetry cannot accommodate the ordinary raucousness of Caribbean life or the ordinary untidiness of tropical nature as it is, without setting it off as iconoclastic, unruly, or exotic, then indeed it is "Poetry," and not the West Indies, that needs to change.[47]

This chapter began with Francis Williams's ode – a special case in which a poem is meaningful as gesture rather than by virtue of its content. So here at the height of the political 1970s, the gesture of writing a poem is attacked and defended quite apart from matters of content. In chapter 1 we followed a debate about what poetry is, and for whom. It is the fruits of that debate that come to the rescue here, to lead West Indian writers out of the impasse of the supposedly "colonial" nature of poetry as such. Here we have been concerned primarily with poets working within a European tradition and then gradually indigenizing the resources of English poetry. That is of course not the only approach taken by writers in the West Indies. The next chapter considers poems more concerned with representing Caribbean people than Caribbean nature. This collateral project is present from the earliest beginnings, but its development is greatly accelerated during the nationalist period, and powerfully reshaped in the 1960s by the West Indian discovery of "Africa," which offered an alternative to "Europe" and in particular induced a new preoccupation with representation of the West Indian voice. As we will see, some writers begin to consider poetry preserved in print as a specifically Western norm; in response they elevate performance over print, orality over literacy, political responsiveness over permanence, a succession of authors over an archive of texts. The enduring consequence of this highly politicized, even ideologically prescriptive, period will turn out to be not any shift in subject-matter so much as the transformation of – the expansion of the resources of – poetry itself in the West Indies.

CHAPTER 5

The relation to "Africa"

The real subject of this chapter is the specifically literary project of enabling actual West Indian people to be seen and heard in poetry, unimpeded by the filter of "Europe." That long-term development of resources is to some extent over-shadowed, however, by a particular episode along the way, the vigorous efflorescence of "Africa" (in various senses of that elusive word). This derives not from the dynamics of literary history but from exterior conditions. After World War II a variety of factors drew attention to Africa and increased actual knowledge of Africa. West Indian self-consciousness evolved within the wider context of American Black Power, transatlan-tic Negritude, African independence, and increasing British racialism (most pointedly legislated in the immigration restric-tions of 1962). Awareness of this context was supplemented by reports of the cumulative experience of Caribbean migrants to the United States and England, and in a more limited way by reports of Caribbean visitors to Africa itself.

As both present-day Africa and its history came to be better known and more positively regarded, they played a potent psychological role for black West Indians. In the course of a development that traces its origins to the work of the Jamaican Marcus Garvey in the 1920s, a complex of ideas about Africa, some accurate and some fanciful, contributed to the West Indian self-image in several ways. It transformed attitudes toward race and color. It limned a history *before* slavery, thereby transforming the Middle Passage from a degraded point of origin to a traumatic but finite episode, on the other side of which a sophisticated culture could be discerned. By imputing nobility and historical depth to the African heritage, this complex enhanced the self-worth of the inheritors. At the same time, establishing the continuity of that heritage into the present provided the support of a second parent-culture, alternative to Europe.

All these have a bearing on the development of West Indian consciousness, but the mirage of "Africa" also had effects on poetry specifically. Though Africa plays a role in the poetry McKay wrote after he moved into the sphere of black America, West Indians seem to have (dis-)regarded him as an American poet until after Independence – few of his poems appear in West Indian anthologies before that date. Similarly, while there are elements of "Africa" in *Bamboula Dance and Other Poems* (1935) by Jose Antonio Jarvis, this book, published locally in St. Thomas, seems to have gone unnoticed in the still-British West Indies. It is not until the 1940s that West Indian poetry attempted to come to terms with the slave past, beyond which Africa itself remained an area of darkness. There was continuing resistance to this effort: "when a West Indian poet in the West Indian context [Eric Roach] . . . wrote of the African element in his cultural and spiritual ethos [in "I am the Archipelago," 1957] . . . he was reproved for harking back to the past."[1] Even in the late 1960s, a commentator as astute as Gordon Lewis could write that "The theme of Africa . . . is not a pronounced element in West Indian English literature."[2] The rapidity of change is striking. Only five eventful years later (1973) a West Indian critic could feel that "There is no need to call attention to the multiple significance of 'Africa' in the Caribbean imagination, for several critics have done so."[3]

Except in Brathwaite's work, African literature (oral or written) is seldom a source of poetic forms for West Indians.[4] Africa is almost never envisioned as a literary tradition, and even West Indian writers with some knowledge of African forms and techniques tend to think of them simplistically (and reassuringly) as a polished body of lore passed on by a neutral process of transmission that discourages modification. Such features as call and response, formulaic improvisation, or the peculiar saltiness of calypso are elements of West Indian folk culture identified as *deriving from* Africa; there are also some formal innovations modeled on vague notions (or imaginary projections) of African practice. "Africa" also supplies subjects for poems, while the increasingly positive attitude toward Africa facilitated addressing distinct but related subjects, such as race, color, and the experience of slavery.[5] West Indian notions of "Africa" have been most important to poetry, however, for what they legitimize: (1) the development of poetry in indigenous rather than metropolitan Standard English – for this the discovery that Caribbean creoles are to varying degrees African in origin was crucial, providing a coherent basis for nation language.[6] And (2) the exploration of "orature," an oral aesthetic for written poetry, which is intimately related to the (re-)definition of audience.[7] This chapter traces these dimensions of "Africa," with particular attention to the emergence of indigenous language as an element of, or vehicle for, poetry.

C. L. R. James's famous pronouncement that "The road to West Indian national identity lay through Africa" suggests the fundamentally dialectical role that "Africa" plays in the region. This is true in literary history as in other spheres. Chapter 4 traced the development of confidence *vis-à-vis* the tradition of English literature. But while access to that English tradition was inestimably important for resources of craft (since it is above all a highly articulated and well-preserved archive of work), the emergence of an identifiable West Indian literature profited from the availability of alternative resources, which provide a kind of leverage. We have seen how Modernism and particularly American Modernism provided a lever by which West Indian poetry could dislodge "Europe" to clear a space for itself, and how Surrealism performed a similar function for writers in French. But those are literary styles. The word "Africa," though ill-defined and idealized, invoked an entire tradition, ranging far beyond the literary. Even writers who knew nothing about Africa were excited by the notion that they had an alternative to the European heritage – a tradition equally venerable and complex, but entirely different. The result is a revolution in poetry.

Writing from this era also reflects an ongoing debate about

the role played in West Indian culture by the complex of ideas and attitudes I am grouping under the term "Africa": Is the role of Africa dialectical, a stage in a progression toward a distinctive West Indian culture that is fully indigenous, a creole culture which includes African elements? Proponents of the dialectical view, however intense their interest in Africa, are committed in principle to the idea that this interest will pass away, reduced finally to only one of the elements in the heritage of West Indian culture, rather than in the culture itself. But we will need to bear in mind an alternative view, according to which the African element is at the root of the indigenous culture, and so represents a rediscovered essence rather than a dialectical lever. Such a view at its strongest implicitly resists creolization as a social or cultural objective; it is most plausible in predominantly black nations like Jamaica and Barbados, most problematic in racially mixed Trinidad and Guyana, where anything like Afro-centrism has been thought to have an incendiary political dimension.

The demographic diversity of West Indian nations brings up another important matter. The most visible poetic developments between 1960 and 1980 were Afro-Caribbean. That is not a statement about the ethnicity of authors, but about the culture in which the poems themselves participate. We have seen that the authors of many "Afro-Cuban" poems were themselves white or (in the case of Pedroso) Chinese – a very Caribbean thing, and quite unlike the atmosphere in North America, where an author who writes in the voice of an ethnicity not his own can expect plenty of vociferous free publicity. In the years when "Africa" dominated Anglophone poetry, writers with diverse backgrounds took part in true Caribbean fashion. Even in Guyana or Trinidad, societies statistically dominated by East Indians, the cultural norm tends to be that of the urban, black, English-speaking population. East Indian West Indians and their culture are well represented in fiction since the era of Selvon, Khan, and the Naipauls, and it is only a matter of time before Chinese West Indians find a voice, but drama and poetry thus far have been dominated by writers who look primarily to the African and European heritages.

Indo-Caribbean poetry – by which I mean poems which explicitly draw upon the cultural heritage of ancestral India – presents something of a special case. East Indian poets have been writing in Guyana since early in the century, but especially since Independence they have been marginalized, not merely by the Black Power tenor of the times, which tended to occlude the concerns of other ethnicities, but also by the increasing isolation of their country from the rest of the West Indies. Moreover, many Guyanese writers have migrated to England and especially to Canada; given the dispersal of the poets, a critical mass of Indo-Caribbean poetry began to accumulate only in the 1980s. Indo-Caribbean poems are now being written also in Trinidad, though the absence of anthologies of Trinidadian poetry has been an obstacle to their circulation. Like the boom in poetry by women, this development thus falls outside the time-frame of this book. Preliminary indications, however, suggest that a discussion of how the African heritage establishes its place in the indigenous tradition will apply *mutatis mutandis* to other heritages whose contributions to the cultural mix are now becoming more prominent in poetry. A few prognostications: the expansion of technical resources from ethnographic representation through dramatic voicing to poems that speak for themselves will probably be traceable in all cases. Neither Indo-Caribbean nor Sino-Caribbean writing is likely to invest heavily in an aesthetic of performance, as Afro-Caribbean writing does; on the other hand we can anticipate very subtle treatment of the dynamics of cultural assimilation and of the implications of exile.

After some account of early techniques for the depiction of Caribbean people in West Indian poetry, this chapter turns to its central question: how does "Africa" contribute to the representation of West Indians? The focus is then on post-Independence poetry, with particular attention to Brathwaite's seminal trilogy *The Arrivants* (1967–69) and its impact on the work of other West Indian poets. This leads directly to discussion of fundamental changes in the language of West Indian poetry, and to the debates about aesthetics which accompanied those changes.

REPRESENTING CARIBBEAN PEOPLE

Chapter 2 recounted how the poets of Cuba and Haiti, themselves generally middle class, became interested in broadening the horizon of their writing beyond the representation of a colonized society by colonized means. As in nineteenth-century Europe, stirrings of national consciousness were nourished in these islands by a revaluation of the vanishing folk: the extinct Amerindian, the black cane-worker or slave, the maroon, the rural peasantry. There is a corresponding phenomenon in the Anglophone Caribbean. While the effort to cultivate a poetry capable of representing Caribbean reality without the filter of Europe applied to the depiction of all West Indians, the greatest challenges (of style, decorum, language) were encountered in the attempt to represent the West Indians least like the poets themselves. From about 1940 well into the 1970s, therefore, technical innovations were usually being worked out in poems concerned with folk figures. Emphasis on the rural peasantry (fishermen, farmers, washerwomen, and the like) was augmented after the 1950s by interest in the urban folk, with their problematically creolized, even cosmopolitan "folkways." When the dust clears, about 1980, an array of new poetic resources is available for depicting the look and sound of West Indians from every walk of life.

An ideologue might insist that identity with the folk is a goal, every other method a falling short, but for a practicing poet there is more accurately an array of resources than a progression; not every poem need be taken over by a vociferous peasant. In the representation of Caribbean people it would be misleading to speak of a sequence of stages of development, because supposedly early stages coexist with much later ones. Poets may become bolder with the passage of time, but earlier techniques do not necessarily become obsolete. There are legitimate effects that can only be achieved by the use of an idealizing distance, and these are most effective when it is apparent that the choice of this distance from among alternative modes of representation has a clear aesthetic motivation. A poem depicting (for example) a middle-class speaker who finally finds the folk remote despite his good intentions, his will to solidarity, can make good use of idealizing effects. Cecil Herbert's "Lines Written on a Train" (1947) does exactly that, as it meditates on the distance between the poet and the peasants he sees through a window, singing spirituals as they reap the sugar-cane.[8] It is appropriate, however, to speak in terms of a spectrum of representation that broadens with time as more of its extent becomes available to writers. Such a spectrum might be said to pass from curiosity through empathy to forced or impersonated identity, and then to genuine identity; from "them" to "us," from "there" to "here." Later in this chapter we will see that this is analogous to the poets' parallel (but independent) exploration of the creole language continuum in the course of learning to bring the least European elements of West Indian language into poetry with assurance.

The first visible band of such a spectrum of representation is ethnographic depiction, the poetic equivalent of *National Geographic*, in which the West Indian of African, or Amerindian, or East Indian heritage is presented as a curiosity. This is the poetry of the museum diorama. Slaves, indentured workers, and Amerindians alike are presented as if they were indigenous populations thoroughly at home in their landscape. The romantic bond between worker and land neutralizes the realities of bondage and eclipses the deracination of Middle Passage. It is as if the people belong in the landscape simply because both are exotic (just as we routinely imagine lions and tigers together in the jungle, though they come from different continents). Such images humanize slaves (an abolitionist agenda) and calm fears of conspiracy to revolt (a planters' agenda). The presence of those motives is supported by an absence: there are as far as I know no corresponding representations of the quaint domesticity of plantation overseers. Some of the very earliest poems published in London, busy reporting the tropics back to England, naturally exhibit this "diorama" mode: Weekes's *Barbados* (1754), Grainger's *Sugar Cane* (1764), Chapman's *Barbadoes* (1833). An example chosen from Grainger virtually at random:

Meanwhile some stripling, from the choral ring,
Trips forth; and, not ungallantly, bestows
On her who nimblest hath the greensward beat,

. . .

A silver token of his fond applause.[9]

Such poems represent their subject in long shot, often in the present tense of ethnography. At the same time a highly conventional poetic diction transforms the events and people described into generic striplings and coquettes cavorting on the lea. The "Ethiops," "dusky swains," and romanticized peasants of verse before the twentieth century were all part of an effort to poeticize Caribbean humanity in metropolitan terms. This was more than mere passive submission to the "filter of England"; there was a positive effort to find West Indian subjects a place in the poetic tradition and thereby to ennoble them (and perhaps make them appear harmless). This occurs most notably in Guyana among the Anglophone territories; Dalton's "The Carib's Complaint" (1858), Leo's "Negro Village" (1883) and his "The Hammock Maker" (1886?) are convenient examples by indigenous authors, each depicting a different ethnic group.

There are obvious parallels with European Romanticism here, and indeed much West Indian poetry before about 1940 is dismissed as imitation Wordsworth. But it is worth asking why he is the model for imitation. Granted that the turn to High Romantic poetry as a model for amateur poets is a matter of schooling in what constitutes "Poetry" and a demonstration of the somewhat belated taste of the colonial. But whether conscious or not, one reason for this choice of model is the parallel of cultural situations. The Romantic era was remarkable for its treatment of and interest in folk culture. The origin of this interest was, among other things, new nationalism, which invested heavily in figures of identity. At the same time industrialization and urbanization physically separated writers from peasantry more sharply than before (as did the general principle of division of labor). These forms of estrangement led writers to establish (or assert) affiliations. Interest in common folk, urban as well as rural, was particularly strong in Words-

worth among the major English poets. In this, as in his
ultimately compromised attitude to social revolution, he bears
a much stronger resemblance to the West Indian poet of the
early twentieth century than does Blake, Byron, or Shelley.
With the passage of time, politics similarly enters the arena
of West Indian poetry. Peasant figures and events are still kept
at a romantic distance by exoticism and idealization, but they
are being developed more pointedly into *icons* of the nation or
culture in question. There is some effort to find subjects that
are not merely interesting, but somehow *characteristic*: fishermen, dancing-girls, market-women; a wedding, a funeral, a
festival. The subject is still viewed from outside and at some
distance, but s/he is now the noble savage, the enduring
peasant, the patient fisherman. The added affective dimension
implicit in those adjectives indicates a sympathy or admiration
not precisely for the individuals, but for values that as icons
they can represent. They are now felt, or made to be felt, as
belonging (in an ambiguous sense) to the poet's circle, to
himself and his audience. Often a first-person narrator appears
as observer in poems of this kind. His presence in the foreground has two functions: it establishes the romantic distance
from the subject, and it informs us of the appropriate attitude
toward the subject. This mode is familiar from West Indian
"yard" novels of the 1930s, and indeed from nineteenth-
century European poetry about humble folk subjects. The
political elements in both cases are analogous – these are icons
in the service of emerging nationalism in nineteenth-century
Germany as in the Caribbean. It is typical of this mode that
poems employing it are, so to speak, proscenium poems or
tableaux vivants, framed as they are with ornamental flowers and
vegetation. Similarly, the frequent presence of a foreground
interlocutor suggests that their subjects are observed; they do
not address us, and we do not participate in their actions,
which are presented in the ethnographic present of habitual,
essential, behavior ("the Carib fisherman mends his nets"). W.
Adolphe Roberts's Petrarchan sonnet "The Maroon Girl"
(1949) depicts an iconic "figure of savage beauty, figure of
pride" in the ethnographic present tense, and the woman

herself is static.[10] She is posed on a lonely forest track in maroon country and framed with orchids, hibiscus, orange and coffee blossoms against a mountain background; the only action she performs in the poem is to "stand." She is being proffered as a national emblem: "She is Jamaica poised against attack." Roberts emphasizes how her fixity embodies contradictions and thereby neutralizes them, relieves potential tensions, reconciles opposites. She combines the blood of black, white, and Arawak; "she is a peasant, yet she is a queen"; she is a maternal figure, yet a beautiful amazon; a madonna and a virgin. And why is she a maroon? Because for Roberts and his contemporaries maroons, though in fact the descendants of runaway slaves, were often treated as surrogate aborigines, an acceptable fiction in the absence of any surviving aboriginal population (we have seen that Cuban nationalists treated blacks as aboriginal in the same way, for the same reason). Thus Roberts and his readers can have it both ways: in the figure of a maroon of mixed race, the creole outcome of Caribbean history can be posited as its origin.

Another Petrarchan sonnet, Eric Roach's "She" (1949), also depicts a physically static, symbolic personage who combines Amerindian, European, African and Asian blood. This woman too is explicitly depicted "in a rare frame of beauty." She is surrounded by immortelle and flamboyant, hibiscus and poui, against a background of sea and sky – apt foils for her pride and passion. Like Roberts's maroon, she is an icon of creole beauty. Unlike Roberts, however, Roach insists upon historicizing:

> She is Caribbean. She is the meaning,
> Flower and fruit of our four centuries
> Of ruthless traffic, of dark uneasy peace
> Among ourselves, of reckless greedy gleaning
> From old continents, and the commingling
> Of our blood with wanton, lustful ease.[11]

The telling enjambments (which recall the characteristic effects of Telemaque's "In Our Land") express the violence of that history. It is apparent from these lines that Roach's investment in the creole icon is more problematic than Roberts's; not surprisingly he was at the same time publishing poems about specifically black beauty ("Dancer," 1950) and even specifically Amerindian beauty ("Anacaona," 1949). Roach's work in the 1940s exemplifies how poets begin to deal openly with several related matters: their growing uneasiness with treating the peasant as decor, and a new urge for some solidarity if not identity with the folk as a premise for what comes to be felt as the poet's responsibility to speak securely of and for the folk, because they define national identity. There is also the clash between European aesthetic habits and what is, by those criteria, the "difficult beauty" (Sam Selvon's phrase) of African, Asian, and Amerindian peoples.

Telemaque's "Adina" (1949) also focuses on the blindness of outsiders to Caribbean beauty:

> They hunt chameleon worlds with cameras.
> . . .
> They have not seen Adina's velvet figure
> Swimming uncovered in our river's bubbles.[12]

"Adina" praises the island's interior secrets, the homely virtue far from the surf and the sights. But it is surprising to find that virtue particularized in a naked native girl, with a sort of Negrista facility that Telemaque usually transcends. The notion that Adina in the river images forth the inherent innocence, simplicity, even virtue of the islands has a certain validity, but it seems hardly possible to extricate that from the more immediate associations of rank tourism: "see the *real* Trinidad – frolicking native girls!" Telemaque does not really want tour buses driving up to Adina's water hole, but the realization of this poem has not moved very far from "dusky swains." It proceeds through all the clichés – Adina dancing, Adina swinging down the road with her basket of fruit – and so stands as an epitome of many poems devoted to uncovering the picturesque beauty of the peasant as an object, just as in Negrismo.

Blindness does not afflict only outsiders. As a consequence of the colonial heritage, British-educated West Indians had to learn to recognize their own beauty, a fundamental step in cultural independence not entirely taken until the repercussions of American Black Power were felt in the Caribbean. So the Barbadian H. A. Vaughan in "Revelation" (1945) accuses West Indians themselves of wearing metropolitan filters:

> Turn sideways now and let them see
> What loveliness escapes the schools,
> Then turn again, and smile, and be
> The perfect answer to those fools
> Who always prate of Greece and Rome,
>
> . . .
> but keep tight lips
> For burnished beauty nearer home.[13]

Though the effect is much more secure, the opening imperative "turn" here corresponds rhetorically to the "but" of the apologetic mode – it marks the same kind of enforced shift of perspective, a self-conscious swerve away from the tradition. Vaughan here is in league with much later poets who work to circumvent the efforts of educators ("those fools"). The West Indian public in all innocence fails to see local beauty for what it is, but the educators, the poet insists, actively suppress it whenever they "keep tight lips." Vaughan's anthologized poems are adept examples of standard rhyming forms – quatrains and sonnets, generally quite regular. But this text is a scamp's sonnet, expressively deformed: tetrameter rather than pentameter, with permissible but inconsistent rhyming patterns, and a sestet that must be described as hyperventilating:

> Turn in the sun, my love, my love!
> What palm-like grace! What poise! I swear
> I prize thy dusky limbs above
> My life. What laughing eyes!
> What gleaming hair!

The sonnet *sounds* complete, in an unsettling way, because the three rhymes expected of a sestet are completed. But in the breathless excitement of the author's swoon we've lost the equivalent of almost two lines. "Eyes," by rhyming with "poise" brings strong closure to a line that is metrically unfinished; the same happens even more precipitously when "hair" rhymes with "swear." We are led to feel that the deformations of traditional form are induced by admiration for beauty that does not obey traditional rules.

Only after the effort to assert Caribbean experience on its own terms engaged received opinion on both these fronts – both the local and the metropolitan blindnesses – did it become possible to celebrate that experience straightforwardly without dialectical preliminaries or metropolitan filtration. This important advance is most apparent in the work of Campbell, M. G. Smith, and other Jamaicans associated with *Focus* – all of them heirs to the social realism of McKay. Campbell's "New World Flowers" (1945) shares themes and procedures with both of the poems just discussed, but "Holy" (1941) is much more representative of Campbell's accomplishment, clearing a space for an assured, expansive, and plainly West Indian poetry. Here Caribbean beauty is taken as a given; no longer an aesthetic taste measured against some standard of uncertain authority, but a holiness, an unmediated radiance, a self-evident beauty. Not more or less admirable than anything else, but autochthonous: "Heads of wheaten gold,/ Heads of peoples dark / So strong so original; / All of the earth and the sun."[14] There may be some lingering question how widely his attitude is shared, how much convincing needs to be done. But there can be no doubt, or even modesty, about his assurance.

The question is: how can West Indian people be presented as mundane and dignified, rather than exotic and theatrical? In their answers Campbell and the *Focus* poets may still protest a bit too much, but within a few years unruffled confidence is the norm. This is true in Roach's depictions of village life, beginning with "The Flowering Rock" and "Transition" (both in 1950), and in Ian McDonald's poems of individual folk figures, which began to appear in *Bim* in the mid-1950s. Forthright portrait-poems are especially prominent in post-Independence anthologies from Guyana. In "Holy" the fact of West Indian beauty is taken as sufficiently established that it is not actually the poem's point, but its premise. The point of the poem is a matter of political idealism: the wealth of a multi-racial creole society. This is very much the orthodoxy of the years before independence; the years *before* the wave of "Africa" caused such creole ideals to be contested by many Afro-Caribbean writers. Most of the poetry published in *Focus* is nationalist and socialist, preoccupied with the politics of class and the celebration of diversity, rather than with race or "Africa." At about the same time, Louise Bennett, usually more interested in the creole nationalist issues of color and race, voices in "Back to Africa" (1947) a respectable middle-class impatience with "Africa" – entirely analogous to that class's attitude toward Garvey a generation earlier.[15]

In the 1930s Una Marson had introduced what Philip Sherlock at the time called "a new issue": race and color (the observation implies, at the very least, that Sherlock either did not know McKay's poetry of a decade earlier, or did not consider it West Indian).[16] This concern appears first in poems of Marson's that anticipate by a decade the work of the *Focus* poets in Jamaica and of Telemaque in Trinidad. Marson offers a compact example of the characteristic recognition of difference, marked with the apologetic rhetoric of "but," in "Another Mould" (1931): "You can talk about your babies / With blue eyes and hair of gold, / But I'll tell you 'bout an angel / That's cast in another mould . . ."[17] This has moved only a short distance from the apologetic manner discussed in the previous chapter, and Europeans still provide the aesthetic reference-point. In her work as a whole, however, Marson initiates the effort of West Indian poetry to recognize distinctively Caribbean beauty as independent of metropolitan standards – a beauty defined by creole standards. This is exemplified in "There will come a time . . .," the final poem of *Heights and Depths* (1931):

> But we who see through this hypocrisy
> And feel the blood of black and white alike
> Course through our veins as our strong heritage
> Must range ourselves to build the younger race.[18]

Most revealing of where she stands in the development of West Indian poetry are her blues poems. We have just seen how nationalist poets frame their beauties in indigenous fruits, or at least make some effort to avoid resorting to any outside frame of reference when establishing the identity of their subjects. In the blues poems (of which more later) Marson's subjects speak for themselves of their intimate concerns, seemingly without such baggage. Her very choice of the blues form, however, situates them explicitly as members of a race, that is, in solidarity with the trans-national African diaspora.

The African strain in the West Indies is present from the very beginning, of course, in real cultural survivals of several kinds among the slaves. This presence is also acknowledged quite early in the history of West Indian self-consciousness – that is, in West Indian writing – where it provides, for example, picturesque ornament in eighteenth-century poems. West Indian awareness of pigmentation, of "shade," as a social index goes back very far too. It is inherent in the taxonomy used under slavery that with terms like "quadroon" and "octoroon" could reach back three and four generations to distinguish degrees of color. Shade is a peculiarly Caribbean preoccupation. Physical differences routinely measure degrees of social status (or sometimes merely mark a horizontal position: this business rather than that, these cultural practices rather than those). But consciousness of race – of being black as opposed to white – comes to the fore through contact with North America and its simple binary view of color, and is sharpened by the experience of emigration to America and of service in the Allied armies in both world wars. In the early 1930s the magazines *Trinidad* and *The Beacon*, whose editors were oriented toward the United States, took a precocious interest in matters of race. The crucial recognition of "Africa" as a ground of identity, as an historical heritage underlying the biological facts, follows after – and helps West Indians deal with – the recognition of race as difference. Consciousness of race is a consciousness of marginality; the discovery of Africa comes as a defensive weapon (as in Negritude), a consciousness of alternative centrality, of race not simply as a mark to bear, but as the mark of a substantial heritage. Such awareness of Africa, and reflection on its implications both as a burden and as a

positive value, first comes to West Indians through their exiles –
workers, soldiers, intellectuals. It seems right to say that
McKay discovered Africa for West Indians (in the same sense
that W. A. Roberts, in his own exile, discovered the Americas
for West Indians). It is easy to treat McKay's writing of sonnets
as an assertion of affinity with the tradition of English poetry;
yet in these same sonnets he repeatedly sets himself apart from
his surroundings, or associates himself with others who seem
set apart, as in "Outcast" (1922) or "The Harlem Dancer"
(1922). Thanks in part to circumstances of the period, he could
trace the root of this Otherness to blackness and so to Africa.
But it was some time before the discoveries of an exile like
McKay could make their way back to the Caribbean itself.

VARIETIES OF AFRICA IN WEST INDIAN POETRY

The word "Africa" has a bewildering array of connotations in
the Anglophone Caribbean. For one thing, different West
Indian writers often have very different parts of the African
continent in mind. For most West Indians, the word "Africa"
initially evoked British East Africa; it comes to refer to the
ancestral west coast surprisingly late – perhaps only after
journalistic attention shifted to Nkrumah's Ghana from earlier
Mau Mau/Rhodesia issues. When C. L. R. James says "Africa"
he is primarily thinking of Ghana, but Walcott and Roach
(among others) more often have in mind the East Africa of
Shaka Zulu and the Mau Mau. A Rastafarian means an
idealized Ethiopia, an "Afro-centrist" means the ancient black
kingdoms of Egypt and the Sudan, while a "Negrista" type
mixes a Congo out of Conrad and the Copacabana. More
significant, however, are the different functions for which
Africa is invoked. Particularly we need to distinguish (1)
"Africa" as historical past, (2) "Africa" as ideal elsewhere (an
alternative world), (3) "Africa" as real elsewhere (a separate
place with its own history), and (4) "Africa-in-the-Caribbean,"
an assemblage of cultural survivals and affinities.

From a fairly early date, the word "Africa" appears often in
the West Indies as the name for a traditional society in the

remote past, frozen in time at the moment of the slave trade (or just before it). McKay provides good examples in "Invocation" (1917) and "Africa" (1921). This is emphatically a noble past, a Golden Age before the Middle Passage, either heroic in its exploits (an empire before any European empire) or Arcadian in the integrity of its civilization. This view owes something to Negritude and to the Harlem Renaissance, in terms of specific literary influences, and is further nourished through the years by pan-Africanism, Black Power, and Rastafarianism. Mythical Africa functioned in the West Indies exactly as it had in Europe after World War I, as the refreshing image of a world success-fully organized along entirely different lines. In the West Indian case, there are several advantages to the frozen Africa. It is easier to utilize "Africa" as a term in a dialectical process if it remains a fixed entity, an invariant cultural norm. Thus the term can generally be relied upon to invoke an image of traditional, pre-colonial Africa.

Another related view of Africa as a feature of the West Indian past reads it specifically as a point of origin – that persistent germ of biological, historical, psychic identity. This view of Africa as home makes possible two quite different sorts of leverage that in recent years have been exploited in the West Indians' relationship to the metropolitan culture. The first can be called "Africa in my blood" – a racial identity, a *négritude*, a state of psyche, the "African personality" (to cite several terms for it). This is the reactive idea of Africa that comes in the wake of a *prise de conscience*. What had been the stigma of difference is reinterpreted by its bearer as a mark of quite specific super-iority: a claim to unmediated contact with emotion, passion, human origins. This Africa, the "tomtoms in the blood," the proud assertion of precisely what white terrified consciousness fears about the archetypal black, functions primarily as a license, invoked to justify everything from irrational behavior to unmetrical verse (the poetry of Laleau discussed in chapter 2 exemplifies such invocation). It is the wild card that suspends the rules and so gives the player room to maneuver. This same conception of Africa as a license can also be invoked as an ultimate authority. At its simplest, this is only a claim of sincerity, as if the poet were saying "my blackness allows me to speak the truth of the human heart in a way inaccessible to rational men" – indeed several poems in French makes precisely this claim to the authority of the primitive, of the chthonic voice. The Negritude movement invoked it as the core of the argument that blacks were not marginal, but centrally human (in contrast to the congenitally alienated whites). This function of Africa is rare in the cricket-playing Caribbean, where a widespread and enduring view of Africa as backward and primitive made it ineffective for anything but the grossest provocation.

But a more sophisticated view of African culture as authoritative, as a second coherent tradition which history makes accessible to the West Indian, has proved especially attractive in the decades since independence. It is not entirely a rigorous notion; the culture in question is a conglomerate of elements from throughout West Africa. It also depends on a revision of typical West Indian thinking about Africa, but this revision is not entirely a correction of that thinking: "Africa" here is a rich, complex, traditional culture, firmly located in the past. An early example is Telemaque's "Poem" (1947), a praise-song which exploits powerful rhetorical parallelisms to assert the affinity of ancient Egyptians, equatorial Africans, and survivors of the Middle Passage.[19] As such a poem makes clear, both Africa as license and Africa as authority give West Indians considerable leverage in the attempt to lighten the burden of the European literary tradition.

If Africa is often seen as the West Indian's past, it can also appear, by the logic inherent in every idealizing edenic myth, as a *locus amoenus* to escape to, as "Africa in my mind," a nourishing parallel world in the imagination, a world of peace, polygamy, and handsome elephants at a safe distance. Many poems reflect this Africa – as we might expect, since escape into nourishing fantasy is a common enough function of poetry. Even poems that attack this conception as enervating or escapist necessarily represent it in the process. So "Africa" becomes a name for heaven, for the Haitian "Guinée," for the Rastafarian "Zion" or "Ethiopia" – an ideal world predestined from the beginning either as transcendent heaven or as earth-bound utopia. This millenarian view of Africa as a realm from which one is absent but in which one's place is kept available, is, of course, most common in the lyrics of reggae songs, and in poems by or about Rastafarians.

Africa as a place in the world with its own historical destiny, interesting to a West Indian in the way that China or Lapland might be, appears in West Indian poetry about as rarely as China or Lapland. The most neutral or objective view that appears with any frequency presents Africa as a distinct place and people with which West Indians have some generalized affinity in the present; that is, affinity as colonials and post-colonials, as people of color, as people of the tropics. Such a perception of Africa is at the heart of Brathwaite's *Masks* (1968), with its searching account of what happens when a West Indian poet's preconceptions adjust themselves to African actualities. Something quite similar is happening in Walcott's earlier poem "A Far Cry from Africa" (1956).[20] Eric Roach, who became progressively better informed about Africa, is aspiring to such objectivity in poems as early as 1953 ("Black Gods" and "In Mango Shade"). His "Senghor Visiting" (*c.* 1964) reverses the scene of *Masks* by situating the encounter between Africa and the West Indies in the Caribbean: "you're farther off from Dakar than you know," Roach warns the visiting Senegalese poet upon his arrival in the Caribbean – "your presence is our past."[21]

Viewed in greater detail, and with an added increment of self-interest, Africa appears as a place and people with which black West Indians shared a history until the era of the diaspora, after which the two have gone separate ways. Writers informed about the attitudes of Africans towards the blacks of the Americas tend to depict the parties as unwilling relatives or actual strangers, moving amid mutual misunderstandings and sharing a recent history that includes such ambiguous elements as black American colonization of West Africa in Sierra Leone and Liberia, movements (like Pan-Africanism, Negritude, and Black Power) that generate entirely external programs and visions for Africa, and Ethiopia's cool reception to the idea of

Rastafarian repatriation there. This discovery of difference is what Brathwaite dramatizes in *Masks*, and he draws important inferences from it. In his later work, he rejects uncritical imitation of African ways, and insists upon the value of learning, through the example of how Africans come to terms with their own environment, how to do what is needed in the West Indies.[22] From this perspective the West Indian is independent of but related to Africa as to Europe, free to choose and adapt elements of the joint heritage that suit indigenous purposes.

Brathwaite's direct experience of Africa enabled him to see the components of West Indian life in a new light. Perhaps the first to make something of this experience was not a West Indian, but the anthropologist Melville Herskovits, who contributed vastly to our sense of the Americas through his work in West Africa and the Caribbean. Brathwaite, in many ways an heir of Herskovits, makes the most substantial recent contribution of this kind. With eyes attuned to Africa, what the observer recognizes when he comes home to the Caribbean is something quite immediate, a large cluster of habits and styles in speech, belief, and behavior integrated into the indigenous culture, but still bearing signs of African origin. This is "Africa-in-the-Caribbean," the most salient evidence that the Caribbean is more than its European history. George Lamming called it "the black rock of Africa," to emphasize its function as a persistent emblem of identity and difference, its lineaments established in the work of Price-Mars and Ortiz, as well as Herskovits, his followers and critics. This cluster links the habits of everyday life to an historically remote past, and interprets the link not as a degradation and forgetting of ancient custom, but as a survival indicating generations of effort in a hostile cultural climate. Africa comes to be read as an element of Caribbean life, the trace of a real and coherent past. It signifies an alternative history that, having been suppressed, can stand as a sign of birthright to be recaptured in the process of achieving independence.

For the most part West Indians are invited to open themselves to influences from the African heritage, rather than from

contemporary African practice. In the realm of literature there
are important exceptions: Walcott read and produced Soyinka's
plays, and even Brathwaite, while his adaptations are almost
always of traditional African materials, was originally affected
by contemporary writing in progress in Ghana during his stay
there. His second trilogy reflects even wider reading in East
African and South African work. In the Caribbean generally,
however, the matter of "Africa" is too readily and too uncriti-
cally assimilated to folk culture. In fact the African element
stands in complex relation to the indigenous tradition, of which
it forms a sometimes refractory part. As we have just seen,
"Africa-in-the-Caribbean" is only part of what the term
"Africa" includes (the courtly Akan ceremonials which
Brathwaite invokes in *The Arrivants* have nothing to do with
African survivals or with folk culture on either side of the
Atlantic). On the other hand, "Africa-in-the-Caribbean" is also
only part of the indigenous cultural tradition, which has been
creolized from the start.

The cross-cultural valuation of the peasantry as the authentic
root which sustains national identity is greatly enhanced by this
conflation with the prestige symbolized by "Africa" in the pre-
Independence West Indies. The turn to Africa can easily have
anti-national consequences, however. The most extreme case is
the Rastafarian who dissociates himself from his Caribbean
environment while awaiting repatriation to Ethiopia, but the
habit of investing in anything but the Caribbean crops up even
among West Indian critics, for example when they speak of
cultural practices as "peasant and *thus ultimately* African."[23]
Poets are not immune. If there is a "filter of English eyes"
which causes poets to see swains on the lea and snow in the
cane-fields, so too there is a "filter of African eyes" which
likewise facilitates representation, but at the price of new
distortions. Sherlock's "Jamaican Fisherman" (1953) is an
excellent example of a poem – yet another sonnet – that
appears to depict another national icon, but differs significantly
insofar as it finds value in a folk figure not because of what he
is, does, or says, but because "Africa" is traceable in his
physique. What the fisherman does in this poem is stride across

the beach, pick up his gear and take it back to his hut. What the poet experiences is quite different: the black body "silently . . . *cried* its proud descent from ancient chiefs and kings; . . . *sang* . . . the velvet coolness of dark forests wide, the blackness of the jungle's starless night."[24] It is especially interesting that this passage is couched in verbs of utterance, for the poem ends noting that the fisherman did not know "how fiercely *spoke* his body then of ancient wealth and savage regal men." The poet knows the peasant better than he knows himself, mirrors him speakingly. The fisherman is not yet speaking for himself, nor is he yet precisely valued for himself. Sherlock's fisherman is a West Indian figure valued because his roots are elsewhere – not in the Caribbean but in Africa.

There is also a body of what can be called interrogative poetry dealing with the matter of Africa – poetry self-conscious about the *prise de conscience*, that problematizes the glance at the iconic figure. This mode appears as early as McKay, precipitated by his experience of the United States. Later, Mervyn Morris is particularly adept in this vein. Vera Bell is remembered chiefly for a single such poem, "Ancestor on the Auction Block" (1948) – a poem whose crux is the poet's troubled relation to the poem's ancestral subject/object. Like Sherlock's fisherman or Roberts's maroon, this ancestor is treated as a mute object – the illusion of dialogue is all by imputation. Unexpectedly, though, the slave ancestor starts to *act* like a subject; the eyes of the ancestor seek out those of the poet, who first turns away, ashamed of the ancestor's humiliation, but also of the "primitive black face."[25] In this situation the poet is, so to speak, the one who blinks first. The continuing gaze compels the poet to see herself as a slave, a slave to shame and ignorance. Bell is here dramatizing in personal terms the larger transformation in her culture's attitudes toward "Africa." In the poem a new level of contact is achieved, though there is as yet no real dialogue. The poet finally returns the gaze, looks upon the slave ancestor with pride, and draws from his (or her?) accomplishments a new sense of mission: "yours was the task to clear the ground / Mine be the task to build." West Indian critics looking back at this poem from a position after Brathwaite's work sniff at its "rather naive solution"[26] or dismiss the poem as "a failure of imagination."[27] But Lamming, writing before Brathwaite's trilogy began to appear, has a better sense of the poem's significance for its time, and for the development we are considering here.[28] For Lamming, Bell's poem has the characteristics of a transitional work: "an uncertainty of tone, an ambiguity of vision, and the psychological timidity that restrains the intellect and inhibits the imagination as it prepares itself for some positive act of cultural commitment" (36). This characterization, along with Lamming's sense of the "inauthenticity" and "embarrassment" that ensue when a poet has the courage to take on a subject which then proves too daunting, situates Bell's poem squarely at a liminal moment in the process of establishing contact with a previously objectified or fetishized Other.

Bell's poem is one of those that light the way to identification with the subject, and make possible a body of pugnacious poems far beyond the defensive gestures of "Jamaica poised against attack." This progression – from the poetry of "here we are" to its extreme, "here we are and what are you going to do about it?" – can be exemplified by such poems as Campbell's "Negro Aroused" (1945), a portrait of the Other as self, and Carter's "I Come From the Nigger Yard" (1954), in which the poet completely absorbs the ancestral figure of Bell's poem.[29] The work of Peter Blackman is especially forward-looking, probably as a result of his own migratory life. Blackman left Barbados, worked as a missionary in West Africa, and then lived in England. Though not as well known as his younger compatriot Lamming, Blackman, like Lamming, associated himself with Negritude. The vaunting tone of the following lines puts a characteristically Eastern Caribbean spin on Negritude's glorification of Africa: "My footprints are nowhere in history . . . / I cast in bronze at Benin when London was marshland / I built Timbuctoo and made it a refuge for learning / When in the choirs of Oxford unlettered monks shivered unwashed."[30] These post-war political poems lead ultimately to the full-blown protest poetry of the 1960s.

This chapter so far has been concerned with poems about

Caribbean people, and poems addressed to them; what has been missing here until these poems of Carter and Blackman is the voice of the Caribbean subject. The next broadening of the spectrum, then, includes poems in which the icons speak for themselves. Such poems occupy several degrees of the scale, beginning with the sort of poem in which, for example, a peasant speaks merely to bring some picturesque turn of dialect into the poem (and there are even a few poems such as Sherlock's "Dinner Party 1940" [1943] which present middle class dialect in the same way.)[31] The sequence extends to the dramatic figure whose consciousness we enter until we see him from within and know the world of the poem only through him. And beyond that, perhaps, we should distinguish poems in which the poet speaks his own language. But what is "his own language"? That is the fundamental question for any poem with a speaking Caribbean subject: what language do West Indians speak, and how do we get it on paper?

FROM DIALECT TO NATION LANGUAGE

The pioneering prose masterpieces of nation language appear virtually together in a neatly representative group: Reid's *New Day* from Jamaica in 1949, Selvon's *A Brighter Sun* from Trinidad in 1952, and Lamming's *In the Castle of My Skin* from Barbados in 1953. It is at first surprising that the appearance of nation language in poetry printed locally comes after these novels printed abroad, but the entry of nation language into published poetry is faced with several obstacles in the West Indies. First, the social stigma attached to it. It is not simply that creole is associated with some picturesque "them," "the little people," the folk; in the West Indies the hierarchies of color, social class, and economic status reinforce one another so thoroughly that use of creole was not merely a generalized sign of lower status, but a fairly precise measure of status. This correlation was naturally reflected in educational practice throughout the islands, which militated against any use of "broken" English. Condemned as "dialect," it remained an intimate language, publicly indulged only by those who could afford to take the risk, or were already sufficiently condemned to low status on other grounds. Any insistence on creole tended to be associated with forms of social aggression: rude boy, calypsonian, saga boy, stereotyped Rastafarian. Increasing nationalism and independence are factors contributing to acceptance of this mother-tongue, but above all it is the slow scholarly identification of the formative role of elements from African languages that makes West Indian nation language acceptable as a language. First, lexical elements were redeemed by this line of argument, then, with continuing sophistication in scholarship, the syntactic and even tonal and rhetorical habits of West Indian speakers.[32] This was the evidence that made it possible to regard Jamaican (for example) not as monstrous defective English, but as the mulatto child of a marriage of Europe and Africa, a new thing.

A second obstacle is the oral nature of nation language. The establishing norm of SE (Standard English) is of course a written norm; the norm for nation language is speech practice, with all its inherent shiftiness. At first, no one is literate in creole – as Louise Bennett notes: "People are not as accustomed to reading the dialect as they are to listening to it."[33] Thus for dialect the point of entry into literature is in the form of transcribed speech; the objective is to present and preserve striking rhythms and locutions – striking because they were colorful bits of folk art, unconscious or inadvertent creations, almost *objets trouvés*. So appear ethnographic poems, those that seem generated from the discovery of a particular turn of folk speech, and from the impulse to preserve it, like any other element of local color or national identity. So too poems *about* class and caste appear; poems that present not just turns of language but also the personae they embody – poems about artisans, servants, fishermen. It is a cross-cultural common-place that dialect first enters any literature as a device for comedy, as an admirable means for depiction in the low mimetic style. Its most obvious value is in the representation of character, and in the directness with which it can distinguish a voice from that of the poet. Dialect is the sound of someone the poet hears, but is not. Thus its close association with dramatic verse, and its natural affinity for comic or ironic contexts –

exploiting the distances between poet, represented character, and audience. The association of dialect with dramaticality and improvisation remains strong even now. Bennett has much to say about this, noting the common (mistaken) assumption by audiences that she did not – in a sense could not – *write* her compositions, but must improvise them on the spot, like a typical unlettered folk genius. When dialect appears in print, it is assumed to be sub-literary, either on purely generic grounds, or because, given the apparently narrow expressive range of dialect (generally assumed to extend from abuse to comedy), the choice to write in it seems a perverse stunt, an indulgence in limitation not unlike setting oneself the task of writing a story without using the letter 'E' (as Georges Perec has so effectively done).

The notion of a text with missing letters points directly to a linguistic stigma, which actually provides the grounds for the social one. Dialect is conceived as a corruption of English, a distortion arising out of ignorance and illiteracy. At the heart of this is a problem of orthography. Jamaican cannot be represented as a version of English, or Haitian as a version of French, without appearing fractured (the ubiquitous apostrophes mark the breaks). A composition that diverges from the linguistic standard, when it appears in print, confesses each and every one of its divergences, branding each with some diacritical mark. The alternative is to generate an orthography that represents it "as it is" and not as a putative tissue of distortions. Nationalism dictates this second choice, but the decision to represent it by means of some conventional phonetic orthography masks the important historical relation to metropolitan languages, and so makes the creole difficult for natives to recognize or foreigners to learn. This alternative, nevertheless, has been adopted by several territories in the region, including St. Lucia. Such an inscribed erasure of heritage may seem unstable and unlikely to survive, but survival is made possible by the isolation such a gesture enhances (as in Europe, for example, French does not become more like Latin with the passage of time).

Papiamento, the creole of Aruba and Curacao, offers a

striking instance of a language made to appear hermetic by its orthography: it sounds like Spanish but comes out looking like a kind of Dutch, in which for example "aki" disguises what "aqui" would make clear to many more readers – and many more Caribbean readers. A convention that makes a language look untouched may also make it unapproachable. Similarly, texts risk unintelligibility not only for a metropolitan audience, but among West Indians, to the extent that the written standards in the region approach SE. Since each nation's – each poet's – orthography is *ad hoc*, each new work constitutes a puzzle of mere notation even before it can be a puzzle of meaning. Any attempt to stabilize an orthography for a language like Jamaican would seem a falsification of a language whose genius and norm is in speech practice, for in fact a nation language exists in as many local forms as did any of its historical analogues, such as Middle English. Spelling the first person pronoun "mi" or "me" or "mih" is of little consequence, but more serious semantic confusions often arise: "deh," "de," and "dey," for example, are all of them possible spellings of "the" or "they" or "their" or "there". But who would undertake to standardize a language identified as nonstandard? Such a project engages with notions of national identity and the relation to the outside world that are sharply political. For individual writers, the practical decision to be made is between writing a "negotiable" language (SE, or a compromise grapholect) and writing a proprietary language, a bearer of national identity which can withdraw into itself so thoroughly as to constitute virtually a cult language. Increasingly precise annotation of actual speech sounds produces an increasingly more arcane text, while an imprecise notation is what makes possible the projection of an unreal but feasible "West Indian" grapholect. In the work of the poets to whom we now turn, we will see a variety of responses to these obstacles.

Nation language does successfully establish itself as a viable medium for poetry. The roots of course are constant: the verbal behavior of West Indians, and the verbal artefacts that arise from it. Of special interest here, however, is the move of nation language into print – that is, into "literature." Nation language first appears in literature of record as "dialect" – not in published sonnets, or any other form that would be regarded as serious poetry, but in a number of settings: (1) Travelers and historians published transcriptions of popular story, ballad, and song for consumption by an audience quite different from the original one. Such publication cast an anthropological or ethnographic aura over the originally popular material. (2) From surprisingly early, poems written in SE include lines or phrases of speech in dialect; quotation marks confine the potentially contagious breaches of the rules. The impulse here is sometimes ethnographic, more often an effort at dramatic characterization, as, for example, in Guyanese poet S. E. Wills's conversation poem "Before and After" (1910). (3) Even in the nineteenth century, some poetry was self-consciously composed in dialect (that is, as opposed to unself-conscious "folk" composition). At first this is verse for newspapers and calendars – comic and cute, sounding dangerously close to the ventriloquized voice of a rustic dummy. But a more substantial version soon develops, chiefly in the form of journalistic verse intended as a vehicle for satire and social commentary, such as that written by Edward Cordle in Barbados and Michael McTurk in British Guiana. All of these instances are "dramatic" in the sense that they project the voice of someone pointedly not oneself.

The poets most consistently interested in accommodating dialect to printed poetry are at first Jamaican. In Guyana and the Eastern Caribbean there are only isolated instances of serious dialect verse until after Independence.[34] Jamaican nationalism and self-consciousness are probable factors in this; so is the unusual scope of the creole continuum available in Jamaica. It is also likely that at least in Trinidad and neighboring islands the impulse was largely deflected into calypso in the early years. The first important figure is McKay, thanks in part to the influence on him of Walter Jekyll, an early transcriber of folk material (*Jamaican Song and Story*, 1907). In his introduction to McKay's first book (that is, *Songs of Jamaica*)

Jekyll maintained that Jamaican speech "refines" SE, and continued, "What Italian is to Latin, that in regard to English is the negro variant thereof."[35] McKay's *Songs* and *Ballads* constitute a real commitment to Jamaican speech as a legitimate means of literary expression. They begin with the usual assumption that the license of dialect can be suitably controlled within sharply defined and relatively simple poetic forms, such as the ballad, and that dialect is most appropriate to the projection of a distinctive persona. This same assumption underlay the dialect poems of Tennyson, or Kipling. But McKay's work is notable for two forward-looking features: a willing identification with the speakers of the dialect poems and a sensitivity to the rhythmic features of the spoken language which made it possible to experiment with them as a potential source of counterpoint for the forms used. Many of McKay's poems are dramatic monologues or songs, but the very first poem of *Constab Ballads* undertakes something more complex, a very forward-looking experiment with relations between nation language and music. "De Route March" effectively reproduces the rhythmic effect of the soldiers' syncopated song acting against the fixed tread of a long march, as, for example, in the third stanza:

> As we tramped on out de dull town,
> Keepin' time so to de drum's soun',
> All de folkses as dey ran out,
> Started dancin' with a glad shout.[36]

As many as four different rhythms vie for attention here: that of the drum, that of the soldiers, that of the spectators' dance, and that of the poetic form. The ballad form suggests a fairly quick tempo, comparable to that of Louise Bennett's ballads. The kind of march indicated, however, sets a long swinging tempo for the poem, which is roughly twice as slow, and so allows room for syncopation. This is an awkward point to make on paper, but it may be enough to draw attention to the rhythmic implication of McKay's placement of the demonstrative "so" in the second line quoted. This is in effect a sharp rimshot on the offbeat – a stroke that illustrates "keeping time" by deliberately failing to do so, and thus a clue to the poem's rhythmic freedom. The trochaic tetrameter implies an impossibly ham-fisted poem, stressed like this: "KEEpin' / TIME SO /TO de /DRUM's soun'." McKay's intended rhythm is probably more like this, in 2/4 time with a steady tempo but with a cluster of small note values after the first beat in the second bar:

> All de / FOLKSes as dey / RAN – / OUT – /
> STARTed /DANCin' with a / GLAD – / SHOUT – /

McKay has depicted a tiny allegory of creole assimilation in the relations between the regular drum, the troops whose mouths keep one rhythm while their feet keep another, and the general dancing based not on the Euro-drumbeats but on the resulting polyrhythms. Brathwaite frequently recalls this as a formative phenomenon from his own youth: the military parade followed by a crowd whose dance "tropes" the rigid beat.[37] But this is not limited to the Caribbean part of the hemisphere; it is depicted frequently, with the same sly Anansi-humor, in the music of the American composer Charles Ives (McKay's contemporary).

McKay's work in this line ends with his own emigration to that America of marching bands, where he abandoned dialect to concentrate primarily on the sonnet. He had no immediate successors, and his innovations lay dormant for some time. Thus Una Marson stands as a fine example of a poet trying to come to terms with the language issue, independent of McKay's work. Her early verse is lightweight but nationalistic nature poetry, with an emphasis on local detail that was precocious in the early 1930s. Her turn to issues of race seems to have been precipitated by her experience of living in England; her first serious treatment of racial matters is the poem "Nigger" (1933) published within a year of her migration to England.[38] But the years in England (1932–36) may also have sharpened her ear and deepened her affection for Jamaican speech. Her third volume, *The Moth and the Star* (1937), includes, along with a new interest in race, several notable experiments with dialect. Here she makes the important step from poems that depict the folk or address them to poems in which they speak for themselves. So "The Stone Breakers" is a dialogue in nation language between two women at work. In another poem a market woman expounds "My Philosophy." Most ambitious is the long dialect poem, "Quashie Comes to London."[39] Evidence that Marson had been dealing with the issue of appropriate language is patent in the contrast of this with an earlier poetic narrative, "The Tidal Wave" (1931), conceived as the reminiscence of a banana-worker about a disaster, but written (after what deliberations by the poet?) in Standard English.[40] Deliberations about appropriate language must also stand behind Marson's blues poems. Such poems as "Kinky Hair Blues," "Brown Baby Blues," and "Canefield Blues" (all in *The Moth and the Star*) make a space for themselves in a very roundabout way by assimilating African-American Modernism's assimilation of the peasant vernacular. Both the form and the diction come from North America; as with Sherlock's "Jamaican Fisherman," the value ascribed to the subject is thus grounded elsewhere – not immanent in the West Indian person as such. But the blues diction itself comes across not with an aura of American value, but almost perversely as dialect, in the sense that it is still presented as someone else's way of speaking – still "in quotation marks."[41]

The poets at home in the West Indies whose attitudes and themes Marson anticipates did not share her interest in pursuing dialect. During the period roughly between 1940 and Independence in the 1960s, the poetic use of nation language progresses unsteadily, by fits and starts. It was taken up usually as a challenge in shaping a single poem, rather than as a writer's concerted project – thus there are isolated poems such as George Campbell's "Me and My Gal" (1933) or Martin Carter's "Shape and Motion Two" (1955). In the mid-1950s, post-war nationalism and the drift toward Independence were accompanied by a burst of poems in which folk characters actually speak their own language to us, but the distance between "them" and "us" is still quite perceptible, coded for example in the vaguely ethnographic implication of entitling these poems "songs" and "ballads": Roach's "Ballad of

Canga" (1955), Evan Jones's "The Song of the Banana Man" (1953), and "The Lament of the Banana Man" (c.1962).[42] The poets of this period are the West Indies' closest parallel to Afro-Cubanism in many respects. Closest of all is Philip Sherlock, in such poems as "Pocomania" (1943) and "Paradise" (1960). The distinctive sound of "Paradise" is probably borrowed from Vachel Lindsay – again as for Marson the model is American rather than Caribbean.[43] "Pocomania" makes some tentative use of nation language and is particularly noteworthy for its use of nation language rhythms both in and out of quotations. But this poem is an exception. In contrast to the Afro-Cuban pattern, rhythmic experiment with the resources of nation language generally comes quite late to Anglophone poetry, in spite of McKay's work in that direction. A sign of the times: "Pocomania" is the only dialect poem included in such canonizing collections as *Focus* (1943), *Treasury of Jamaican Poetry* (1949), and *Kyk-Over-Al* (1957).

In this period the writer with the greatest impact is Louise Bennett. Building on her experience in radio and theatre (and owing something to the British music-hall tradition), she emerges as a performer of dialect verse satire in rhyming quatrains of various shapes. In spite of frequent publication during the 1940s, in the Jamaican *Sunday Gleaner* as well as in several books, beginning with *Dialect Verses* (1942), she was thought of primarily as an "artiste." It seems that none of her work appeared in an anthology of poetry until the Jamaican Independence anthology of 1962, but this canonization was followed at once by critical recognition from a younger generation of poets, especially Mervyn Morris and Dennis Scott. Recordings soon became widely available, and what had first been presented, by the poet herself, as dialect could thereafter be read (and heard) as nation language. Bennett is apparently the first to use what is still perceived as dialect to make explicit claims for the dignity of nation language. In her "Bans o' Killing" (1944), a piece of "popular" discourse speaks from a full consciousness of its historical antecedents in the emergence of English as a literary language:

Dat dem start fe try tun language,
From de fourteen century,
Five hundred years gawn an dem got
More dialect dan we!

Yuh wi haffe kill de Lancashire
De Yorkshire, de Cockney
De broad Scotch an de Irish brogue
Before yuh start kill me!

Yuh wi haffe get de Oxford book
Of English verse, an tear
Out Chaucer, Burns, Lady Grizelle
An plenty o' Shakespeare![44]

We can get some sense of the measure of her accomplishment by comparing the handling of dialect in the thoroughly text-oriented work of Walcott from this period. Walcott from the very beginning trained himself to be a part of the European tradition, but his linguistic setting in St. Lucia presents an extreme form of the general West Indian case. There the descent from SE is marked at a certain point by a quantum leap downward into French creole, in those days far inferior socially to even the freest forms of English creole. Walcott's earliest uses of dialect are two simple instances of local color: a hint of calypso in " . . . fragment" and a bit of Jamaican dialect in "Kingston – Nocturne."[45] By the late 1950s however there are indications that he is working toward a generalized "West Indian," an accessible grapholect, hinging especially on syntactical features common to several islands. For general readers of English such texts can "pass" for SE, but West Indian readers will have most of their own rhythmic and syntactical expectations fulfilled, so they will not perceive the author as having chosen to use SE instead of nation language. With the appearance of *The Castaway* (1965), dialect is superseded by a new colloquial voice for the poet himself. This is flexible nation language, strongest in satirical contexts and recognizably Trinidadian. The French creole of St. Lucia (not after all the poet's own mother-tongue) only appears in the poetry with *Another Life* (1973) and "Sainte Lucie" (1976). In the plays, French creole appears early, in *The Sea at Dauphin* (1954), *Ti-Jean* (1958) and *Malcauchon* (1958); but it is almost entirely ornamental – that is, confined primarily to expletives that provide color but take no expository role. The audience is not required to understand this language, only to hear it. There is frequent use of creole song (e.g. *Ti-Jean* and *Malcauchon*) but this is still clearly an alien element, a separable insert. To that extent it should still perhaps be regarded as dialect rather than nation language, still in implied quotation marks. Even on stage, it is rare that Walcott's characters turn to creole simply because it is the best way to say their say. There are some cases in which Walcott reduced the level of nation language when revising his work for publication.[46] It is easy to lay the blame for this sort of thing on overseas publishers worried about obstacles for their readers. This is not a problem solely *vis-à-vis* the metropolis, however; Bruce King notes repeated complaints by West Indian reviewers of Walcott's plays about the incomprehensible accents of the Trinidadian actors.[47]

Walcott's handling of nation language was not programmatic, and the nature of his early reputation was such that West Indian poets looked to him for features other than his use of nation language. Since language issues are central to Bennett's work, she remained the preeminent influence and inspiration in that regard. She is important for confronting various obstacles to the use of dialect in poetry, and to its reception by the local audience; for making the crossover from voice to print, from entertainment to art; and also from representation of a character to expression of a sensibility. Only in her work is the specific effort begun in McKay finally brought forward. The distinction between Walcott's plays and his poetry points to the general distinction between nation-language work written for performance (though it may also be published), and that written essentially for the page (though it may also be performed). It is Bennett, however, who substantially contributes to both developments, and it is really her work that first makes such a distinction necessary.

Bennett has counterparts throughout the region, composers of dialect verse who perform their own work. Some of them, like Bruce St. John of Barbados and Paul Keens-Douglas in Trinidad, along with many younger Jamaican poets, frankly acknowledge their debt to Bennett. This social niche of popular, almost cabaret poetry is neighbor to the calypso of the Eastern Caribbean. The calypsonian shares Bennett's manipulation of tone and satirical edge in a way that Jamaican song does not, at least since the overshadowing of mento by the more serious, often frankly religious, tone of reggae. The lyrics of calypso are on the whole much more substantial and rhetorically interesting than those of reggae and reward critical attention copiously, as Rohlehr's studies in particular have demonstrated. There are also parallels in the realm of rhythmical experimentation. Bennett's performance "breaks out of the strict metrical limitations of the quatrain,"[48] and this is one of the ways in which she carries on experiments initiated by McKay. But Rohlehr argues that the same sort of development occurs independently in calypso: "In Sparrow, metre exists as a powerful force which the singer cannot afford to ignore, but which he needs to conquer and against which he must establish such strong rhythmic patterns as the sense of what he is saying demands. Sparrow seems to be continually at war against the confining strictures of the basic beat. It is this which has made his contribution to the rhythm of calypso no less than revolutionary."[49]

There are significant differences, of course: the work of Bennett and her followers is dramatic comedy, while calypso moves beyond satire to a form of political action. The established calypsonian speaks with considerable personal authority, as is apparent in the interjections (e.g. "I lie?" and "Ah tell yu") and claims ("If Sparrow say so is so") that typically pepper calypso texts. Indeed, after the American intervention in Grenada, there was much speculation about the position Sparrow would take in that year's calypso. Warner's careful comparison of the calypsonian to the West African griot suggests the unique position of the calypsonian in Trinidadian society.[50] On the Jamaican music scene only Bob Marley has had this authority, or this kind of direct link to politics.

But calypso is beyond our scope here; the essential interplay between nation language and musical forms would take us too far afield and require too much quotation. For this reason, for its extreme topicality, its evanescence, the difficulty of access to recordings, and the virtual absence of transcriptions, I here refer the interested reader to the excellent indigenous criticism.[51] Perhaps it is enough for our immediate purposes to note that this is where calypso fits in. Topical like Bennett, it is popular performance art and has popular ritual associations as well: the link of calypso to carnival and its annual competitions is at least palely reflected in the link of Bennett's work to the seasonal Jamaican pantomime. It is worth noting too that both delightfully acknowledge the creolization of West Indian speech, making much use of the rapid shifts of diction exploited with such sophistication by West Indian speakers. The extreme shifts that occur in calypso – for example from Oxbridge British to military American to creole Chinese – reflect the tremendous ethnic diversity of Port-of-Spain. In ethnically homogeneous Jamaica there is probably the greatest refinement of this exploitation of minute adjustments of diction and intonation.

I have been speaking of Bennett's influence on performers, but her impact on "writers" is also significant. Most likely we have her to thank for the occasional dialect poems, often very successful and even ground-breaking, of poets like A. L. Hendriks, John Figueroa, Andrew Salkey, James Berry, or their younger contemporaries Mervyn Morris, Dennis Scott, and Edward Baugh – all of them Jamaican. These are, incidentally, the writers who first discuss the use of dialect critically; for them reading Bennett seriously was a step toward writing "dialect" seriously; that is, toward writing nation language.[52] In all of these poets, nation language is thought of as an enabling element of dramatic monologue, or occasionally dialogue. Their poems broaden the range of dialect beyond comedy and pathos to the representation of complex emotions, making the case against the common assumption that people speak dialect only when drunk, angry, or addled. Baugh's "The Carpenter's Complaint" (1986) is a good example of a poem which is an experiment within this tradition, rather than an innovation on it: his dramatic monologue issues from a character who is both drunk and angry, but the poem is about grief unexpectedly complicated by an encounter with the consequences of class and color.

BRATHWAITE'S *THE ARRIVANTS*

The publication of Brathwaite's first trilogy, beginning in 1967, is the single most *consequential* event in the history of West Indian poetry to date. These poems, along with the position they earned the poet on the literary scene, had profound effects on the poets of his own generation and of the following one. The first volume, *Rights of Passage* (1967), marks the crucial moment, heralded in single poems earlier in only a limited way and for a more limited audience. Here Brathwaite shows the way to make entire poems speak nation language. In the charged atmosphere of the late 1960s, what excited metropolitan reviewers was the theme of black rage; for West Indian critics, by contrast, the impressive thing was the extraordinarily subtle and wide-ranging use of what they still called dialect. Indeed, many of the poems that comprise *Rights* are still, taken alone, dialect poems, dramatic presentations of personae. But the commonplace representational mode of dialect is here self-conscious and self-critical. Many of these poems are frank self-dramatizations, revealing the various masks worn by male West Indians (for example "All Gods Chillun," "Folkways," "Wings of a Dove"), but these jazz solos (as it were) are set in a matrix, and the voice of the poem itself (it is awkward to speak of a "narrator" for *Rights*) exploits virtually the entire expressive range accessible to West Indian speakers, from SE to Rastafarian argot. There are North American speech-styles as well, not very different from the heavily Americanized voices that daily exert their influence on West Indian radio. Only deep rural speech is absent from this primarily urban poem, though the absence is not very noticeable.

For its plastic, inventive, yet faithful handling of the sound of West Indians, for its demonstration of the close relation between musical behavior and speech behavior, for its definitive ennobling of the taproots in folk life, *The Arrivants* is for its time and place a functional equivalent to the work of Dante or Chaucer. It offers the foundational compendium of the resources of what Dante calls the *"volgare illustre"* – the literary idiom of the vernacular. Suddenly, West Indian poets were in possession of a wide-ranging primer for nation language poetry, not only for the syntax and diction of it speech registers, but for its rhythms and, perhaps most innovative, for its forms.

It is fair to talk of a simmering "revolution in rhythm" that Brathwaite brings to the boil. Brathwaite has listened to jazz all his life, and his ear for rhythm is extraordinary. The range of his rhythms is most apparent in comparing those of the matrix voice of *Rights* (audible in such framing passages as "Prelude," "Postlude/Home," and "Epilogue"), with the more relaxed, slower, weightier (but less stressed) voice so common in *Masks* – a representation of an African voice. The voices of *Rights* and even more obviously those of the third volume, *Islands*, are by contrast distinctly West Indian: nervous, abrupt, full of syncopations and extra stresses. Brathwaite can securely establish such a contrast, with its structural implications for the poem, without jeopardizing his access to rhythms deriving from all over the black diaspora.

Brathwaite's rhythmic sense is a talent, not something imitators can simply pick up from his example; form is a craft that can be learned. Most previous nation-language poetry developed within ballad or song forms (forms with "folk" associations in the European tradition) that provided a ground for confrontation, compromise, or polyphony between the language and the formal tradition. The turn to take "dialect" seriously involves a turn to indigenous sources for *forms* as well. The germs of new, characteristic forms lie in daily verbal behavior; that is, in toasts, dubs, speeches, prayers, either adapted wholesale or, with more sophistication, quarried for features that could be refined into thoroughly new poetic forms. Various poets of the 1940s and 1950s (including those who resemble the Afro-Cubans) sensed that folk linguistic behavior was least contaminated in ritual situations. On that basis they experimented with poems that invoked nation language within a religious context. A number of successful poems resulted: Sherlock's "Pocomania" (1943), Shake Keane's "Shaker Funeral" (1950), Eric Roach's "Black Gods" (1953), Owen Campbell's "Shango Drums" (1954).[53] For the development of West Indian poetry, this gesture had an unexpected advantage. Ritual offers readymade formal coherence; the point was not lost on Brathwaite, whose individual poems are frequently grounded on rites as diverse as cricket ("Rites"), carnival ("Jou'vert"), the limbo ("Caliban"), and spirit-possession ("Shepherd").

West Indian poets writing about Brathwaite invariably singled out "The Dust" as the first great achievement: this companion piece to the male monologue of "Rites" presents the sustained interplay of female West Indian voices. Both the vitality and the individuality of their language is apparent on the page, as several women speculate in a shop in Barbados about a mysterious blight on the crops ("greens swibble up an' the little blue / leafs o' de Red Rock slips gettin' dry / dry dry").[54] Overcoming the usual restrictions of dialect, this discussion is serious and substantive, in that it draws upon their knowledge of their own land, their notions of science, and their religion. There is even a rueful joke about the chauvinism of small islanders, when one woman explains that the cause is a volcano "in one o' them islands away / where they language tongue-tie / an' to hear them speak so / in they St. Lucia patois / is as if they cahn unnerstan' / a single word o' English." This is the first of many poems in which the integrity of Brathwaite's transcription makes possible poetic effects and even statements that would simply not be possible otherwise. After three decades, Brathwaite remains the most uncompromising reproducer of speech among the major poets, and his advocacy is reinforced by the remarkable poetry this practice has allowed him to transcribe and make durable. David Dabydeen, looking back in 1990 on Brathwaite's use of nation language, calls it "polite" and "conventional" because it does not "take the language to the very edge of the boundaries of expression."[55] But Brathwaite's own achievement creates the position from which that observation is possible. It was

Brathwaite, really, who moved the boundaries of expression to their present position, and thereby liberalized the climate of taste and critical judgment in which all West Indian poets work.

AFTER BRATHWAITE: NATION LANGUAGE AND CODE-SWITCHING

Brathwaite's poems provoked and in many ways transformed the writers of his own generation. This was especially true in Jamaica – because he lived there, and no less because of the strong tradition of dialect experiment among Jamaican poets. Since these poets were his first reviewers, they read his work very thoughtfully, and learned much from it about what was possible, about what worked (and what did not). Brathwaite's technical innovations did not appear in a vacuum, but rather coincided with the cultural imperatives associated with Independence and the high water mark of Black Power in the Caribbean. In that setting, the recuperation of nation language, at first narrowly identified with peasant speech, entailed a kind of hypercorrection, by which the inherited opposition between SE and "distorted" local speech was reinterpreted as an opposition between "alien" SE and indigenous nation language. The underlying polarization remained in effect, and if anything became even more highly charged in the 1960s and early 1970s. In those times, some West Indian writers (Walcott prominent among them) found themselves forced to defend the use of SE. Since then, however, the notion of polarity has largely been supplanted by one of continuum. SE has come to be recognized again as a component of nation language. The notion of a creole continuum has found broad acceptance, and there has been one very important consequence for poetry. Once habitual code-switching along the creole continuum has been recognized as a feature characteristic of West Indian speech at all social levels, it becomes available to writers as a rhetorical technique.[56]

It has certainly encouraged a robust development of what might be considered the old ways of using nation language, which continue to be used, but now more thoughtfully and pointedly. So "Fragments to a Return" and "Lusca," fine poems by John Robert Lee, embed French creole terms, phrases, and occasional scraps of dialogue in an SE matrix.[57] But here the maneuver is purposeful, linked directly to how Lee situates himself as a poet in the unusually complex language situation of St. Lucia. In Trinidad, there has been a resurgence of poems that similarly enshrine bits of language, but these come from very diverse sources, reflecting the poets' increasing engagement with their country's multicultural heritage. Thus Joya Gomez's "Swahili Love-Call" showcases some Swahili words, just as Rajandaye Ramkissoon-Chen uses Hindi terms in an SE matrix in "Baara-Wala" and in her quintessentially Trinidadian poem, "When the Hindu Woman sings Calypso" (all 1990).[58] Poets also continue to exploit the specific thematic associations of particular forms of speech. Kendel Hippolyte's work is notable for the number of poems in which the appearance of nation language is explicitly linked with some musical context, such as "Madrigal," "Worker Chant," "Last Waltz," and "The Muse's Complaint."[59] Poets also continue to cultivate nation language as a medium for dramatic monologues. David Dabydeen is particularly adept at this in poems like "Coolie Son (The Toilet Attendant Writes Home)" (1984), but there have been many recent successes in this vein, such as John Agard's "Listen Mr Oxford Don" (1985). Here the Guyanese immigrant to England is accused of mugging the Queen's English armed only with his human breath, and his creole defiance is laced with grammatical puns:

> I ent serving no jail sentence
> I slashing suffix in self-defense
> I bashing future wit present tense.[60]

Robert Lee's "Letter" (1974) employs a self-consciously "dialect" voice for a frankly comic purpose, made more comic by its setting in a library – the great archive itself – and by the nature of the addressee: he's explaining to Queen Elizabeth that he won't be marrying her daughter because he's met another girl: "And your highness / how I want she! / Yes your

highness / is bad I need she! / And your highness / Is have I
goin' have she!"[61]

As the conception of a continuum of language choices has
become more familiar, poets have been quick to explore it. The
juxtaposition of different registers proves to be an effective way
to differentiate characters. In John Croal's "Meditation"
(1980), for example, the narrator, a poor man living in a one
room shack, speaks SE, while the dog and the roaches speak
nation language.[62] A similar effect appears in Mervyn Morris's
sequence *On Holy Week* (1976), where only the crucified thieves
speak nation language (and the good thief's speech is Rastafarian).[63] The *locus classicus* of this effect is Figueroa's "Portrait
of a Woman (and a Man)" (1971), in which the two characters
meet in the center of the continuum. The man has descended
from a level that includes Latin quotations from Virgil, while
the woman's code-switching is abrupt: "Doan mek mi do it /
mek mi / laard; / You see I intend to be /a nurse."[64] Code-
switching by a single dramatic character, often in response to
different auditors, is a useful tool for satire. Not surprisingly, it
was pioneered as a poetic technique by Louise Bennett. In her
"Candy Seller" and "South Parade Peddlar," street higglers
address prospective clients in language adjusted to the clients'
apparent social station, while all are abused *sotto voce* in the
higgler's "own" language.[65] Empirically, of course, this type of
code-switching is familiar to anyone who has ever noticed what
happens to a West Indian waiter's speech as he circulates
between dining-room and kitchen.

A new area is staked out for West Indian writing when poets
following Brathwaite's lead demonstrate that nation language
can provide not only linguistic objects to be enshrined in a
poem, or the means to create a poem of characters, but the
material of the poem itself, its own voice, its logos. Once the
poem itself, rather than a voice represented in it, can be said to
be speaking nation language, then the value of that language as
a mode of expression is established. It is among the poets of
Brathwaite's own generation that poetic resources expand
beyond dialect as a mode of representation to explore nation
language as a mode of expression. The poet can write verse

that actually takes shape in West Indian language, and can discover what his language can say that cannot be said in SE – can discover, in other words, the poetic resources of his own language, the genius of his language. There have been major accomplishments in this vein recently, though it is of their nature not to be ostentatious. Anthony McNeill's "Who'll see me dive" (1971) exemplifies a voice at the higher end of the continuum. Disguised by its explicit allusion to Lowell, it can pass for SE, but there are many Jamaicanisms, unobtrusive (perhaps merely colorful) to international readers but signals of rhythm and tone to West Indians.[66] Closer to creole is something like the finely tuned Jamaican language of Baugh's "Getting There" (1988).[67] Closer still is much of the poetry of Dennis Scott. We have already seen his engagement with Rastafarian language in "More Poem"; his "Uncle Time" (1960) remains one of the most haunting realizations of measured Jamaican speech:

> When im play in de street
> wid yu woman – watch im! By tomorrow
> she dry as cane-fire, bitter as cassava,
> and when im teach yu son, long after
> yu walk wid stranger, an yu bread is grief.[68]

Even closer to the sound of the street, but still unquestionably literary (not popular, or oral) are such poems as Opal Palmer's "Koo de Man," and "Shame ole lady" (1979).[69] For purposes of illustration I have just cited a series of Jamaican examples, but a similar range of expression would be apparent in Guyanese poetry (especially because of the extent to which "Guyanese poetry" is now poetry written by Guyanese whose language has been affected by living abroad). David Dabydeen, who lives in England, writes poems in his own voice from various points across a wide range of language. For example, the child-narrator's voice in "Catching Crabs" (1988) ("Ruby and me stalking savannah / Crab season with cutlass and sack like big folk") is decidedly closer to SE than that in "Coolie Mother" (1988), which describes how a woman works for her son's future: " . . . he *must* read book, / Learn talk proper, take exam, go to England university, / Not turn out like he rum-sucker chamar dadee."[70]

Many poets write poems situated at various points along the continuum from creole to SE, but do not particularly explore or depict individual speakers in the act of code-shifting along the continuum. Nevertheless, such shifting has been an important feature of Walcott's poetry since long before *The Arrivants*. "Tales of the Islands VI" (1958) offers the most talked-about early instance, at the moment when the creole narrative voice quotes the code-shifting of a "black writer chap": "Each generation has its angst, but we has none." Fluent code-switching is crucial to the moulding of Shabine in "The Schooner *Flight*" (1978), and therefore to the substance of the poem, which he narrates. There are plenty of stark juxtapositions of register in the course of the poem, but most characteristic is a passage like this:

> My first friend was the sea. Now, is my last.
> I stop talking now. I work, then I read,
> cotching under a lantern hooked to the mast.
> I try to forget what happiness was,
> and when that don't work, I study the stars.[71]

Here lexicon ("cotching"), verb tenses, and even the rhymes ("was / stars") work to weave a sheer fabric of nation language. By contrast, the code-switching in "The Spoiler's Return" (1981) is intentionally rougher and more homespun – the result of pulling together the language of Dante, Lord Rochester, and calypso.[72] Such code-switching, which quite accurately reflects West Indian speech habits, is chronically misunderstood by critics outside the region. Convinced that no one could actually speak like this, they find the texts artificial and "macaronic" because they do not abide by the decorum that segregates poetry in creole from that written in SE.[73]

Quite a few West Indian poets do write in SE, of course. In Trinidad poets of the calibre of Victor Questel, Dionyse McTair, and James Aboud do so with only rare exceptions. Though Martin Carter's language is often idiosyncratic (as in the opening of "Black Friday"), it is almost always standard, and the same is true of other noteworthy poets in Guyana: Milton Williams, Mahadai Das, Brian Chan, and even Fred D'Aguiar. In fact, a look at some representative anthologies confirms the impression that writing in SE continues to dominate the field, even (perhaps surprisingly) among younger poets. In Seymour's *Treasury of Guyanese Poetry* (1980), though there is much reference to African, East Indian, and even Amerindian cultural fields, the language is overwhelmingly SE and the diction often self-consciously poetic.[74] There are only two poems in which Guyanese nation language is used dramatically: Mahadai Das's "Me and Melda" and Croal's "Meditation." Similarly the language of the anthology that features the generation of St. Lucian poets after Walcott is almost unswervingly SE. Jane King has a poem here about the dub poet Jean Binta Breeze, but "Intercity Dub, for Jean," while it very effectively catches Breeze's rhythms and rhymes, is composed entirely in SE.[75] Even in *Creation Fire* (1990), an ambitious regional anthology of poetry by women, with a few exceptions the only poems in nation language are by poets from Jamaica and Trinidad (roughly half a dozen from each). In practice, then, printed poetry tends to occupy the SE end of the spectrum; to put it another way, after the turmoil of the 1970s SE is no longer *infra dig*. This need not be interpreted as a slide backward into conventionality; it may very well reflect changing conditions, consequent on the shifting balance between micro-nationalism and internationalism in the poets' own outlook. More and more good poets travel extensively, and the impulse to maintain a base in SE may reflect their experience of international English.

AFTER BRATHWAITE: MEDIA ISSUES

Code-switching has to do with ways of getting West Indian speech onto paper. An equally important preoccupation of West Indian poets "after Brathwaite" is that of getting poetry *off* the page – not only of realizing it in a reading, but of conceiving poetry as a form of vocal performance, rather than as a form of inscription. Writers of the younger generation responded not only to the poems but to Brathwaite's personal charisma. For them his authority was greatly enhanced by his status as "been-to" and *houngan*, bearing concrete knowledge of West Africa and perceiving, celebrating, the continuities between the ancestral land and the Caribbean. In his multiple roles as poet, historian, literary editor, and cultural instigator, he inspired a flood of poems by new poets, some of them boldly innovative, and some better left unwritten. But Brathwaite was also a performer, and *The Arrivants* was not merely published; it was also issued as a set of LPs (1972–73). In this form the trilogy reached a general audience that no publication of poems, local or metropolitan, could hope for. Thus Brathwaite offers his fellow poets not only a body of poetry, inspiration and personal support, but a newly trained audience, primed by his work and the rewards of adjusting to it on its own terms. The lesson was not lost on the young.

Extensive groundwork had been laid even before *The Arrivants*. Thanks to the BBC "Caribbean Voices" program, much West Indian poetry during the 1950s was heard rather than seen; West Indian poets and listeners had grown accustomed to spoken poems, and so in a limited way to the aesthetic of oral conception and presentation. The "Caribbean Voices" program was instrumental in developing the West Indian ear, but it also inclined poets to think in terms of voices, rather than print. So, as we have seen, did the work of Louise Bennett. Other contributing factors include advances in recording technology, ease of access to that technology, and developments in the music industry in Jamaica and Trinidad. Thus some of the most exciting recent developments in West Indian poetry, and in West Indian theorizing about poetry, have come out of the interplay of speech and writing as models for the production of poetry. Post-colonial theory invites us to concentrate on how writers in the region are feeling out the relation of their work to the metropolitan tradition of literature in English. But that is in some ways old news. What engages – and energizes – many West Indian poets is the matter of situating their work in relation to improvisation, to oral composition, to orature, to poetry written as a script for performance, to poetry written (or improvised) for distribution through recordings, and to poetry written for performance with music (as distinct from songs *per se*).

The groundwork for these developments in poetic practice was being articulated simultaneously with ACLALS. Appearing as an issue of *Savacou*, the anthology entitled *New Writing 1970* precipitated an important critical debate about the relation of folk art and of Africa to West Indian literature, and their joint characterization (and valorization) as a Little Tradition. Brathwaite was the force behind it; assembled just before and published just after the ACLALS Conference, it could hardly avoid being taken to represent the hard literary currency behind the formulations and assertions made at the Conference. Brathwaite's "Foreward" [*sic*] is unusually defensive. He writes that while there is "revolutionary questioning" here, there are no "polarizations." "The miracle is . . . that despite the racial/colour/class bases and stereotypes on which our society is built, explorations of it, by West Indians, have on the whole, been conducted in the most humane and generous context imaginable. This is because the dream of wholeness has (so far) dominated over the fragments, the pebbles, the divided islands of the selves."[76] The anthology was an augur's gamble. Over half the contributors were Jamaican, outnumbering any other nation four to one. Several contributors were undergraduates; a few were even younger. Brathwaite took pains to put in perspective the strong element of Black Consciousness subjects and rhetoric in the collection, and concluded by affirming the solidarity of writers and audience.

If the writing was predominantly Jamaican, the critical reaction was Trinidadian. The debate over the vision of West Indian poetry projected by the *Savacou* anthology articulated fundamental issues for West Indian literature, and it was carried on by poets and critics of the highest stature (Brathwaite, Eric Roach, Wayne Brown, Roger McTair, Gordon Rohlehr, Kenneth Ramchand).[77] One reaction was surprise that a selection dominated by recent Jamaican writing would not automatically be representative of the region as a whole; surprise at how much diversity the concept of West

Indian literature was going to have to accommodate. Where ACLALS had been concerned with the identity of the literature, Brathwaite's "dream of wholeness" defined by its difference from external entities, *Savacou* 3/4 raised the question of its internal integrity, as a congeries of diverse writing from independent nations. Beyond that, the debate about the anthology concentrated on three objections: this poetry was too "black," too political, too inept. As Brathwaite had anticipated, there was a fierce reaction (from Eric Roach) to the suggestion that Black Consciousness constituted the thrust of West Indian writing: "To thresh about wildly like [Audvil] King and [Bongo] Jerry in the murky waters of race, oppression and dispossession is to bury one's head in the stinking dunghills of slavery."[78] The political climate is an important factor here. The rhetoric of Black Power in overwhelmingly black Jamaica served constructively in achieving national self-consciousness and self-respect, but in racially mixed Trinidad at the time of the February Revolution it could appear irresponsibly inflammatory. The canonization of Africa was still new, and Roach was only one of many fervent nationalists, long aware of the African heritage, who objected to the Black Power movement (and particularly to its rhetoric) on the firmly nationalistic grounds that it was a piece of the old mimicry, a slavish importation of the North American version of ideas which had actually originated in the Caribbean of Césaire, Fanon, and James.

The question of poetic craft, really of *degree* of craft, largely took the form of a generational debate: was this verse original and experimental, or hasty and inept? In fact the anthology called itself "New Writing," and much of its contents was amateur and half-baked, potential poems ripped untimely from workbooks, with high marks given for good intentions. The weak poem "Mother to Child," for example, would probably never have been included if it did not attempt creole. Issues regarding the level of craft in poetry were closely related to the political questions, chiefly by way of an assumption shared by most of the participants that the more political a poem was the less crafted it would be. The debate was thus concerned with what degree of license could be tolerated, whether urgency and finish were incompatible, and especially whether print had different standards than performance.

In the early 1970s, then, "orality" and "orature," like "nation language" itself, were becoming powerful shibboleths. Pantin speaks for many of the region's younger poets of that era when he declares that "the poetry of the Caribbean must be the poetry of the spoken word, the so-called vernacular."[79] Even if Pantin actually meant "the spoken word," the "vernacular" – that is, nation language in the wide sense – he was generally understood to mean specifically "creole." The inherent confrontation between "creole" and "standard" poets was aggravated by a further tendency to associate oral practice with visions of a traditional, usually African, society. This meant that advocacy of either speech *or* writing as a model for poetic practice carried a strong political charge. At the most extreme, writing itself was considered too "European" for West Indian languages, inexorably bringing with it an aesthetic of permanence and hierarchical ordering, a notion of the artefact as transcending history, and a notion of tradition as archive rather than as craft training, a matter of books rather than authors. In the debates of the 1970s, rejection of writing (and so of standard English, of "Europe") entailed an "African" aesthetic of transient performances and disposable artefacts (the carnival mask was often proposed as a touchstone). This particular invocation of "Africa" illuminates some of the background for the rejection of "Poetry" (by some of the same writers) mentioned at the end of the previous chapter. That critique of aesthetics is very nearly Brechtian: politics and social injustice make poetry an anachronism, or an unjustifiable indulgence. Once West Indian poets began to associate the term "poem" narrowly with "printed poem," they had a way to circumvent what was after all a very European critique. Rejecting the associations of print, they embraced a (supposedly) African model of oral, performed poetry – which incidentally features the commanding presence of the poet.

Among a variety of performance-oriented poetic practices arising in the midst of this debate, Jamaican dub is preeminent.

It is what results when experimentation with nation language goes on in the context of local Jamaican traditions, particularly Rastafarian language and drumming, the culture of reggae, and the boasting improvisations of Jamaican DJs (not unlike those of rappers in the United States). Notwithstanding its roots in pop culture, and its interest in reaching a wide audience, dub regards itself very seriously as poetry, not popular entertainment. The foundational text is probably Bongo Jerry's "Mabrak" (1971), and there are many practitioners.[80] Onuora, Mutabaruka, and Jean Breeze have already been mentioned in these pages, but the most important dub poets to date are probably Michael Smith and Linton Kwesi Johnson.

Linton Kwesi Johnson, though he has lived most of his life in England, has produced some of the richest dub poetry. His texts succeed even in cold print and reward repeated readings. Of course, what is prominent on the page does not correspond precisely to what is prominent for a listener. In "Five Nights of Bleeding" (1974), for example, silent reading emphasizes the repetition of rhetorical structures visible on the page, while to the ear those structures constitute a background against which significant variations occur. The effects in "Dread Beat an Blood" (1974) are apparent even in brief quotation. A reader sees thirty-one present participles in a twenty-two–line poem of very emphatic trochees and dactyls; into the sound-world created by those features break these closing lines:

> rage rising out of the heat of the hurt;
> and a fist curled in anger reaches a her,
> then flash of a blade from another to a him,
> leaps out for a dig of a flesh of a piece of skin.
> and blood, bitterness, exploding fire, wailing blood,
> and bleeding.[81]

Here after a distinct change of rhythm the poem's only finite verbs ("reaches," "leaps") correspond to the climax of the action. Yet even before the consequences of the violence have played themselves out in the meaning of the lines, the dread beat of the numbing present participles quickly reasserts itself to conclude the poem. What a silent reader does with these details is unpredictable; in Johnson's own performance with music, that final "bleeding" unequivocally constitutes a return to the tonic – to the catatonic.

Perhaps the greatest dub poet to date is Michael Smith, murdered in 1983 and widely perceived as a martyr to freedom of expression. His reputation is by no means merely a byproduct of his tragic death. With his remarkable voice, his ear for rhythmic subtleties, and his dramatic training, Smith was a stunning performer of texts which often do not seem very promising on the page (he reportedly drafted his poems on a tape recorder rather than on paper). He appears to have left fewer than thirty poems, but luckily several of his performances were captured on records before his murder. Without them a later generation would not understand his contemporary reputation. Only occasionally does a hint of the freedom and sophistication of his performance survive on paper, as perhaps it does in these lines from his emotionally exhausting masterpiece, "Me Cyaan Believe It" (1979):

> Me daughter bwoy-frien name Sailor
> an im pass through de port like a ship
> more gran-picni fi feed
> an de whole a we in need
> what a night what a plight
> an we cyaan get a bite
> me life is a stiff fight
> an me cyaan believe it
> me seh me cyaan believe it.[82]

Some dub poets come at you with a blunt instrument; Smith is the Olympic boxer of dub. If print conveys little sense of the compelling power of his performances, at least his footwork is sometimes apparent, as in this passage. The detached indulgent ease of the opening lines quoted gives way when the burden of an unwanted child is (quite literally) brought home. For four lines the rhythm tightens up and the rhymes jab more frequently until the pounding double dactyls are brought up short. The complex rhythmic shuffle of "me life is a stiff fight" pulls back from the clinch, and with an effort that is both physical and psychological, makes the metrical transition to the poem's dazed, incredulous refrain.

Precisely to the extent that these are West Indian poems, they assume (and depend upon) a West Indian voice and a West Indian ear, familiar with a Caribbean field of allusion and familiar above all with a variety of rhythms in the West Indian air. This brings up again Dabydeen's notion of "boundaries of expression." Both Walcott and Brathwaite have had occasion to comment on how different West Indian material sounds outside the region.[83] Even West Indian poets sometimes have trouble hearing local poems from cold print. Mervyn Morris had to hear Bongo Jerry's "Mabrak" performed to catch "the rhythms . . . which had escaped me on the page."[84] The boundary in question is orthographic. Performance finesses the problem of orthography, by making it merely an instrumental medium rather than the inky embodiment of the text. But as long as literary recognition comes only with publication, poets will need to choose some relation to print. The orthographic problems that arise are not different in kind from the ambiguity as to performance that is the price of free verse. Many West Indian poems encounter the problem in both areas. The experience of controlling free verse so that its movement can be reproduced by a reader other than the author usually comes first, and so forearms the West Indian poet for the touchier problem of finding an "objective correlative" for his spoken language. I adopt Eliot's term here in part as a reminder that this is the area of Eliot's peculiar influence on West Indian poetry: first as the master of a free verse that embodies its own scoring quite successfully and then as a vernacular, jazz poet. In *The Waste Land* Eliot famously writes "O O O O that Shakespeherian Rag" and leaves us to decipher the rhythm of the first four words – or leaves us perhaps to recognize it: we may require the support of an oral tradition or a recording to read it properly. The risks Eliot takes and the assumptions he makes in such an instance epitomize the risks and assumptions of the West Indian poet as he seeks means to get his language reliably and transitively onto paper.

Some poems that attempt accurate notation can be performed by readers other than the writer ("like a normal poem" so to speak), but others can be spoken only by the poet himself, or by someone trained by him (or imitating his performance), rather than strictly read off the page with any confidence in the notation. The reader is presumed to know that certain rhythms are being employed; there is no attempt to embody them in the notation. The layout on the page of "Mabrak," for example, accomplishes the feat (of dubious value in this context) of transforming a poem aurally conceived into a visual poem that addresses the reader (as it were) ideographically. Its highly visual organization offers hardly any clues for enacting the poem aloud. On paper, it has become a different poem. In this "Mabrak" is not an isolated sport. Chapter 4 cited a simple instance from Mutabaruka's "call me no poet," and much of Brathwaite's recent poetry (such as *Barabajan Poems*, 1994) is visually transformed by the capabilities of his computer (just as the late work of Henry James was transformed by the type-writer). The result is texts whose variety of fonts and formats resemble medieval manuscripts – texts whose appearance on the page bears no relation at all to performance. This is instead a kind of shaped poetry, whose visual effects function – remarkably – as a metaphor for orality.

One can step back from that extreme and still end with a paradox. Compositions are being published as poems, but hardly travel well, because arcane notational systems make not just performance but even sense inaccessible. On the other hand, these same compositions, recorded as song or as melo-drama (i.e. as accompanied or unaccompanied recitation), can reach and interest a wide international audience without compromising their distinct, almost militant, West Indian character. Is that vast audience experiencing poetry, or has the language been reduced to a strand in an exotic, but effectively inarticulate, music? Time will tell. This chapter has been tracing a wide variety of responses to the challenge of repre-senting West Indians in poetry. After decades of exploration, West Indian poets find themselves in secure possession of an impressive array of techniques for that purpose. Dub poetry, whatever place it finally takes in the spectrum of West Indian poetic practices, is most noteworthy for its persistent affirmation of the presence of the poet/performer, and of his or her authority to put himself into his own words. Where else is the West Indian subject so vividly seen and heard?

CHAPTER 6

The relation to "America"

Chapter 4 examined poetry associated with a nationalist agenda which is anti-colonial and committed to establishing difference from "Europe." Such an agenda is inherent in the situation of West Indian territories early in the twentieth century. Chapter 5 considered poetry associated with the West Indian embrace of "Africa." This opportunity does not derive from any logic or dynamics inherent in the nationalist project or even the West Indian situation; rather, external conditions dropped "Africa" (that amorphous complex of information, attitudes, and values) into the lap of West Indian intellectuals. The paths of these two developments often crossed, and sometimes merged. The efforts to move further from one parent-tradition and closer to another were not necessarily coordinated, but they often overlapped, for example with respect to the high valuation of the peasantry and of folk culture – a feature of nationalism strongly reinforced by the prominence of language and folkways in the perception of "Africa." So "Europe" provides the occasion for the process of negative definition, via opposition, rejection, and critique. "Africa" makes possible a dialectical definition. The elaborate assertion that the West Indies is less European and more African comprises the main thrust of West Indian thinking in the middle of this century. The renegotiation of relations with metropolitan culture only occasionally took the extreme form of rejection, just as the rediscovery of cultural contact with Africa only occasionally took the extreme form of unconditional identification with Africa. Instead both maneuvers contributed mightily toward the common aim of establishing a space for distinctly West Indian writing.

Even so, West Indian poets sometimes expressed discomfort with this indirect way of establishing a space for themselves. They sought a more immediate way of coming to terms with their place – their creole America. Some worried that such a project was eclipsed by the encounter with "Africa," and the confrontational politics that happened to coincide with it. Wayne Brown is one who warns that preoccupation with "Africa" makes it easy to overlook West Indian experience and history: "In claiming historical identification with ancient Africa, the poet maneuvers himself out of having to examine that section of his lineage which is most suspect, namely, the three hundred years of Afro-Caribbean transplantation."[1] Indeed, awareness of this elision of history in America is expressed almost four decades earlier by McKay: "I am as conscious of my new-world birthright as of my African origin, being aware of the one and its significance in my development as much as I feel the other emotionally."[2] Antithetical definitions by nature only demarcate an area in which principles of identity might be sought. They must be accompanied by efforts at *positive* definition, the identification and assertion of some essential characteristics, some central self. A very rudimentary form of this move is apparent in some of Walcott's earliest poems. "Prelude" (1948) is one of several poems to express anxiety that islanders can define themselves only from the perspective of a passing ship, that the people of the islands are to be "found only in tourist booklets . . . found in the blue reflection of eyes that . . . think us happy here."[3] A decade later, "Islands" (1962) advances from that negative definition to a positive assertion of identity grounded on independent agency: "Islands can only exist if we have loved in them" (CP 52).

Here the development of Negritude offers a parallel which is especially pertinent for the point at which the parallel breaks down. Negritude begins in an orgy of negations: "we refuse to be ashamed of what we feel" (*Légitime défense*), "Eia for those who never invented anything" (Césaire). But even this dialectical movement had to devise a central identity for itself, in the myth of the "African Personality." Negritude was influential because it was not just a reaction against the current state of French culture; it was a reaction by another distinct entity. The intellectual position asserted a dispersed black nation as its defining human base. A young French poet might have precisely the same reaction to his culture, but he could not be part of this movement without that central self; without *négritude* – without being black. The case is clear for the Senegalese whose established culture was colonized and made superficially French only relatively recently; but the Caribbean case is different. Caribbean attention to "Africa" cultivates pride which can be pride in *place* as well as in heritage, and in that way "Africa" both makes way for recognition of West Indian realities, and also gives force and weight to what is recognized: an indigenous culture built entirely by immigrants, who have been thrown together under various degrees of duress. There are many black people in the Caribbean, all of whom share in the heritage of the diaspora; but even for recent Yoruba immigrants to Trinidad, to the extent that they identify themselves as Trinidadian or West Indian, the "central self" of that identity cannot be *négritude*; it must be culturally even if not biologically creole.

Attention to the creolized new world of the Americas constitutes a third path, a third strand in the fabric of West Indian poetry: thus this chapter considers poets in the act of coping with the place where they are "on its own terms," in full knowledge of how that phrase is problematized by the interventions of Europe, Africa, Asia, and North America. This is a quest not for what the pristine place once was, but for what it uniquely is, in the aftermath of those interventions. What people have grown out of this place and its weathers? What gods have grown out of these people? It is in the nature of the case that this third strand cannot always be disentangled from the others. "Europe" is inherent in the languages and the cultural tradition, "Africa" is inherent in most of the people themselves and to some extent echoed in climate and topography. But "America" is the discovered place, the strand of the stranded, and that is the key to an array of attitudes. The valences of "Africa" have received the most explicit attention from West Indian writers, while the valences of "America" have rarely been addressed directly. Yet those valences (if not the term itself) have been important to the development of West Indian poetry – most especially as it has been conceived as a regional expression, rather than a local one.

Exploring the valences of "America" in West Indian poetry will be the business of this chapter, and they can be summarized briefly. Most straightforwardly, "America" designates the attractive nuisance of North American culture. One way in which Caribbean poets have come to terms with its blandishments is by cultivating a broadly hemispheric view of "America." In such a view, the term "America" might be said to designate a shared condition of "discoveredness," of being a new world. As complex as "Africa," such a conception of "America" presents to the imagination (as the continent did to the first European explorers) a paradox of fullness and emptiness. Walcott puts it succinctly in "Air": "There is too much nothing here" (CP 114). The Europeans found in the Caribbean their earthly paradise, their virgin land, and subjected it to a regimen which remains the defining gesture of one of the things we mean by "America": admire it, bulldoze it, and then stock it with entirely new plants, new animals, and new people. The Caribbean is thus an empty site where everything can happen for the first time, but it is also a site choked with the fragmentary detritus of many cultures.

West Indian poets investigate both sides of the paradox. We have seen how the "filter of Europe" enabled writers to look at the Caribbean and see not only English countryside but Greek city-states, and how the "filter of Africa" enabled writers to see previously invisible cultural survivals. The idea of "America" is associated with the ideal of seeing without any filter – associated, that is, with the prospect of awakening to this place as it actually is. This is an aspiration to set aside history and its burdens and to begin with the poetics of place, of geography and geology. It is most prominent in Walcott's work of the 1960s, a time when the sparse decor of his poems led him to be characterized as the poet of "nothing."[4] During the same period the principle is equally crucial for Brathwaite, who insists at the heart of *Islands* that, "the eye must be free / seeing."[5] It is in just these terms that Walcott in *Another Life* praises the untutored "aboriginal force" of paintings by his friend Dunstan St. Omer (called "Gregorias" in the poem) (CP 201). Both poets are voicing the same faith that unprejudiced perception of the a-historical immediacy of Caribbean experience promises to have revelatory consequences. Such perception also promises to be impossible; no one can see simply what is there. When Columbus first looked at the Caribbean and repeatedly described it as resembling "Andalusia in spring," the process of filtration was already complex. He was not merely, ineluctably, seeing with the eyes of Europe. He himself was Italian; his simile strongly suggests that he put on a "filter of Spain," in order to see with the eyes of the Spanish monarchs whose servant he was. Even if it were possible to describe without a political subtext, description is hard pressed to proceed without similes. The drive to assimilate new experience to old experience is especially insurmountable for poetry, which does so much of its work by metaphor. The slippage from resolutely unmediated vision to the implementation of metaphor is one way that the notion of "America" as elemental *produces* poetry. There is another very productive slippage here. Walcott has said that poetry is what happens *after* you describe the landscape, and it comes as no surprise that poems depicting even an elemental landscape soon introduce the barely accommodated man that such a place implies.[6] In the period when Walcott is the poet of the empty beach and the uninterrupted horizon he is also the poet of the castaway, the solitary, the almost Emersonian I/eye on the beach. Poetry may start with elemental landscape, but a human figure soon materializes, and human language interposes itself.

The language that generates metaphor also generates myth, and that commonplace leads to the other side of the paradox of the new found land. West Indian poets – often the very same poets – are driven to articulate the *fullness* of Caribbean experience. They respond to a pressure to fabricate or tease out a mythology by finding the local gods, the spirits of the place. For that reason they are concerned not only with generating myths of the place, and myths of the people in the place, but also, necessarily, with justifying mythopoesis within the inhospitable conceptual framework of a post-modern world. America is indeed a new place where you can start from zero, from the "nothing" right before your eyes; but it is also a kind of Sargasso into which everything has drifted, and in which everything has been changed. To begin at the beginning is always to start with what is already here, washed up on this beach. That is the nature of creole space, and the imagination that corresponds to it is preeminently adaptive. This defining feature of creole cultural work has been characterized in a variety of ways which reflect the attitudes of the commentators: as apeish mimicry, craven assimilation, or bold appropriation. Each of those characterizations, however, emphasizes the relation to metropolitan cultures and so emphasizes the belatedness of creole imagination, struggling to make something out of what are only the haphazard leavings of coherent cultures elsewhere. In other words, what "America" is full of is "Europe," "Africa," and "Asia." Such a perspective makes this chapter's project of disentangling "America" from other strands appear hopeless. But the poets who invest in the "American"-ness of the Caribbean – Walcott and Brathwaite foremost among them – repeatedly insist that all cultural materials have undergone a sea-change coming to the Caribbean. Everything the beachcombing poet finds in the sea-wrack on the elemental beach *used to be* something else, but though he knows that, what he perceives is not a daunting hodge-podge of other people's castoffs, but something new.

The operation of the creole imagination in its own space, at home in the Caribbean, is best described as *bricolage* – the inspired tinkering that ingeniously works with what is at hand.[7] This is the essential skill for castaways, and its patron saint is Robinson Crusoe. Walcott has written frequently about Crusoe, and that figure of the *bricoleur* accommodating himself to a new world is subsumed under Walcott's fundamental myth of a "second Adam," who wakes in a paradoxical second Eden where the as-yet-untasted apples have "the tartness of experience."[8] Likewise, Brathwaite's *The Arrivants* is full of imminent or deferred beginnings which depend upon "sea-changes," transformations of consciousness or perception; thus the entire trilogy ends with a vision of carnival revellers waking on Ash Wednesday morning, but waking with "hearts no longer bound to black and bitter ashes," and in this new day "making with their rhythms something torn and new" (*Arrivants*, 269–70).

These then are the valences of "America" to which we now turn: the looming North American presence, the more benign fraternity of the hemisphere, and two complementary views of the New World – as a place so new that it reveals itself to the eye in its most rudimentary elements, and as a place so cluttered with miscellaneous importations that it can only be grasped by mythopoesis.

NORTH AMERICA

The American occupation of the West Indian imagination began with the movies. Among the urban poor, this meant an identification with stars like George Raft and Humphrey Bogart that is reflected in fiction ("Bogart" is the first story in Naipaul's *Miguel Street*), in the street-life of Kingston and Port-of-Spain, and in the first West Indian feature film, *The Harder They Come*, perhaps inevitably a homage to the Hollywood B-movie. Considering the pervasive influence of the United States on popular culture – especially advertising, film, and music – its impact on poetry is curiously limited. It is indicative that (North) American music has affected Jamaican music, but not particularly the dub poetry which is otherwise so closely associated with the music. American (that is, United Statesian) poets are important if intermittent influences. Claude McKay of course, virtually becomes an American poet. We have already found the fingerprints of American and specifically African-American Modernism on West Indian poetry of the 1930s and 1940s. The American connection is strongest in Trinidad, and was first established through *The Beacon*, and later developed as a by-product of US war-time occupation.

The influence of American writing is much more attenuated in Jamaica, Guyana, and the smaller islands.

The poetry of Robert Lowell eventually plays an important role in Walcott's development, but Lowell must take his place in a large circle of diverse influences. The Beat poets made some impression on Brathwaite (he would have been attracted by their association with jazz, and by their appreciation of performance and improvisation). An argument might be made for echoes of Hart Crane in Brathwaite, McNeill, and perhaps Victor Questel; Walcott published a poem *about* Crane as early as 1951. A number of younger poets – McNeill, Scott, and Goodison, among others – have lived or studied in the United States, but their work seems affected by the experience more than by American poetry. On the whole, echoes of North American voices are heard only in specific poems. Most surprisingly, Wallace Stevens seems to have inspired no one, despite his close attention to hemispheric–colonial issues in a poem like "The Comedian as the Letter C" (*Harmonium*, 1923), and despite his preoccupation with "nothing."

The intermittence of influence reflects the fact that West Indians are positioned to perceive American literature in quite different ways: as a facet of an oppressive, colonizing culture; as a liberating alternative to British writing; or even as a fraternal enterprise, a (post-)colonial literature that has only recently made its own way out from under metropolitan models. The shiftiness of the relations based on these perceptions seems to make poets less vulnerable to American poetry. The relationship between T. S. Eliot and Brathwaite best illustrates West Indian handling of a potentially overpowering influence. We tend to look back at Eliot as the authoritative theorist of relations between "tradition and the individual talent," and as a poet whose works enact allusive homage to the Great Tradition. But we need to historicize; in its time, the vast majority of the allusions in "The Waste Land" were to unfamiliar, marginal texts. Only Eliot's *use* of them has made them famous. The attempt to shore up his ruins with fragments from, say, the obscurer plays of Middleton exemplifies the desperate *bricolage* behind the cultural project of Eliot's poem. It is not decked out with immortal lines of Sophocles and Shakespeare, but instead seems to reflect the omnivorous, almost indiscriminate, reading of an autodidact. In this as in other respects it is a very American – very creole – poem.

This, and not cultural authority, is what the young Brathwaite responded to when he perceived Eliot as colonial, colloquial, and musical. What he learned from him offers a clear case for distinguishing creole appropriation from passive assimilation. Most of Brathwaite's earliest work comes in sequences of eight or ten lyrics, often quite different in form but integrated by diction or theme. The overwhelming influence on the form and diction of these poems is Eliot (particularly "The Waste Land" and "Four Quartets"). In the case of "Shadow Suite," the shadows themselves, the High Church liturgical diction and decor, even the cats, all seem to come from Eliot.[9] By contrast, only two of the poem's eight sections include recognizably Caribbean details, and these are stereotypical palm trees, sand, and surf. With time, Brathwaite's diction gradually moves from that of the oracular Eliot to that of colloquial Eliot, while the musical modeling gravitates specifically to jazz.[10] From such beginnings, Brathwaite grows toward trilogies that pursue Eliot's interest in complex rhythms of structure, in the architectural possibilities (and problems) involved in making large poems of free-standing lyrics. The poet himself has written that "The only 'European' 'influence' I can detect and will acknowledge is that of T. S. Eliot. The tone, the cadence, and above all the *organization* of my long poems . . . owe a great deal to him."[11] Perhaps more importantly, Brathwaite drew inspiration from an Eliot almost forgotten in Anglo-America: the jazz poet, explorer of the whole gamut of colloquial American voices and their rhythms, whose phonograph recordings of his work inspired Caribbean poets to shape their own speech into poetry.[12] What a jazzman does with the old standards is for Brathwaite also a model for what the West Indian poet, indeed any (post-)colonial poet, can do with Standard English and its tradition. Brathwaite later described his goal in these revealing terms: "I'm trying to outline an alternative to the English Romantic/Victorian cultural tradition which still operates among us and on us, despite the 'colonial' breakthrough already achieved by Eliot, Pound, and Joyce; and despite the presence among us of a folk tradition which in itself, it seems to me, is the basis of an alternative."[13] Brathwaite, in effect, constructed for himself precisely the Eliot he chose to imitate.

"OUR AMERICA"

Walcott's essay "The Muse of History" is an exhortation to take command of history and tradition in just that way. His proposition that "maturity is the assimilation of the features of every ancestor" envisions a successful confrontation with fictions about the past, successful *bricolage*.[14] A central project of the essay, however, is to orient West Indian poetry toward the hemisphere generally, and away from Europe and narrowly United Statesian models, by parsing the term "America" as hemispheric in scope and mythic in its force (encompassing as it does the whole history of discovery and colonization). Walcott emphasizes not so much the styles as the visions of the most ambitious poets. To read Whitman, Neruda, Borges, Perse, Césaire, or Guillén is to learn how to be of the place, of the vast America their imaginations inhabit. The hemispheric perspective, by minimizing the prominence of North America, helps poets view what is directly before them as "new," part of a "new world." West Indian writers gain from the expansiveness of a hemispheric perception, but their own reality is not a continent. On small tropical islands the vistas are not of the place, but of the sea, tempting the eye away from the place. With a history of migration and rootlessness, writers in that situation search for ways to belong to, and take possession of, the place where they are. What they begin with is dispossession: life in an empty house, in a place without a history, in an artificially contrived landscape, where everyone is an alien. When poets in that situation are under additional pressure to eschew both sensuous detail (which risks exoticism) and figurative language (which risks introducing the trappings of "Europe"), they often produce stylistically minimalist poems, the landscape pared down to its elements: beach, surf, sea grape. The Caribbean bereft of exoticism can appear brutal, "the merciless idiocy of green, green" ("Guyana," CP 115). It will become clear however that the effort to start with rudiments leads quickly to the presence of man, and the exposure of a political posture – a reminder that the urge to begin with the most elemental is often a response to pressures that politicize the work of poetry.

H. D. Carberry's "Silhouette" (1943) exemplifies severe minimalism, with just a tinge (in the placement of the word "only") of the apologetic trope so common in the period. It opens like this: "There is only the red sky / The green tree / The brown grass . . ."[15] The very next line, however, changes the atmosphere of the entire brief poem by adding a different *kind* of element: ". . . And my dreams." That move firmly situates the poem as an expression of the nationalist idealism of the PNP poets. Indeed, less extreme examples of this combination of sparse diction and idealism could be found in the work of M. G. Smith, K. E. Ingram, and George Campbell. Quite different in texture, the poems of Eric Roach could never be called minimalist, but they frequently set out from elemental topographies of wind, earth, ocean. These lines from "March Trades" (1949) are typical:

> The trade winds wake
> and shake their mane
> on earth and ocean.
> Fast flows the long green wave
> Hurried by their urge
> To crash their flowing strength
> On furrowed rock and shoaling sand.[16]

The poem as a whole envisions a generalized Caribbean island as a "ship-shape" vessel on its voyage through history, and again the generalization has a political dimension. Roach was a supporter of Federation during the 1950s, and his rudimentary, non-specific island landscapes reflect his conviction that the individual islands have much in common. Very seldom does Roach ever describe any particular place, or even the specific conditions of any one island; he wants to create landscapes that are representatively "West Indian." Over just such landscapes soar Roach's hawks and eagles, the bird/bards which are his habitual symbols of the poet in poems like "Beyond" or "Frigate Bird Passing" (both 1950).

Particularly in Jamaica and Trinidad, the 1970s were another decade of parsimonious poems, and the parsimony was again often related to political pressures. Anthony McNeill's "Residue" (1972) begins with wind, sea, and flowers in the grass, and the first stanza ends: "The grass itself shines and is precious."[17] But after thoughts of Columbus, and the sight of tourists taking possession of the beach just as he did, the poem ends by recasting that line in the light of new-found independence: "The grass is precious / merely because it belongs to us." Another minimalist Jamaican poem of the 1970s, Orlando Wong's "Scene" (1977), bears an especially striking resemblance to Carberry's poem of a generation earlier. Here is the entire text:

> blue
> sky
> white
> clouds
> green
> trees
> earth
> red
> blood red.[18]

It would seem difficult to imagine a more generic poem than this. What is there for analysis to grasp here? Yet it could in fact be *more* generic than it is. Instead of the three closing lines there could be only two: "red / earth." When "earth" is instead followed by "red," the reversal of the established "adjective + noun" sequence has great force in so laconic a poem, and it deftly sets up the grammatical ambiguity of the final line: "blood red" is heard as a compound adjective, but also as a "noun + adjective" phrase. To attach a meaning to this rhetorical gesture requires placing the poem in a fairly specific Jamaican context. There is a pun in the title which depends upon familiarity with Rastafarian speech. "Scene" refers to the depicted landscape, of course, but it also says "Seen," the usual Rastafarian expression by which one signifies comprehension of something just presented (equivalent to "understood"). That pun very economically signals the context of Rastafarian issues in which the evident emotional force of the closing lines takes on articulable meaning. The earth is red with the blood shed under slavery and colonialism, but also with the blood newly shed in the political tribalism and social conflict of the 1970s. Moreover, much of Jamaica's earth is literally red, rich with bauxite, and that evokes images of the wounded earth, of the newly independent land itself being sold off as a commodity for export.

The specific reference of Wong's poem to Jamaica is not apparent on the page; Roach, though often described as a landscape poet, seldom wrote about particular places. Walcott, by contrast, has always written poems in which specific settings are quite recognizable. He is a poet of immanence, of "natural supernaturalism," but in the works of the 1960s which culminate in *Another Life*, the holiness of West Indian landscape is the holiness of the "nothing," the holiness of a black hole which swallows both people and their history. The jaws of the Guyanese rain forest devour "two minor yellow races, and half of a black" ("Air," CP 113), and the "tribal memory" of West Indians is locked up in "that grey vault," the sea ("The Sea is History," CP 364). All history comes down to this moment's surf on this present shore ("Sea Grapes," CP 297). The climax of *Another Life* is a celebration of the holiness of Rampanalgas, but the specificity of setting seems futile in the face of what that sea serves up to the shore (and to the man on the shore):

> the silver-hammered charger of the marsh light
> brings towards us, again and again, in beaten scrolls,
> nothing, then nothing,
> and then nothing.   (CP 287)

Walcott's concern is not with describing the nothing as a fundamental condition of Caribbean life, though he does that, but with responding to it – for example, by asserting its holiness. Sometimes this elemental nothingness of the Caribbean is overwhelming. In "The Castaway" (1964), "the starved eye devours the seascape for the morsel of a sail," but nothing disrupts the infinite horizon, and the observer remains inert (CP 57). At other times, Walcott makes it sound invigorating, a blank canvas of infinite possibility: "If there was nothing, there was everything to be made."[19] This attitude underlies his praise for the painter Gregorias, with his "Adamic," untutored approach to the representation of West Indian landscape. It is pertinent that the "nothing," whether daunting or inspiring, is something Walcott arrives at *after* that wide-ranging apprenticeship of his earliest, unashamedly imitative poetry. It is not a beginning, but specifically a *new* beginning, as these lines from "Winding Up" (1976) make clear:

> I live on the water,
> alone. Without wife and children.
> *I have circled every possibility*
> *to come to this*:
>
> a low house by grey water,
> with windows always open
> to the stale sea.   (CP 336; emphasis added)

"CARIBBEAN MAN"

Those lines make something else clear as well: crucial to Walcott's "nothing" is his own presence in it. The presence of a sail is important in "The Castaway" because it could confirm the presence of the poet who looks for it. It would function like Friday's footprint – the trace of the Other against which identity can be defined. Without that trace, the poet remains attentive but immobilized. The objective in reducing experience to the elemental, after all, was to find a resonance, a *meaning*, for the Caribbean "nothing" and the Caribbean man barely accommodated in it: "The mind, among sea-wrack, sees its mythopoeic coast, / Seeks, like the polyp, to take root in itself. / Here, in the rattle of receding shoal, / Among these shallows I seek my own name and a man" ("Origins," CP 14).

The elemental landscape reveals the unmediated nature of the place, but by inviting mythopoesis, it also provides a setting which the castaway can make his own, and in which he can therefore see himself reflected.

In search of models for imagining Caribbean man as the castaway who makes a new beginning through his *bricolage*, Walcott and other West Indian poets have explored several archetypes. Some of these liminal figures are borrowed from European tradition: most obvious are Adam and Crusoe, whose significance Walcott has explored in poetry and essays. There is also the biblical Noah, who plays a crucial role in Brathwaite's *Rights of Passage*, and Virgil's Aeneas, who in some respects offers the richest analogue. It is worth considering Virgil, for a moment, in a post-colonial light. Like that of a West Indian poet resisting "Europe," his poetry demonstrates not only his own competence but that of his language; in subjecting his Latin to Greek form and Greek meter, he proves that his language can support a literature by using it to do what Greek does in Homer. But the issue is not superiority or even equality; the central imaginative claim of his *Aeneid* is difference. It was Roman culture's sense of marginality with respect to its metropolitan (Greek) culture that led it to embrace the imaginative claim that Romans were descended from the Trojans, rather than the Greeks (just as in West Indian literature it can be enabling to insist that West Indians are African, not European). Virgil's *Aeneid* (his *Arrivants*) depicts its hero at sea between his Trojan heritage and his Roman posterity. The question that haunts Aeneas in his wanderings, the question he asks when he goes to the Underworld in Book vi, is: when do we stop being Trojans and become Romans? Brathwaite and Walcott are concerned with very similar questions: when do we stop being Africans, Europeans, Asians, and become West Indians? By what means do we cease to be colonized by our own history, and begin to pursue our own separate fate? Aeneas looks most West Indian at the moment when he flees the conflagration of Troy, encumbered with his past (his father Anchises) and his future (his son Ascanius), bereft of his wife, and carrying only his defeated gods and some fragments of his possessions. What better emblem of the traumatic sea-change after which one can wake to a new world than Aeneas – an Asian disinherited by Greeks, and then helped by Africans to become a Roman? "Of his bones are coral made" – so Shakespeare symbolizes the sea-change in *The Tempest*. There are bones and coral again when Walcott, in his most elated language, celebrates his own conception of the sea-change:

the possibility of the individual Caribbean man, African, European, or Asian in ancestry, the enormous, gently opening morning of his possibility, his body touched with dew, his nerves as subtilized to sensation as the mimosa, his memory, whether of grandeur or of pain, gradually erasing itself as recurrent drizzles cleanse the ancestral or tribal markings from the coral skull, the possibility of a man and his language waking to wonder here.[20]

Walcott wants West Indian poets to respond to the weight of the present rather than the burden of the past (that is one of the motives for his invocations of "America"). Occasionally he puts a mythopoeic spin on that distinction by speaking not of the "present" but of "presences," as, for example, when he urges a vision of Caribbean man as "a being inhabited by presences, not a creature chained to his past."[21] At such moments Walcott, poet of immanence, sounds unexpectedly like the much more theologically inclined Brathwaite. Brathwaite for his part matches the paradox of a second Adam in a second Eden with his own emphasis on the need to discover "*local* primordial man."[22] As in Walcott, the delineation of a representative "Caribbean man" is essential to the process of taking possession of the place, and the medium of the process is language: "the recognition of an ancestral relationship with the folk or aboriginal culture involves the artist and participant in a journey into the past and hinterland which is at the same time a movement of possession into present and future. Through this movement of possession we become ourselves, truly our own creators, discovering word for object, image for the word."[23] In context Brathwaite is speaking particularly of Guyana, the only West Indian territory that actually has an aboriginal culture. Even so, it is clear that he is describing an artistic, rather than an ethnographic, project. Only the imagination can create a setting in which it is meaningful to say, "We become the Maya who were already us."[24] Thus for most West Indians the discovery of "local primordial man," urgent as it is, can only be a poetic invention.

Such invention is in fact successfully under way in the West Indies, as can be illustrated by examining poems about three different poetically "primordial" figures. Two – the eighteenth-century maroon leader Nanny, and the contemporary Rastafarian believer – are real people who have inspired poems, while the third is a unique ancestral figure imagined in a poem of Frank Collymore's. All of these poems invite comparison with the early, erotically charged icons of national identity discussed in chapter 5. The conventions of that genre have been both a goad and an inspiration to West Indian poets. We saw those conventions being deconstructed, with respect to history, as early as Roach's "She" (1949), and they are challenged in a variety of ways in the poems to which we now turn. Yet the icon-poem has continued to provide a resource for poets far beyond the narrowly nationalist agenda out of which it originates. Walcott's magnificent poem "The Light of The World" is fundamentally a complex reinscription of the genre: another celebration of the immobile female beauty who is somehow the spirit of the place.[25]

Nanny, now a National Hero of Jamaica, was not a passive beauty but a very active historical figure who hardly fits the mold of the genre. Yet at least one poem about her, Grace Nichols's "Nanny" (1990), has strong affinities with the earlier icon-poems. Like Roberts, Nichols presents a static figure, and wants her maroon leader Nanny to be both African ("Ashanti") and maroon. Like Bell's "Ancestor on the Auction Block" this poem is addressed to her without allowing her to speak for herself, and without quite coming to terms with her – the poem is a predictable description of Nanny which ends rather oddly with this question: "Is that you Nanny – Is that you Nanny?"[26] Lorna Goodison and Honor Ford-Smith have written revisionist accounts of the maroon icon. Goodison's "Nanny" (1983) deconstructs it specifically with respect to gender; this Nanny is neither a mother nor an erotic object. In Goodison's version, she is not a spirit of the place, but a transitional figure, first trained in Africa and then purposely sent to the Caribbean to become a leader for those who had been enslaved – to become (in effect) West Indian. As a result of her training she "became most knowing and forever alone," because her personal desires must be sacrificed to serve a larger cultural purpose.[27] This icon speaks for herself, and when she does so the diction of the poem even appropriates a boasting style which in the West Indies is traditionally a male prerogative: "my womb was sealed with molten wax of killer bees for nothing should enter nothing should leave." This diction, by its manipulation of gender cues, further underscores Goodison's point that Nanny's is "the condition of the warrior." Like all boasting, this has a defensive edge to it, and that draws attention to the element of self-dramatization in Goodison's Nanny.

By contrast, Ford-Smith's maroon leader in "Message from Ni" (1990) does *not* believe her own legend, and in fact actually debunks the stories that have grown up about her. She is less than noble about the sacrifices she has made ("I cursed the people / they say I led . . . I longed for lovers or children"), insisting that she trembled in battle, vomited at the sight of death, and fainted at the smell of blood.[28] The honesty, the terror, even the rage, which she reveals in her confession humanize the icon without interfering with the process by which she becomes her own legend. The breach in the legend that this poem has enacted (by exposing Ni's fears, her lies, her weaknesses) is itself sealed with the closing litany of praise-names:

> It was terror of terror that drove me on
> Till it was all over and I heard
> I was Ni
> eye of change   leadress   path
> finder   healer of the
> breach.

In this way the poem justifies its own potentially risky procedure: it is possible to attain greater human knowledge of the person and still leave the legend intact.

The overt theme established in Frank Collymore's "Flotsam" (1948) seems quite remote from the tradition of the icon-poem. The opening lines take up the elusive relation of language to experience:

> WORDS – words are the poem,
> The incalculable flotsam;
> That which bore them vanished beneath
> The hurrying drift of time.
>   . . .
> Words float upon the surface, a broken
> Message.[29]

The central symbolic work of the poem, however, hinges upon its two voyages: a first that ends in the shipwreck which produces the flotsam and a second which is the voyage of the reader. This second voyage is of course the act of reading the poem, but it is also figured within the fiction of the poem, in the innocent ship that comes upon the "broken message" of the flotsam. The sea-wrack bespeaks an event; looking down from our own ship, we read wrack as wreck. But in making out what it means, we are drawn to make out what it means to us, about ourselves. So Collymore asks: does the flotsam direct our attention onward or downward? Does the flotsam encourage us to continue our own interrupted voyage anew, the wreck a sign men have come this far and can come farther? Or should we stop to "peer / Below the restless surface, discerning, / Tangled among the seaweed and obscured, / A shape that might have been a man?" The poem, in asking, attends to both alternatives, but seems most troubled by the descent to the obscured, possibly human, shape beneath the surface. The emotional weight of this poem is concentrated in that final question, so tentative and so obstructed in expression, and that weight suggests that the alternatives are not truly equal. The tangle in the seaweed fathoms beneath the tangle of the flotsam exerts an irresistible magnetism.

Flotsam as the ultimate detritus of a man is the image through which Collymore thinks about poetry, expression, and authorship. But there is another level on which the poem invokes the history of the West Indies and its trajectory into the future. It was Césaire who called the West Indies "the greatest shipwreck in world history,"[30] and that catastrophe is at the heart of the West Indian quarrel with history discussed by Edward Baugh.[31] The simple dilemma is the one raised here – delve into the past or move on – but those alternatives are hotly contested and variously interpreted. Martin Carter provides a convenient text for comparison. His poem "Fragment of Memory" (1956) concentrates on the same situation as "Flotsam": a voyage to the New World interrupted by shipwreck. But Carter is a deeply political poet working in a setting of sometimes fierce racial politics, so the voyage he dwells upon is explicitly part of the Middle Passage, not of the Discovery. Even setting aside the poem's specifically Guyanese details, it is apparent that Carter reads the whole event with a very different emphasis than Collymore:

> In the ships coming, in the black slaves dying
> in the hot sun burning down –
> We bear a mark no shower of tears can shift.
> On the bed of the ocean bones alone remain
> rolling like pebbles drowned in many years.[32]

Out in Carter's ocean there is nothing but bones, and as he presents them they have been leached of all humanity. They are stark and matter-of-fact, while Collymore's "shape" is organic, almost fertile, and for that reason an emotional focus. In Carter the traumatic mark is not on the sea (or on time, or on history) and merely come upon by the contemporary West Indian; instead it is actually inscribed on the West Indians of the present. Carter's eye is on man at the end of the voyage, not at its origin, and his attention is narrowed to certain men, those who have been marked not by a failed voyage but by a successful one – those whom the poet sees, at least in this instance, not as readers of history but as in effect its very documents: "The ships are gone and men remain to show / with a strong black skin what course those keels had cut."

By contrast, Collymore's poem is notable for the ambivalence and difficulty of its final question. For him, the pathos we read in the scattered débris originates in the submerged human factor we guess or discern beneath it. But this is only barely, only putatively, human. The final image is a demythologized version of Ariel's song, in which the sea-change is rudely natural, the rough magic of time and dissolution. All marks of race and rank are gone, and it is impossible to tell from the shape or from the splinters what sort of voyager this was – slaver, discoverer, settler. As a result we lack the clues to know how we are expected to feel about the wreck, the voyage, and its human agents. Without access to those politicized stock responses, this flotsam can stand as emblem for the whole history of the place, the entire vexed human effort that created the West Indies, and indeed put all of us here in the Americas. In that obscured shape beneath the flotsam Collymore has envisioned an impossible creole ancestor; not one of the grand-fathers polarized into black or white, master or slave, Indian or invader, but that psychic necessity, the common ancestor of West Indians as West Indians – a shared ancestor who can exist only as myth. Unlike Roberts's "The Maroon Girl," which envisions the maroon as a product of problematic differences of race and class, Collymore glimpses a common ancestor somehow innocent of them. Collymore's mind is perhaps still on *The Tempest*, where vengeance turns to reconciliation, and the sea-change of the father stands for the redemption of the past, of ancestral crime and faction.

Collymore's obscure ancestor is a purely literary invention. By contrast, Jamaican Rastafarians are real, highly visible people, but both the invention of the Rastafarian religion itself and the extensive body of poetry that takes the Rastaman as its subject are of interest here. Rastafarianism presents itself as a salient example of the impact of "Africa" – a faith grounded on the recovery of African roots and the hope of repatriation to Ethiopia. But despite appearances it is a profoundly creole creation, a triumph of *bricolage*, an instance of making something *here*, out of the materials at hand. It combines the English Bible, nonconformist religious culture, sometimes-fanciful African additives, and very West Indian habits of "grounda-tion" (a kind of sociable debate on philosophical topics in which there is usually some element of self-dramatization – Plato's *Symposium* is not too remote an analogue). After the sea-change, all this has been integrated into something unique.

A key to this particular *bricolage* is the role of the Bible for West Indian culture at large. While the Bible is of course at the heart of the Great Tradition, to the extent that it is memorized rather than read, it exists also as an *oral* resource, and in that form it can often be found functioning as an important feature of the Little Tradition. This curiously double role of the Bible deserves some further explanation, particularly since it is analogous to the double role of "Africa," which it can thus help to clarify. In the Protestant Caribbean, it is the Bible in English that belongs to the Little Tradition; thanks to years of non-conformist and revivalist emphasis the book as a whole is identified with its apocalyptic parts, which were absorbed into the popular imagination (and diction) before literacy became widespread. On the other hand, it is the Bible as a European book that forms a cornerstone of the Great Tradition, and, speaking very loosely, a writer who turns to the Bible as a literary text, rather than as a body of oral lore, is construed as working in (and committing himself to) the Great Tradition. In the poetry of Figueroa, for example, where turns of phrase from the Bible appear among quotations from Horace and Terence, readers tend to take them as literary, while in Bongo Jerry, where biblical phrases jostle with nursery rhymes, they are construed as oral. In short, though the Bible is in fact the root of the colonial cultures imposed in the Caribbean, it functions in the islands as part of the alternative popular tradition.

This has as much to do with West Indian techniques of appropriation as with the Bible itself. The same phenomenon is apparent, on a much smaller scale, in Brathwaite's treatment of T. S. Eliot as an oral resource, and, on a much larger scale, the case of "Africa" is also parallel. The body of cultural material referred to as "Africa," like that accumulated around the Bible, constitutes an independent Great Tradition. As it happens, both have been absorbed through the West Indian Little Tradition, primarily as a result of British colonial policies

which discouraged both African cultural survivals and orthodox Christian religious practice among the slaves. Thus the
West Indian artist can resort to each in its fullness. Since the
Bible is squarely in the Little Tradition, he can exploit parts of
the text or even of the traditions surrounding it that are not in
practice part of the Little Tradition. Similarly the presence of
"Africa-in-the-Caribbean" allows the artist to exploit features
of African culture itself and still be perceived as invigorating
the indigenous culture, rather than as polluting or diverting it
with mimicry of alien and potentially stultifying material.
Rastafarianism adds another twist. The religion is not very
strict about codifying its doctrine, but there is a view that the
English Bible is in fact a corrupt version, rewritten to suit the
needs of colonizers and slave-holders. Through inspiration, the
Rastafarian believer can discern beneath its distorted surface
the so-called "Maccabee" version, the original scripture given
to the true chosen people, who are black Africans.[33] The
situation is quintessentially creole: the basis for the religion is a
reconstructed "African" version of a "European" text, which in
fact only exists in the West Indies.

In part because Rastafarianism is a very West Indian creation, its adherents have proven very attractive as subject-matter
for poetry. These poems might fairly be regarded as another
variant of the nationalistic icon, but it should be borne in mind
that the motivation for them is not initially literary; they do not
arise as revisions of poems, but as depictions of actual West
Indian people, who have developed a new mechanism for
coming to terms with the place, through the creative cultural
work which produces Rastafarianism. Up until the early 1960s,
Rastafarians were marginalized objects of derision and fear.
Attitudes toward them changed so rapidly in the early years of
Independence that soon the Rasta, even more than the
maroon, came to be envisioned as what Walcott calls a "race-
containing symbol," the creole *creation* of an aboriginal figure, a
new Adam.[34]

These poems are not necessarily written by Rastafarians;
other writers are attracted by the Rastafarian's picturesque
demeanor and language, and stimulated by a fundamental

dilemma in the valuing of both rootedness and escape which was an especially prominent feature of the Rastafarianism of the 1960s and early 1970s – this was the form of the belief system that most influenced poets who were themselves often making decisions about migration. The most common scene in these poems is the solitary Rasta smoking his ganja as sacramental escape from the conditions of his life, while he awaits the expected coming of the ship that will repatriate him to Ethiopia. Brathwaite's "Wings of a Dove" (1967) is the model for a proliferation of poems on this subject in the 1970s. Usually written in SE, most come from Jamaica, though some have been written in the Eastern Caribbean and even Guyana (often, it should be said, by poets who studied at the University of the West Indies in Jamaica). Anthony McNeill's poems about Rastafarians are sympathetic, but the attraction he obviously feels to the Rastas is reined in by skepticism. "Saint Ras" treats the Rastaman as a social misfit, always out of step in a world which is not his own – but the title at least hints that this is a common-enough attribute of saints. In "Ode to Brother Joe" the Rasta is arrested for smoking his weed, and the poem ends with Joe in his cell, repeating the "magic words" of his faith: "Haile Selassie I / Jah Rastafari." But McNeill has already commented that "Selassie is far away / and couldn't care less"; despite the magic and the faith, "the door is real and remains shut."[35] "Straight Seeking" presents a more sacramental view, but again the speaker of the poem distances himself from the Rastas worshipping their god:

> Tonight, Jah
> rears in a hundred tenements
> missed by my maps.
> Still compassed by reason,
> my ship sails, coolly, between
> Africa and heaven.[36]

Mervyn Morris's "Rasta Reggae" takes a perspective very much like McNeill's. Here what seems to be an expression of orthodox Rastafarian faith is suddenly reduced by the turn of the poem's final phrase: "let my people go / home to Ethiopia

/ in the mind."[37] McNeill and Morris are representative of a number of poets whose attraction to Rastafarian ways is tempered with discomfort at the prospect of grounding so much on a pipe dream. By contrast, the linguistic code-switching of Opal Adisa Palmer's poem, "Ethiopia under a Jamaican Mango Tree," reinforces her positive account of the personal, and societal, value of the Rastafarian's ritualized escape to his dream of Ethiopia.[38]

Chapter 4 referred in passing to early West Indian complaints about religious poetry, and even today self-consciously devotional poetry (like self-consciously political poetry) is often clumsy if not insipid. Rastafarian poets are among several strong exceptions to that characterization (others would include Robert Lee, Anson Gonzalez, Lorna Goodison, and a number of East Indian Guyanese whose field of reference is Hindu). The nature of the impediment to successful religious poetry may be illuminated by a paradox in the verbal arts of Jamaican Rastas. Rastafarianism has developed a powerful religious prose, especially in a number of prayers that can compete in vigor with the Latin prayers of the early Christian church. It has also produced in classic reggae a remarkable kind of genuinely religious popular music. Both of these forms are grounded in speech rhythms and in a deeply ingrained habit of biblical diction. However, Rastafarian lyric that presents itself as poetry rather than as song still tends to follow colonial models, gravitating toward a generalized "poetic diction" and to the measures of hymn tunes. This poetry is on the whole technically naive, and in its extreme conventionality bears the marks of the colonial heritage more visibly than any other aspect of the Rastafarian movement.[39] Strangely, this verse is not modeled on speech. By contrast, secular West Indian poets often recognize Rasta speech as the germ of powerful poetry. There are several fine examples in Dennis Scott's collection of poems from the 1970s, *Dreadwalk*.[40] Lorna Goodison's "The Road of the Dread" (1980) is an effective projection of Rastafarian consciousness in modified Rastafarian language – an inhabiting of the figure, that is neither a description nor an uneasy impersonation. Kendel Hippolyte's

"Zoo Story – Ja. '76" (1976) uses unmediated Rastafarian language to write about a resonant incident, the story of a Jamaican who died after jumping into the lion's cage in the Kingston zoo. Despite strong competition from Mikey Smith, Bongo Jerry's "Mabrak" (1971) is perhaps still the finest Rastafarian poem that has found its way into print. A number of promising poems (for instance Audvil King's "Big Wash") are weakened by giving in to the kind of extemporaneous sprawl that "Mabrak" so carefully controls. Bongo Jerry's command of form and rhetoric here are impressive, but the poem's greatest achievement is its articulation of a compelling eschatological myth out of materials provided by Rastafarianism and Jamaican culture generally.

MYTHOLOGIZING

The figure of the Rastafarian is distinctive in that it emerges from a fully developed creole religion, and in becoming available to poetry makes the mythological resources of the whole faith available as well. But that is a special case. "Caribbean man" was meant to make sense of the place, also, by his coming to terms with it, imposing himself on it; how do poets move from solitary "Caribbean man" to secular myth, larger-scale imaginative structures that can indeed make sense of the place? In Brathwaite, the castaway imposes himself on the world, creates the world, through poetic language: "I / must be given words so that the bees / in my blood's buzzing brain of memory // will make flowers, will make flocks of birds, / will make sky, will make heaven, / the heaven open to the thunderstone and the volcano and the un-folding land" ("Negus," *Arrivants*, 224). The articulation of the elemental landscape comes from within. Brathwaite's faith in this ordering power of language is affirmed in the large-scale movement of *Arrivants*, which comes to "the brink of vision" when the solitary fisherman flings his net out over the water in "Vèvè." This act of containment symbolizes the imposition of order, of understanding, on a sea which is both the elemental Caribbean place and its history:

> The net drifted downward,
> through tides and reversals
> of shell-clinking water,
> through time and the hopes
> that were drowned in the deep.   *(Arrivants,* 263)

The implication is clear. The lines of the net will cut through the shifting "tides and reversals" to recover the drowned hopes and the lost history. But at the end of the trilogy the net has still not been pulled in, so the question remains open: what kind of net will work?

Haiti has a living mythological order in vodun, and it is not surprising that West Indian poets have borrowed from it when trying to respond to the dearth of indigenous mythological foundation available in the Anglophone Caribbean. Taking a different approach, Wilson Harris, in his early poems, makes use of classical Greek mythology, and Walcott has often done the same. The most familiar example is the catalogue of St. Lucians in chapter 3 of *Another Life*; they are presented in alphabetical order (a straightforward enough framing device), and most of them are either named after, or associated with, human characters from Greek myth (CP 158–64). Walcott seems worried about the effect, however. The passage ends with a self-denigrating shrug – "These dead, these derelicts, / that alphabet of the emaciated, / they were the stars of my mythology" (CP 164) – and he raises the issue of possible disproportion between these West Indian people and classical stature later on (CP 183). In *Omeros* (1990) he no longer pretends to apologize for an account of St. Lucia resonant with the names of Greek heroes, though he remains finicky about gods, whether Greek, African, or Christian.

Brathwaite, of course, is entirely comfortable with gods of all sorts, and his two massive trilogies weave the most elaborate net yet devised for the comprehension of West Indian realities. *The Arrivants* proceeds fairly simply. In the first volume, *Rights of Passage*, the central figure is Tom, the representative survivor of the Middle Passage who is at once the last African and the first "New World Negro." Brathwaite appropriates this character from the seminal North American novel *Uncle Tom's Cabin* and strenuously re-imagines him. The provocative results recall (and perhaps inspired) Ford-Smith's willingness to explore without prejudice the true complexity of Nanny. Tom here is often treated as if he were a male solitary, but he is also a problematic parent (like Aeneas rather than Crusoe), and his isolation is redeemed as the poem progressively weaves him into a mythological fabric of Afro-Caribbean gods. For the purposes of the poem Tom has one single cultural possession, a memory of the golden age of the Ashanti Empire under Osai Tutu, a painful and apparently useless story he cannot meaningfully pass on to his children. The volume ends by associating Tom with "Old Negro Noah" who, like Tom, steps into a new world, like him lives to be mocked by his own sons, and like him bears the responsibility to make hard choices for the descendants whose survival he has just assured.

The first half of the next volume, *Masks*, traces the migration of a desert people across the savannahs to their "final" settlement in the forests of West Africa. This is presented not only as a pre-history of displacement before the great displacement of Middle Passage, but also as a lesson in cultural adaptation. Brathwaite's point is the transformation of culture that results from an adjustment to radically new conditions, and especially the transformation of religion from the monotheistic response to the sun in the desert to the animism of dense forest where "leaf eyes shift, twigs creak, buds flutter, the stick becomes a snake" (*Arrivants*, 115). In the second half of *Masks* the West Indian protagonist of the trilogy travels to Africa and makes a pilgrimage upcountry to Kumasi, the old imperial capital of the Ashanti, which culminates in a vision of Osai Tutu and his court. Here we see enacted the events that Tom in *Rights* had compressed into a memory: Tutu's consolidation of the Ashanti empire through the unifying symbol of the Golden Stool. But the vision discloses not only the glory, the imaginative victory that surely was, but the expedient sacrifices; unexpectedly, the poet sees his own tribe brought in as captives and sold to slavers. Tom's treasured African memory is revealed as already a slave's memory of his master. The poet, the New World descendant of Tom, is imaginatively present at the event, and sees not just the central ritual but its grimmer context. He is forced to accept the totality of African experience, not just the ideal, and to accept in addition the West Indian's severance from all that. The volume ends as the orphaned poet returns to basics, to the earth, and that means not the African earth, but the Caribbean.

Islands then grounds itself in the Caribbean, where "the gods have been forgotten or hidden" (*Arrivants*, 164). Bereft of mythology or native language, objects have no meanings, or remain the property of the master who names them. With eyes freshened by the experience of Africa, Brathwaite surveys the Caribbean for its repressed culture, its survivals from Africa, its indigenous innovations – the psychic furniture that might make it a comfortable home. Eventually the poet's clearing vision recognizes continuities in his own relatives, his ancestors, and out of the background Tom begins to emerge again in a new light. Tom's empty cabin progressively decays as *Rights* proceeds ("The Cabin"), while around it the Caribbean is transformed to a cheap imitation of the metropolis in steel and concrete. It is only through the imaginative work of *Masks* and then *Islands* that the cabin is symbolically resurrected as the sacred space of possession ritual ("Anvil") – the site where ancestral presences, African or American, can make their presence felt. The sea change is a dominant motif of *The Arrivants*, and Tom, who has the complex relation to memory characteristic of a "second Adam," represents the liminal figure who ceases to be an African and becomes something else – West Indian, American, creole.

The second trilogy (it has no collective title) differs from the first primarily in its scope and in the boldness of its *bricolage*. The first two volumes of this new trilogy gradually delineate a vast mythic frame conceived on the scale of geologic time, and inhabited by characters who have in effect both human and geologic (or astronomical) aspects. "My mother, Barbados" is both the setting and the central character of *Mother Poem* (1977). She is a pool, but also the cloud that evaporates from the pool, and the porous limestone through which the falling rain percolates; she is the island, a stone shaped like a liquid tear. In much the same way that *Rights of Passage* meditates on Tom by turning attention to his children, *Mother Poem* depicts its central figure by sketching her relations with the men in her life (husband, parson, teacher, debt collector . . .). All of them are broken or distorted by the heritage of colonialism, so that she must somehow find ways to support them at the same time as she resists their demands on her. As so often in *The Arrivants* the momentum of the poem leads to a final "beginning" through spirit possession, which is at once an escape, a grounding, an empowerment and an act of resistance. Finally, through the "birth" which is her death she is metamorphosed from natural to mythic mother. When the volume concludes we have learned how she became the pool/rain cloud of the opening; the flow of her *words*, which in fact have dominated the poem, fills the island's watercourses that had been dry so long, "travelling inwards under the limestone / widening outwards into the sunlight / towards the breaking of her flesh with foam."[41]

In contrast, *Sun Poem* (1982) elaborates upon the linear career of the father, figured variously as the trajectory of the sun from dawn to dark, the sequential colors of the rainbow, and the journey of an African spirit swept westward from home to be cast up on the island's Atlantic shore. *Sun Poem* complements the female landscape of its predecessor with the corresponding *male* history; the sun that rises and sets over the island, alternately warming and then abandoning it, enacts the male lifecycle from child to husband to grandfather. The poem's central character is a boy called Adam, who in the course of the story moves from the west coast of Barbados to the east. Within the symbolic framework of the poem the boy's eastward movement, contrary to the progress of the sun, is a movement back to origins (similarly Brathwaite's own notes to the poem describe the fifth section, "The Crossing," as "the Middle Passage in reverse").[42] Thus the poem's visionary center (section VI, "Noom") recounts the story of how the African god Legba once emerged from the Atlantic of his own Middle Passage on this coast of Barbados (as Brathwaite often reminds us, it is the part of the Caribbean closest to Africa).

Sun Poem ends away from both coasts in the center of the island, at the country house where Adam witnesses his grandfather's funeral and as a result becomes conscious of the cycle of Caribbean manhood, perceived in a cosmic context. The cycle of the poem ends in night, but it is a night full of stars, and the volume concludes with an extraordinary creation song that envisions a god, "nameless dark horse of devouring morning" arriving out of the east to bring the dawn: "out of that brass / that was beating its genesis genesis genesis genesis / out of the stammering world / . . . my thrill- / dren are coming up coming up coming up coming up / and the sun / new."[43] (The contrast between ideas of the fullness and the emptiness of "America" is stark in the juxtaposition of this mythopoeic "genesis genesis genesis" with Walcott's image of the charger of the marsh light bringing "nothing, then nothing, / and then nothing" [CP 287].)

The setting of *Mother Poem* and *Sun Poem* is Caribbean, but *X/Self* (1987) stages a coup and turns to "Rome" – for once, Europe is treated as myth. If *The Arrivants* can be described as investigating the realities under our familiar myths of Africa as the "dark continent" symbolized by the jungle, *X/Self* correspondingly proposes that we consider Europe under the figure of the Alps. Thus Mont Blanc is the center and central image of Europe, its hub and holy mountain. Its counterpart is Mount Kilimanjaro, the African hub of histories. The human imitation of the one is the Roman Empire and its successors, of the other the kraal and the village compound. One is the industrial furnace, missile-oriented, while the other is an agrarian center, surrounded by the diverse life of the savannah. *X/Self* accumulates an impressive array of such oppositions – male and female, aggressive and patient, stable and unstable, linear and circular, cultures of the "projectile" or of the circular "target." Brathwaite envisions history as a cycle of changing relations between these opposites; the kind of cycle he calls "tidalectics," an ebb and flow of antithetical ideas or processes, as distinct from the usual three-stage progression of dialectics. *The Arrivants* undertook a careful questioning of assumptions behind the idealization of Africa, an exhaustive investigation of issues of origin. The pointed and provocative repositioning of Uncle Tom and the similar re-evaluation of Tutu and glorified Africa have their counterparts here, for example in *X/Self*'s complex rehabilitation of "Rome" – for the purposes of the poem it is in the vacuum left when Rome burns that slavery begins.

There is ambivalence too inherent in the central character of this volume. The mythic apparatus of the first two volumes becomes itself the subject of *X/Self*, whose multi-form eponymous hero is the "child" of that sun and mother. Altogether, this is a trilogy of ancestral/mythic figures; after mother/island and father/sun, the third volume presents X/Self as a crossing-point of the others, the heroic/unheroic sons of those parents. The result is a small but intensely resonant pantheon. One of its manifestations, for example, is the family group Prospero, Sycorax, and Caliban/Ariel. "X/Self" is in a way the name of a tribe: the resistant selves on the margins of empire. They represent the creole presence both within and over against empire. Thus the volume starts with a letter from an inconsequential nephew of the emperor. But the emperor is Severus, and that choice initiates the play of centrality and margin: he is the first African to become emperor, thereby bringing his marginality to the center of Rome, and in the end bringing his centrality to the margins, to die at York, a place that was then on the edge of the world. "X/Self" is the name for Severus, and his nephew, and all the obscure populations who could only be perceived as monkeys or savages, gorillas or guerrillas.

The scope of this work is enormous and has not yet been fully absorbed into Caribbean discourse. What has attracted attention, however, is the trilogy's mythic nuclear family. Feminist critics have raised questions, and Brathwaite's long-time advocate Gordon Rohlehr has extravagantly praised *Mother Poem* as "perhaps the most varied kaleidoscope of female experience that yet exists in West Indian literature."[44] But though the children are dispersed and the marriage is rocky, the trilogy makes us sharply aware that there have been no Eves in the poems of the Caribbean's second Eden. It cannot be coincidental that sterility is an attribute of so many castaway figures. Of those we have been considering, only Noah and Aeneas are functionally parents. The historical Nanny was married, and even in the poems Rastamen often have shadowy families, but poets almost always present them as isolated and even self-absorbed. West Indian poetry has had difficulty making the step from the castaway to the couple, the first parents.

Brathwaite seems to be aware of this. The epigraph for *Mother Poem* comes from Wilson Harris's novel *The Whole Armour* (1962), a remarkable early attempt to envision a mythic family. The words are spoken by Christo to his pregnant girlfriend Sharon: "we're the first potential parents who can contain the ancestral house."[45] Unlike those around them, who still think of themselves as aliens and new arrivals, Christo and Sharon are the Adam and Eve appropriate for a new Eden. They are the first inhabitants who are not looking back, or living in the past, but instead bringing the past forward into the future: "we have begun to see ourselves in the earliest grass-roots, in the first tiny seed of spring . . . We're reborn into the oldest native and into our oldest nature."[46] Brathwaite had already been influenced by this conception of Harris's when he wrote "Timehri"; it is what enables him to assert that "We become the Maya who were already us." Fulfillment of an "American" vision of the West Indies would seem to require the vigorous imagining of these paradoxical first parents; both Harris and Brathwaite have made significant progress in meeting that need. Achievement of such a goal, however, requires attention not only to myth, and to ideas of "America," but to the West Indian family. That is a task that the region's poets are only just beginning to take up. At the end of Harris's novel, after all, Christo is arrested for a capital crime, and pregnant Sharon is left in the care of Christo's overbearing mother; Brathwaite's trilogy itself might reasonably be described as an account of the detonations of the nuclear family.

Male poets of domestic life like Morris and Scott tend to start at least from a premise of the family man as dutiful husband and doting parent. Yet despite "the steady glowing power / that makes a man feel loved, / feel needed . . . ," the husband in Morris's "Family Pictures" (1973) cannot repress an urge to become the castaway:

> to go alone
> to where
> the fishing boats are empty
> on the beach
> and no one knows
> which man is
> father, husband, victim,
> king, the master of one cage.[47]

As a result, this ends up resembling Walcott's "Winding Up" and is consistent with other poems in which Morris emphasizes the confinement of domesticity, such as "At Home" and "Interior."[48]

For their part, female poets often present instead the brave mother and the womanizing father. Some of these poems are frankly retributive, but others have great imaginative subtlety. For example Goodison's "For My Mother (May I Inherit Half Her Strength)" (1986) presents the standard West Indian philanderer from the perspective not of his wife but of his perceptive girl-child, and the result is compelling. This is a celebratory poem about the mother's courtship, marriage, and widowhood. At one point the surface breaks and Goodison describes a special place in the marriage, "a country where my father with the always smile / my father whom all women loved, who had the perpetual quality of wonder / given only to a child . . . hurt his bride. // Even at his death there was this 'Friend' who stood by her side, / but my mother is adamant that that has no place in the memory of my father."[49] Even at this point the description of the father is admiring. The forbidden phrase "hurt his bride," though it "has no place" in the memory of the father, does have a place here, in this memory of the mother. And because it is set off by Goodison's own ellipses we realize that it matches in rhythm and rhyme another phrase in the poem, the words "and she cried," which appear at three crucial points in the text: at her wedding, when she finally mourns her husband weeks after the funeral, and in the final line, "and she cried also because she loved him." The strength of the poem derives from the same candid integrity we saw at work in Ford-Smith's treatment of Nanny or Brathwaite's of Tom.

This chapter has come by a very roundabout route, through epic voyages and geologic time, to arrive at poetry of ordinary domestic life. To some extent that accurately reflects historical developments. In the course of the 1980s West Indian poets, after having to grapple with an assortment of pressing responsibilities (to "Europe," to "Africa," to "America," to societies in the throes of independence), emerged at yet another new beginning: the freedom to write straightforwardly of their own lives. There have always been West Indian poets writing intimate and even confessional poetry, but this book has been tracing developments in West Indian poetry during an era dominated by issues of nationhood, Federation, and West Indian identity – an era when such work was hard pressed to justify itself as part of the very public and indeed political mission of West Indian poetry. But after all that, and especially after "Africa" does its work, in regional politics as well as in literary history, poets seem to feel less obligated to be representative. The masculine nationalist stance of speaking for and to the society remains available, of course; but the wish to have the whole society as an audience no longer necessarily entails addressing all of it at once. One can write "I" and not mean "we." Poets may have legitimate roles which are not always so literally functional, of such direct social relevance, as conditions around Independence made necessary. Even Brathwaite, the model of the communal voice in *The Arrivants*, has become in recent years much more intimate, isolated, and even reclusive as a poet. His later autobiographical work, including the second trilogy, remains enormously ambitious in conception, but is much less representative than even Walcott's supposedly "confessional" poetry.

The nature of Lorna Goodison's collection *Heartease* (1988) is relevant here. In these poems "Heartease" is Goodison's word for an abode of peace and illumination, a kingdom to which we will come. What is pertinent is not so much the precise meaning of the term as its function. Half a dozen of these poems ("Some Nights I Don't Sleep," "Heartease I," "Heartease III," "Heartease New England 1987," "Come Let Your Eyes Feel," "A Rosary of Your Names") end with "Heartease" in the final line – in several cases it is the final word.[50] The effect is incantatory, but not always persuasive. "Heartease" sometimes comes across as a privately achieved satisfaction which the poems attest, but not as an outcome to which the poem has effectually brought the reader. This is consistent with Goodison's handling of other important recurrent figures in her poems, such as the Mulata, the Wild Woman, and the King of Swords. No one would call this "mythopoesis," but Goodison has no interest in assembling a mythology for West Indians to inhabit; instead her goal is to cultivate private symbolism in a way that is accessible to individual readers. The same might be said of an older poet like McNeill or Gonzalez; the significant change is that *no* poet of the generation after Walcott and Brathwaite has yet written poetry even as mythopoeic as Goodison's. Out from under the pressure to be "representative," to "function" for society, younger poets may have suspended or set aside large mythopoeic ambitions. West Indians seem to feel free to write as they wish, rather than as they must. Perhaps thanks to the austerities of the 1960s and 1970s, West Indian poetry can afford to invest in something that had been regarded as a luxury: the psyche and experience of the private citizen.

The 1980s brought other changes to West Indian poetry. Now that issues of Federation and Independence have had their day, recent poetry demonstrates an increasing awareness of *local* identity, reflected in choices made about language and field of reference. Women's voices are increasingly audible, as are the voices of ethnic minorities. The consolidation of localized and minority identities may suggest the coming of *new* fragmentations (so that we now speak, for example, of "Afro-Caribbean" or "Indo-Caribbean" poetry). But at the same time the great resourcefulness of creole culture, and especially of creole language, is uncontested. Further, the rise of very local consciousness is contemporaneous with the experience and articulation of diasporic identity, as more and more West

Indian writers live with one foot squarely planted abroad. These seemingly antithetical tendencies probably do not stand in need of reconciliation: "local" and "diasporic" work can equally well find a place in the now very wide continuum of West Indian poetic practice.

Prognostication is a mug's game. A sublime epic may appear tomorrow, signed with an unfamiliar name. The purpose of a book like this is not to foresee the future, or even to explain the present, but to lay a foundation that will sustain and enhance the reading of West Indian poetry, present and future. This book ends having reached a point from which it is possible to say this much: nourished by the initial *prises de conscience* of nationalism and "Africa," West Indian poets are at this moment writing unself-consciously from, about, and for the place where they find themselves, whether that place is in the West Indies, or in one of its new cultural colonies.

Notes

I WEST INDIAN POETRY AND ITS AUDIENCE

1 My account of the conference draws primarily upon two reports: C. D. Narasimhaiah, "A.C.L.A.L.S. Conference on Commonwealth Literature: Kingston, Jamaica, 3–9 January, 1971," *Journal of Commonwealth Literature* 6:2 (Dec., 1971), 120–26, and an anonymous "Statement of Position to the Commonwealth Literature & Language Conference – Mona, January, 1971," *Journal of Black Poetry* 1:17 (1973), 29–32. Though the catalogue of the Radio Education Unit at UWI Mona lists recordings of all the conference sessions, neither tapes nor transcripts seem to be accessible there. An incomplete set of presented papers is preserved at the Institute of Jamaica.

2 For consistency, I have followed the somewhat idiosyncratic use of the term "folk" which functions as the norm in West Indian literary criticism. Established primarily by Gordon Rohlehr's influential essay, "Literature and the Folk," first presented at ACLALS in 1971, this rough taxonomy identifies a "middle class" (moneyed rather than landed, and therefore essentially urban) and the "folk," a term which included both the rural "peasantry" and what might with circumspection be called the urban proletariat.

3 George Lamming, "The Negro Writer and His World," *Caribbean Quarterly* 5:2 (1958), 112–13.

4 Anon., "Statement of Position," 29.

5 Louis James, ed., "Of Redcoats and Leopards," *The Islands in Between: Essays on West Indian Literature* (London: Oxford University Press, 1968), 64.

6 Brathwaite, "Foreward," *Savacou* 3/4 (Dec. 1970/Mar. 1971), 9.

7 Derek Walcott, "West Indian Poetry – A Search for Voices," part five of the series, "The State of the Arts in Jamaica," UWI Radio Education Unit transcript of a Mona seminar (Mar. 14, 1965), 1.

8 Mervyn Morris, "Some West Indian Problems of Audience," *English* 16 (1967), 129.

9 Sylvia Wynter, "Reflections on West Indian Writing and Criticism," *Jamaica Journal* 2:4 (Dec. 1968), 23–32 and 3:1 (1969), 27–42; Edward Baugh, "Towards a West Indian Criticism," *Caribbean Quarterly* 14:1&2 (1968), 140–44; Kenneth Ramchand, "Concern for Criticism," *Literary Half-Yearly* 11:2 (1970), 151–61 (reprinted *Caribbean Quarterly* 16:2 [1970]); Rohlehr, "West Indian Poetry: Some Problems of Assessment," in *My Strangled City and Other Essays* (Trinidad: Longman, 1992), 133–41 (originally published serially in *Tapia* 1970/71).

10 Anon., "Statement of Position," 29.

11 *Ibid.*, 32.

12 Quoted by Mervyn Morris, "Some West Indian Problems of Audience," 128.

13 Quoted in *Commonwealth Caribbean into the Seventies*, A. W. Singham, ed. (Montreal: McGill University Press, 1975), 40.

14 Reprinted in *Public Opinion* 30 (June 10, 1966), "Roger Mais Supplement," 7.

15 Parallel quotations from Eric Williams, C. L. R. James and Martin Carter are cited in Gordon Rohlehr, "The Creative Writer and West Indian Society," *Kaie* 11 (August, 1973), 64.

16 George Lamming, *The Pleasures of Exile* (1960; reprint. London: Allison & Busby, 1984), 42. Mervyn Morris also comments upon the perverse philistinism of the new left, especially at university. As a reader of examinations he notes "the dangerous view, so popular with students in the Social Sciences: 'an artist who appeals to a limited circle is not an artist of real value'" ("Derek Walcott and the Audience for Poetry," *Caribbean Quarterly* 14:1&2 [1968], 9). This attitude would scotch the effort to broaden audience before it began, as at the other ideological extreme would the attitude of Naipaul.

17 Mervyn Morris, "Some West Indian Problems of Audience," 130.

18 Mervyn Morris, "Walcott and the Audience," 7.

19 Brathwaite, "State of the Arts," REU (1965), 3.

20 As recounted in Morris, "Walcott and the Audience," 10.

21 Morris calls them "self-denying ordinances indeed, for a poet of any subtlety" ("Walcott and the Audience," 11); for Walcott's comments see "Walcott on Walcott" (interview with Dennis Scott), *Caribbean Quarterly* 14:1&2 (1968), 79.

22 Ramchand, quoted in Narasimhaiah, "A.C.L.A.L.S. Conference," 121.

23 *Freedom Has No Price* (Bridgetown: Modern Printing and Graphics,

1980); "Forward" is a cyclostyled sheet stapled into the front cover.

24 See Roger D. Abrahams, *The Man-of-Words in the West Indies: Performance and the Emergence of Creole Culture* (Baltimore and London: The Johns Hopkins University Press, 1983).

2 THE CARIBBEAN NEIGHBORHOOD

1 J. Michael Dash makes a compelling case for a parallel period of Haitian literary consciousness in the 1830s, marked also by the presence of Indigenist, African, and anti-European cultural elements, and in its turn rejected as "exoticism" by its descendants ("Haitian Literature – A Search for an Identity," *Savacou* 5 [1971], 81–94).

2 Hannibal Price, quoted in G. R. Coulthard, *Race and Colour in Caribbean Literature* (London: Oxford University Press, 1962), 63.

3 Antenor Firmin's *De l'égalité des races humaines* (Paris, 1885) takes the dialectical course later followed by exponents of Negritude and argues racial equality by asserting the high civilization of ancient Africa. J. Michael Dash makes it clear, however, that the resemblance goes no further: Firmin and his contemporaries felt no commitment to identifying African survivals in their culture (*Literature and Ideology in Haiti, 1915–1961* [Totowa NJ: Barnes & Noble, 1981], 16).

4 Naomi Garrett, *The Renaissance of Haitian Poetry* (Paris: Présence Africaine, 1963), 135.

5 Garrett (*ibid.* 65) cites "La littérature d'hier et celle de demain," P. Thoby-Marcelin and Antonio Vieux, *La Nouvelle Ronde* (July 1925), 28–31.

6 Coulthard, *Race and Colour*, 65.

7 Garrett, *Renaissance of Haitian Poetry*, 94 (my translation).

8 Walt Whitman's *Leaves of Grass* provides a salient North American instance; for examples from the other end of the hemisphere see Jorge Luis Borges, "The Argentine Writer and Tradition," *Labyrinths* (New York: New Directions, 1964), 177–85.

9 Garrett, *Renaissance of Haitian Poetry*, 142; translation by Ellen Conroy Kennedy, *The Negritude Poets* (New York: Viking, 1975), 15.

10 Garrett, *Renaissance of Haitian Poetry*, 111–12; translation by Langston Hughes, in Kennedy, *Negritude Poets*, 22.

11 Price-Mars adopts this expression from Jules de Gaultier's work on Flaubert: Price-Mars, *So Spoke the Uncle* (Washington: Three Continents, 1983), 231.

12 The Nicaraguan Rubén Dario established this usage in the 1890s,

for example in his description of the end of the Spanish-American war as "the triumph of Caliban" (for Dario see Jose Augustin Balseiro, *The Americas Look at Each Other* [Coral Gables: University of Miami Press, 1969], 60–65). Instrumental in the semantic reversal were Césaire's revision of Shakespeare's *The Tempest* (Paris: Editions du Seuil, 1968) and the treatment of the theme in *The Pleasures of Exile* (London: Michael Joseph, 1960), by George Lamming, the West Indian writer most closely associated with the Negritude movement.

13 Dash cites an interview of 1927 in which Roumain urged Haitian literature to reorient itself toward the "flourishing black poetry" of the United States (*Literature and Ideology*, 73).

14 Bibliographic information in this paragraph derives from Garrett, *Renaissance of Haitian Poetry*, 77–80.

15 Price-Mars, "A propos de la 'Renaissance nègre' aux Etats-Unis," *La Relève* (July 1932), 15–19; (Aug.), 9–15; (Sept.), 8–14.

16 The full title, *Les Griots: La revue scientifique et littéraire d'Haiti*, was meant to indicate the assimilation of ethnographic and literary interests (July/Sept. 1938, 17). It was published again between 1948 and 1950.

17 These expressions used by F. Duvalier and Lorimer Denis in "La tendance d'une génération" (1934) are quoted in J. Michael Dash, "The Way Through Africa – A Study of Africanism in Haiti," *Bim* 58 (1975), 128. In this article Dash emphasizes that the road to Africa was meant to lead to Haitian national identity, while I am suggesting that it unavoidably tended to deflect attention from immediate realities. Chapter 5 will return to this difference between Africa-in-the-Caribbean and Africa-in-the-mind.

18 Morriseau-Leroy, *La Relève* (Aug./Oct. 1938), 24.

19 Dantes Bellegarde, *Haiti et ses problèmes* (Montreal: Editions B. Valiquette, 1941), 95.

20 C. H. Hirsch, "Revue de la quinzaine: les revues," *La Mercure de France*, Oct. 1938, 179–82 (quoted in Garrett, *Renaissance of Haitian Poetry*, 146). On the political consequences of Africanism for Haitian conditions in the 1930s and after, the best analysis is that of Dash in "The Way Through Africa," 127–31.

21 Coulthard, *Race and Colour*, ch. 1.

22 Dennis Sardinha, "Cuba – the Negrista Movement," *Bim* 58 (June 1975), 112.

23 Janheinz Jahn, *Neo-African Literature: A History of Black Writing* (New York: Grove Press, 1961), 219.

24 Luis Palés Matos, "Towards a Cuban poetry" (1932), as quoted in Coulthard, *Race and Colour*, 31.

25 Both quotations are from Juan Antonio Corretjer, "Spengler – A Creole Projection," *El Mundo*, 1938 (Coulthard, *Race and Colour*, 54). Emphasis added.

26 Jahn, *Neo-African Literature*, 232. As the involvement of the Puerto Rican Palés Matos suggests, poetry in a Negrista style was also cultivated and published in Puerto Rico and the Dominican Republic. For the purposes of this chapter, however, a consideration of the Cuban case suffices.

27 Rachel Benson attributes to Palés Matos a view strikingly similar to that of Price-Mars in the passage about aridity quoted above: "In the thirties . . . [Palés Matos] began to see in the mixture of Negro and Spanish culture that is specifically Antillean a way of expressing a simple strength – poetic, religious, and physical – that might oppose twentieth century complexity and apathy," *Nine Latin American Poets* (New York: Las Americas, 1968), 136.

28 The title of Ronald Firbank's popular 1924 novel was actually provided by Carl Van Vechten, a white writer and critic whose association with the Harlem Renaissance put him in a position quite analogous to that of a white Afrocubanist. On 'danza negra' stereotypes see Coulthard, *Race and Colour*, 31–33.

29 As quoted by Dennis Sardinha, "Cuba," 113.

30 Jorge Luis Morales, *Poesía afroantillana y negrista* (Rio Piedras: University of Puerto Rico Press, revised edition, 1981), 79; translation: Jahn, *Neo-African Literature*, 220.

31 *Selected Poems of Claude McKay*, Max Eastman, ed. (New York: Harcourt Brace, 1953), 61.

32 Morales, *Poesía afroantillana*, 341.

33 Richard L. Jackson, *Black Writers in Latin America* (Albuquerque: University of New Mexico Press, 1979), 87.

34 Jackson quotes Guillén's characterization of Afro-Cubanism as "circumstantial tourism which never penetrated deeply into the human tragedy of race, being more like excursions organized for photographing coconut trees, drums and naked Negroes" (Jackson, *ibid.*, 83).

35 "Prologue" to *Sóngoro cosongo*, as translated in Jackson, *Black Writers*, 83.

36 Hughes, "The Negro Artist and the Racial Mountain," *The Nation* (June 23, 1926), 692–94.

37 "Conversation with Langston Hughes (1929)," *Caliban* 2:1 (1976), 123–26.

38 Sardinha, "Cuba," 114.

39 Aimé Césaire, *Cahier d'un retour au pays natal* (Paris: Editions Présence Africaine, 1971), 116–17 (Emile Snyder trans.).

40 Césaire, *Discourse on Colonialism* (1955; Joan Pinkham, trans. New York: MR, 1972), 72.

41 Nardal, "Editorial," *Revue du monde noir*, 1 (1930), 1.

42 Lilyan Kesteloot, *Black Writers in French: a Literary History of Negritude*, Ellen Kennedy, trans. (Philadelphia: Temple University Press, 1974), 4.

43 *Revue du monde noir* 1 (1930), 8 and 32, respectively.

44 Melvin Dixon, "Toward a World Black Literature and Community," *Chant of Saints*, Michael S. Harper and Robert Steptoe eds. (University of Illinois Press, 1979), 176.

45 Summarizing here the contents of two articles in *Légitime défense*: Ménil, "Généralités sur l'écrivain de couleur antillaise", 7–9, and Léro, "Misère d'une poésie," 10–12.

46 James Arnold quotes Senghor ("Claude McKay can rightfully be considered the true inventor of Negritude") in the course of demonstrating that, while Afro-Cubanism and even the Haitians had virtually no impact in Paris in the 1930s, the Harlem Renaissance poets "enjoyed heroic status among black intellectuals" – *Modernism and Negritude: The Poetry and Poetics of Césaire* (Cambridge: Harvard University Press, 1981), 27–28.

47 As quoted in Kesteloot, *Black Writers*, 15.

48 *Ibid.*, 45; Césaire, *Discourse*, 68. Césaire speaks extensively about his relationship to surrealism in an interview with Sonia Aratan, "Negritude," Lloyd King, trans. *Voices* 2:3 (Mar. 1973), 9–20.

49 I have been unable to see a copy of *L'etudiant noir* – Dathorne, Jahn, and Kesteloot seem also never to have seen it; they rely on later accounts of it by the participants. Césaire characterizes the precursor Martinicans (Léro, Ménil, and company) as indistinguishable from French communists; they were "forgetting our special situation as black men" (Aratan, "Negritude," 11–12).

50 Claude Lévi-Strauss, *Tristes Tropiques* John and Doreen Weightman, trans. (1955; New York: Washington Square Press, 1973), 12.

51 This is recounted in Breton's "Un grand poète noir," his preface (dated 1943) to Aimé Césaire, *Cahier d'un retour au pays natal* (Paris: Editions Présence Africaine, 1971), 9–16. James Arnold points out that the parts of *Cahiers* most commonly regarded as surrealist were all added after the war (*Modernism and Negritude*, 147). To put it another way, they come *after* the intervention of Breton.

52 Arnold, *Modernism and Negritude*, 15.

53 O. R. Dathorne, *The Black Mind* (Minneapolis: University of Minnesota Press, 1974), 309.

54 "Césaire's Africa is . . . a willed construction of his creative

imagination . . . not very different from that which a white would or does construct for Africa; not an experience which has been lived through," Roger Bastide, "Variations on Negritude," quoted in *Negritude: Essays and Studies*, Albert H. Berrian and Richard A. Long, eds. (Hampton, VA: Hampton Institute Press, 1967), 77.

55 Dash, "Marvellous Realism – The Way Out of Negritude," *Caribbean Studies* 13:4 (Jan., 1974), 60.

56 Sartre, "Preface," in Frantz Fanon, *The Wretched of the Earth* (New York: Grove, 1966), 17.

57 George Lamming, "The Negro Writer and His World," *Caribbean Quarterly*, 5:2 (1958), 109.

58 Jean-Paul Sartre, *Black Orpheus*, Samuel Allen, trans. (Paris: Présence Africaine, 1976), 60.

59 Fanon, after reading *Black Orpheus*: "The generation of younger black poets has just suffered a blow that can never be forgiven": *Black Skin, White Masks* (New York: Grove, 1967), 133. C. L. R. James writes that Sartre's "explanation of what he conceives Negritude to mean is a disaster": *The Black Jacobins* (New York: Vintage, 1963), 401. For Soyinka's critique, see *Myth, Literature and the African World* (Cambridge: Cambridge University Press, 1976), 126–39. In what follows I will be emphasizing the West Indian critique of Negritude.

60 Sartre, *Black Orpheus*, 15.

61 Sylvia Wynter, "Reflections on West Indian Writing and Criticism, Part I," *Jamaica Journal* 2:4 (Dec., 1968), 30.

62 Ralph Ellison's phrase in *Shadow and Act* (New York: Signet, 1964), 255.

63 Dathorne, *The Black Mind*, 308.

64 Dash, "Marvellous Realism," 64.

65 *Ibid.*, 61.

66 In his report on the First Congress of Negro Artists and Writers (1956), James Baldwin quotes a typically Afrocentric comment by Césaire: "Wherever colonization is a fact the indigenous culture begins to rot. And, among these ruins, something begins to be born which is not a culture but a kind of subculture, a subculture which is condemned to exist on the margin allowed it by European culture." Baldwin objects: "he had not raised the central, tremendous question, which was, simply, what had this colonial experience made of them and what were they now to do with it?" "Princes and Powers," in *Nobody Knows My Name* (New York: Dial Press, 1961), 34, 36. Dash summarizes the Haitian critique of Negritude in "Marvellous Realism," 62–64.

67 See chapter 9, Joseph Owens, *Dread: The Rastafarians of Jamaica* (Kingston, Jamaica: Sangster, 1976).

68 The appearance of Edward Kamau Brathwaite's *The Development of Creole Society in Jamaica 1770–1820* (Oxford: Clarendon Press, 1971) is pivotal in this regard. Notions of "America mestiza," which trace back at least as far as Martí, are hardly to be found in the Francophone Caribbean before the Martinican writer Edouard Glissant; see Beverly Ormerod, "Beyond Negritude: Some Aspects of the Work of Edouard Glissant," *Savacou* 11/12 (Sept. 1975), 39–45.

69 Alioune Diop, "Niam n'goura ou les raisons d'être de Présence Africaine," *Présence Africaine* 1 (Nov.–Dec. 1947), 8.

70 Angel Flores, "Magical Realism in Spanish-American Fiction," *Hispanica* 38 (1955), 187–92.

71 Jacques Nantet, *Panorama de la littérature noire d'expression française* (Paris: Fayard, 1972), 211.

72 Jacques Stephen Alexis, "Du réalisme merveilleux chez les Haitians," *Présence Africaine* 8–10 (June–Nov., 1956), 263.

73 Alejo Carpentier, "De lo real maravillose americano," *Tientos y diferencias* (Montevideo: Arca, 1967), 108.

74 George Irish, "Magical Realism: A Search for Caribbean and Latin American Roots," *Revista Interamericana*, 4:3 (1974), 413.

75 Carpentier, "Do lo real maravillose americano," 112.

76 *Ibid.*, 109.

77 Irish, "Magical Realism," 420.

78 See Michel Fabre, *From Harlem to Paris: Black American Writers in France 1840–1980* (Urbana: University of Illinois, 1991) and Paul Gilroy, *The Black Atlantic* (Cambridge: Harvard University Press, 1993). Surprisingly, Gilroy mentions both McKay and Hughes only once (13).

3 OVERVIEW OF WEST INDIAN LITERARY HISTORIES

1 *West Indian Literature*, Bruce King, ed. (London: Macmillan, 1979), 8.

2 Henry Swanzy, "The Literary Situation in the Contemporary Caribbean," *Books Abroad* 30:3 (1956), 270.

3 Frank Collymore called it "a school of lady poets" in "Writing in the West Indies: A Survey," *Tamarack Review* 14 (1960), 114–21; Edward Baugh, *West Indian Poetry 1900–1970* (Kingston: Savacou Publications, 1971), 5; Derek Walcott, "Some Jamaican Poets," *Public Opinion* (Aug. 3, 1957), 7.

4 J. E. C. McFarlane, *A Literature in the Making* (Kingston, Jamaica: Pioneer Press, 1956), author's note, unpaged.
5 *Ibid.*, 66.
6 *Ibid.*, 91. But note McFarlane's insistence that McKay should return to Jamaica for the sake of his work (80).
7 Wycliffe Bennett, "The Jamaican Poets," *Life and Letters* (April, 1948), 60.
8 E.g. *The Caribbean* (New York: Bobbs Merrill, 1940). On this aspect of Roberts see G. R. Coulthard, "The Literature of the West Indies," *The Commonwealth Pen*, A. L. McLeod, ed. (Ithaca: Cornell University Press, 1961), 190–91.
9 McFarlane, *Making*, 93.
10 Quoted in Ramchand, *The West Indian Novel and Its Background* (London: Faber and Faber, 1970), 54–55. See also Mervyn Morris, "The All Jamaica Library," *Jamaica Journal* 6:1 (1972), 47–49.
11 McFarlane, *Making*, 7.
12 *Ibid.*, 2.
13 J. E. C. McFarlane, *A Treasury of Jamaican Poetry* (London: University of London Press, 1949), 6.
14 Reinhard Sander, *From Trinidad* (London: Hodder and Stoughton, 1978) offers a selection of work from the early magazines. There are several accounts of the circle by its chief participants: C. L. R. James, "Discovering Literature in Trinidad: The Nineteen-Thirties," *Savacou* 2 (1970), 54–60; Alfred Mendes, interview with Clifford Sealy in *Voices* 1:5 (Dec., 1965), 3ff.; Albert Gomes, *Through a Maze of Colour* (Port of Spain: Key Caribbean Publications, 1974), 16–26.
15 *The Beacon* 3:4 (1933) notes the role of other predecessors: A. M. Nolte's *The Quarterly Magazine* and *The Royalian* (magazine of the Queens Royal College Literary Society).
16 The phrase is from Gomes, *Through a Maze of Colour*, 18.
17 James stresses the importance of Learie Constantine's *Cricket and I* (1933): "To the general it was merely another book on cricket. To the West Indians it was the first book ever published in England by a world famous West Indian writing as a West Indian about people and events in the West Indies," *Beyond a Boundary* (London: Hutchinson, 1963), 124.
18 As quoted in *West Indian Literature*, Bruce King, ed., 54.
19 C. L. R. James, "Beyond a Boundary," transcript of broadcast (Radio Education Unit, University of the West Indies, Mona, 1965), 1.
20 C. L. R. James, "The Artist in the Caribbean" (1959), in *The Future in the Present* (Westport, CT: L. Hill, 1977), 186–87.

21 C. L. R. James, "Discovering Literature," 54.
22 C. L. R. James, *The Black Jacobins*, revised ed. (New York: Vintage, 1963), 402.
23 *West Indian Literature*, Bruce King, ed., 57. Some small groups were active during this period, among them the Cellar Club, the Trinidad Readers and Writers Guild. For the 1940s see Michael Anthony, "Growing Up With Writing," *Savacou* 2 (1970) 61–66, and remarks by Telemaque in Anson Gonzalez, *Trinidad and Tobago Literature: On Air* (Port of Spain: National Cultural Council, 1974), 36.
24 Reprinted in *Caribbean Voices*, vol. II, John Figueroa, ed. (London: Evans Brothers, 1970), 182–87.
25 J. D. Elder, *From Congo Drum to Steelband* (St. Augustine, Trinidad: UWI Press, 1969), 15–20.
26 Lloyd Brown in his generally comprehensive *West Indian Poetry* (London: Heinemann, 1984) gives more space to Sparrow than to any Trinidadian poet before Independence, while of the younger poets he treats only Wayne Brown. On Sparrow see Gordon Rohlehr, "Sparrow and the Language of Calypso," *Savacou* 2 (Sept., 1970), 87–99.
27 Gordon Rohlehr, "Withering into Truth," *Trinidad Guardian* (Dec. 10, 1969), 18.
28 The anthology *Corners Without Answers* was to have been published by Scope in Trinidad. Rohlehr's introduction appears as "My Strangled City" in *Caliban* 2:1 (Fall–Winter 1976), 50–122.
29 *Washer Woman Hangs Her Poems in the Sun: Poems by Women of Trinidad and Tobago*, Margaret Watts, ed. (Tunapuna, Trinidad, 1990).
30 For example, C. L. R. James in *Kas-Kas*, Reinhard Sander and Ian Munro, eds. (Austin: University of Texas, 1972), 28.
31 Norman Cameron, "Introductory Essay," *Guianese Poetry 1831–1931* (Georgetown, Guyana: Argosy, 1931), 1.
32 *Ibid.*, 93–94.
33 *Ibid.*, 4.
34 A. J. Seymour, "Introduction to an Anthology of Guianese Poetry," *Kyk-Over-Al* 6:19 (1954), 62.
35 Ian McDonald, "The Unsteady Flame: A Short Account of Guianese Poetry – Part I," *New World* (fortnightly) 1:17 (June 25, 1965), 22.
36 A. J. Seymour, "Editorial," *Kyk-Over-Al* 1:1 (Dec., 1945), 7.
37 For an account of *Kyk*'s achievement and dynamic, Edward Kamau Brathwaite, "*Kyk-Over-Al* and the Radicals," *New World Quarterly* 2:3 (1966), 55–57.
38 A. J. Seymour, "Editor's Note," *Kyk-Over-Al* 2:7 (Dec., 1948), 2.

39 A. J. Seymour, "Preface to the First Edition," *Kyk-Over-Al* 7:22 (1957), viii.

40 A. J. Seymour, "Editor's Note," *Kyk-Over-Al* 2:7 (Dec., 1948), 2.

41 Michael Swan, *The Marches of El Dorado* (Boston: Beacon Press, 1958), 19.

42 *Voices of Guyana*, Donald Trotman, ed. (Newtown, Guyana: International P.E.N. Guyana Centre, 1968) and *My Lovely Native Land*, Arthur and Elma Seymour, eds. (London: Longman Caribbean, 1971).

43 See the account of Harris's lectures in Andrew Salkey, *Georgetown Journal* (London: New Beacon, 1972), 154–55, 169–71, 180–82.

44 George Lamming, quoted in John Wickham, "Introduction," *Bim: The Literary Magazine of Barbados* vol. 1 (Millwood, NY: Kraus-Thomson, 1977), iv.

45 According to Brathwaite's bibliography, *Barbados Poetry: A Check List* (Mona, Jamaica: Savacou, 1979).

46 Even Baugh, hardly a spurner of the past, equates the record of *Bim* with the history of West Indian literature, "since what went before is almost a kind of pre-history." "Frank Collymore and the Miracle of *Bim*," *New World Quarterly* 3:1&2 (1966), 130.

47 Baugh, "The Miracle of *Bim*," 130.

48 Frank Collymore, "The Story of *Bim*," *Bim* 38 (1964), 68.

49 *Bim* 7 (1946), 1.

50 Collymore, "The Story of *Bim*," 68.

51 Derek Walcott, "Leaving School," *London Magazine* 5:6 (1965), 4–14; "Meanings," *Savacou* 2 (1970), 45–71; "What the Twilight Says: An Overture" in *Dream on Monkey Mountain and Other Plays* (New York: Farrar, Straus & Giroux, 1970), 1–40.

52 Walcott, "Meanings," 45.

53 *Confluence: Nine St. Lucian Poets*, Kendel Hippolyte, ed. (Castries: The Source, 1988).

54 For a review of writing in St. Lucia before and after Walcott, see Elaine Campbell, "The Third Wave of St. Lucian Literature," *Studies in Commonwealth Literature*, Breitinger and Sander, eds. (Tübingen: Gunter Narr, 1985), 115–21.

55 Alan McLeod, "The English Literature of Belize," *World Literature Today* 56:3 (Summer, 1982), 439–43.

56 *Vincentian Poets: 1950 to 1980*, Anthony Joyette, ed. (St. Laurent, Quebec: AFO Enterprises, 1989).

57 J. J. Thomas, *Froudacity: West Indian Fables Explained* (London: New Beacon, 1969), 179.

58 W. F. Elkins, "Revolt of the British West India Regiment," *Jamaica Journal* 11: 3&4 (1978), 73–74.

59 *From Trinidad: An Anthology of Early West Indian Writing*, Reinhard Sander, ed. (London: Hodder and Stoughton, 1978), 30–31.

60 Esther Chapman, "The Birth of an Idea," *West Indian Review* 1:1 (Sept. 1934), 7.

61 Bryan King, "What Poetry Means to Me," *Bim* 7 (1946), 45.

62 Peter Blackman, "Is There a West Indian Literature?," *Life and Letters* 59 (Nov. 1948), 96 and 102.

63 Henry Swanzy, "Caribbean Voices: Prolegomena to a West Indian Culture," *Caribbean Quarterly* 1:2 (1949), 22–23.

64 Ellsworth Keane, "The Contribution of the West Indies to Literature," *Bim* 14 (1951), 103.

65 *Ibid.*, 106.

66 Holder, *Bim* 14 (June, 1951), 141–42.

67 Henry Swanzy, "Writing in the British Caribbean: A Study in Cultural Devolution," *West Indische Gids* ('s Gravenhage: M. Nijhoff, 1952), 227.

68 The history of A. J. Seymour's regional anthology is a case in point. He and the Jamaican Philip Sherlock had considered the possibility in 1944. In 1946 Seymour tried unsuccessfully to interest T. S. Eliot at Faber, and a sampler of their selection finally appeared as part of Langston Hughes, *Poetry of the Negro*, in 1949 (ironically all the West Indian poets had been deleted some time before the edition of 1970).

69 This complaint is heard as early as Tom Redcam. See H. P. Jacobs, "Tom Redcam Re-assessed," *Public Opinion* (Mar. 30, 1957), 7.

70 John Hearne, "Who Killed the King?," *Focus* (1960), 137, 140.

71 *Ibid.*, 139.

72 R. J. Owens, "West Indian Poetry," *Caribbean Quarterly* 7:3 (1961), 127.

73 *Ibid.*, 120.

74 *Ibid.*, 122.

75 *Ibid.*, 127.

76 On CAM see Ann Walmsley, *The Caribbean Artists Movement: 1966–1972* (London: New Beacon, 1992).

77 Walmsley, "First C. A. M. Conference," *Bim* 46 (1968), 83.

78 *Ibid.*, 82.

79 Edward Kamau Brathwaite, "Timehri," *Savacou* 2 (Sept., 1970), 40.

80 Arthur Drayton, "Editorial," *Literary Half-Yearly* (Mysore) 11:2 (1970), v.

81 *West Indian Literature*, Bruce King, ed., 8.

4 THE RELATION TO "EUROPE"

1 Houston A. Baker Jr., *Modernism and the Harlem Renaissance* (Chicago: University of Chicago, 1987), 86.

2 *Ibid.*, 92–93.

3 Arthur Drayton, "West Indian Consciousness in West Indian Verse: A Historical Perspective," *Journal of Commonwealth Literature* 9 (July, 1970), 70–73; Lloyd Brown, *West Indian Poetry*, second ed. (London: Heinemann, 1984), 21; S. E. Ogude, *Genius in Bondage* (Ile-Ife, Nigeria: University of Ife, 1983), 21–29.

4 Edward Long, *The History of Jamaica* (London, 1774), vol. II, 478. Text and translation of the ode, 479–81.

5 G. R. Coulthard, *Race and Colour in Caribbean Literature* (London: Oxford University Press, 1962), 116.

6 A. N. Forde, "Across a Fisherman's Net," *Bim* 13 (Dec., 1950), 33.

7 *Guianese Poetry*, Norman E. Cameron, ed. (Georgetown: Argosy Co, 1931, 1970), 6–12.

8 *The Penguin Book of Caribbean Verse in English*, Paula Burnett, ed. (Harmondsworth: Penguin, 1986), 131.

9 *Voices from Summerland*, J. E. C. McFarlane, ed. (London: Fowler Wright, 1929), 62–67.

10 *Ibid.*, 82–84.

11 "Caribbean Poetry," *Sunday Gleaner*, June 13, 1948, 9.

12 *New Writing in the Caribbean*, A. J. Seymour, ed. (Georgetown: Guyana Lithographic, 1972), 87 (originally in *Belizean Poets*, 1965).

13 Michael Anthony's story "Sandra Street" is a classic instance: see *Sandra Street and Other Stories* (London: Heinemann, 1973).

14 *From Trinidad: An Anthology of Early West Indian Writing*, Reinhard Sander, ed. (London: Hodder and Stoughton, 1978), 212–13.

15 *A Treasury of Guyanese Poetry*, A. J. Seymour, ed. (Georgetown: Guyana National Lithographic, 1980), 107–08.

16 *Selected Poems of Claude McKay*, Max Eastman, ed. (New York: Harcourt Brace & World, 1953), 31.

17 *From Trinidad*, Reinhard Sander, ed., 210–11.

18 *Ibid.*, 209–10.

19 John Barth, *The Friday Book* (New York: G. P. Putnam's Sons, 1984), 46.

20 *Guianese Poetry*, Cameron, ed, 163.

21 Slade Hopkinson, *Literary Half-Yearly* (Mysore) 11:2 (1970), 149.

22 Keith Warner, *Voices* 2:3 (Mar., 1973), 21.

23 For example, C[lytus] A. Thomasos, "Tropic Sun," *Beacon* 1:4 (1931), 20; Wynn Rutty's poem beginning, "But you must love her

/ my little sea-girt isle," in *The Year Book of the Poetry League of Jamaica 1941*, Archie Lindo, ed. (Kingston, 1941), 9.

24 H. D. Carberry, *Focus* (Kingston: City Printery, 1943), 73.

25 Daniel Williams, *Caribbean Voices*, vol. II, John Figueroa, ed. (London: Evans Brothers, 1970), 81–82.

26 A. N. Forde, *Bim* 12 (June, 1950), 341.

27 H. M. Telemaque and A. M. Clarke, *Burnt Bush* (1947; reprint. Nedeln: Kraus, 1973), 11 (emphasis added).

28 *Ibid.*, 12.

29 *Ibid.*, "Introduction."

30 *Ibid.*, 17.

31 Neville Dawes, *Prolegomena to Caribbean Literature* (Kingston: Institute of Jamaica, 1977), 13.

32 Dawes's reading may be affected by developments since the poem's composition; West Indians now do "make emblazonry of lions" thanks to the combined effect of Garveyism and Rastafarianism, as a result of which the lion is no longer an Imperial icon to be avoided, but an African one to be cherished.

33 Anson Gonzalez, *Trinidad and Tobago Literature: On Air* (Port of Spain: National Cultural Council, 1974), 37.

34 H. D. Carberry, "I Shall Remember," *Focus* (Kingston: City Printery, 1948), 167; emphasis added.

35 Herbert, *The Poems of Cecil Herbert*, ed. Danielle Gianetti (Port of Spain: The College Press, nd), 25, my emphasis.

36 *Breaklight*, Andrew Salkey, ed. (New York: Doubleday, 1973), xvii.

37 J. E. C. McFarlane, *A Literature in the Making* (Kingston: Pioneer Press, 1956), 66.

38 McKay, *Selected Poems of Claude McKay*, Max Eastman, ed. (New York: Harcourt Brace & World, 1953), 13.

39 Rohlehr, "My Strangled City," *Caliban* 2:1 (1976), 50–122.

40 Mutabaruka, *Mutabaruka: The First Poems (1970–1979)* (Kingston: Paul Issa, 1980), 35.

41 Orlando Wong (now known as Oku Onuora) *Echo* (Kingston: Sangsters, 1977), 44.

42 *Ibid., Echo*, 43.

43 Mutabaruka, *Mutabaruka*, 17.

44 Dennis Scott, *Dreadwalk: Poems 1970–78* (London: New Beacon, 1982), 35.

45 Edward Baugh, *A Tale from the Rainforest* (Kingston: Sandberry Press, 1988), 33.

46 Mervyn Morris, *Caribbean Voices*, vol. II, 181.

47 Aldous Huxley deserves credit for seeing the problem early: "The Wordsworthian adoration of Nature has two principal defects.

The first . . . is that it is only possible in a country where nature has been nearly or quite enslaved to man. The second is that it is only possible for those who are prepared to falsify their immediate intuitions of Nature" ("Wordsworth in the Tropics," *Collected Essays* [New York: Harper and Brothers, 1958], 3).

5 THE RELATION TO "AFRICA"

1 Arthur Drayton, "West Indian Fiction and West Indian Society," *Kenyon Review* 25:1 (1963), 132.
2 Gordon Lewis, *The Growth of the Modern West Indies* (New York: Monthly Review, 1968), 21.
3 Mark Kinkead-Weekes, "'Africa' – Two Caribbean Fictions," *Twentieth Century Studies* 10 (Dec. 1973), 37.
4 Edward Brathwaite, "The African Presence in Caribbean Literature," *Daedalus* 103:2 (1974), 73–109; Maureen Warner-Lewis, "The African Impact on Language and Literature in the English-Speaking Caribbean," in *Africa and the Caribbean: The Legacies of a Link*, Margaret E. Crahan and Franklin W. Knight, eds. (Baltimore: Johns Hopkins Press, 1979), 101–21.
5 On "Africa" as subject-matter see especially: Anonymous, "'Africa' in West Indian Poetry," *Caribbean Quarterly* 4:1 (1955), 5–13; George Lamming, "Caribbean Literature: The Black Rock of Africa," *African Forum* 1:4 (1966), 32–52; Arthur Drayton, "West Indian Consciousness in West Indian Verse," *Journal of Commonwealth Literature* 9 (July 1970), 66–88.
6 See Mervyn Alleyne, "The Linguistic Continuity of Africa in the Caribbean," *Black Academy Review* 1:4 (Winter 1970), 3–16.
7 Kamau Brathwaite popularized the use of the term "orature" in the Caribbean, borrowing and adapting it from Ngugi wa Thiong'o and Pio Zirimu. See Chinweizu, Onwuchenkwu Jemie, and Ihechukwu Madubuike, *Towards the Decolonisation of African Literature* (Washington, DC: Howard University Press, 1989), 2.
8 Cecil Herbert, *Bim* 10 (June, 1949), 110.
9 *The Penguin Book of Caribbean Verse in English*, Paula Burnett, ed. (Harmondsworth: Penguin, 1986), 105.
10 Adolphe Roberts, *Life and Letters* 57 (April, 1948), 61.
11 Eric Roach, *Trinidad Guardian*, February 6, 1949, 14.
12 *The Poetry of the Negro*, Langston Hughes and Arna Bontemps, eds. (Garden City: Doubleday, 1949), 349.
13 H. A. Vaughan, *Sandy Lane and Other Poems*, second edition (Bridgetown: *Bim*, 1985), 1.

14 George Campbell, *First Poems* (Kingston: City Printery, 1945), 34. Dated "1941" in the text.

15 Louise Bennett, *Jamaica Labrish* (first published 1947) (Kingston: Sangster's Book Stores, 1966), 214.

16 Philip Sherlock, "Introduction," in Una Marson, *The Moth and the Star* (Kingston: Gleaner Co., 1937).

17 Una Marson, *Heights and Depths* (Kingston: Gleaner, 1931), 77.

18 *Ibid.*, 95.

19 H. M. Telemaque, *Burnt Bush* (1947; Nedeln: Kraus Reprint, 1973), 28.

20 Originally in Walcott, *Public Opinion* (1956); republished in *In A Green Night* (London: Jonathan Cape, 1962), 18.

21 E. M. Roach, *The Flowering Rock: Collected Poems 1938–1974* (Leeds: Peepal Tree Press, 1992), 191–93.

22 See particularly "Timehri," *Savacou* 2 (1970), 34–44.

23 See this locution for example in Maureen Warner-Lewis, "African Impact," 108, 111 (emphasis added).

24 Philip Sherlock, *Ten Poems* (Georgetown: Master Printery, 1953), 9 (emphasis added).

25 Vera Bell, *Focus* (1948), 187–88.

26 Gordon Rohlehr, *Pathfinder: Black Awakening in The Arrivants of Edward Kamau Brathwaite* (Tunapuna, Trinidad: author, 1981), 190.

27 Wayne Brown, "Poetry of the Forties: Part VI," *Trinidad Guardian* (Oct. 18, 1970), 6.

28 Lamming, "Caribbean Literature," 34–38.

29 George Campbell, *First Poems* (Kingston: City Printery, 1945), 28; Martin Carter, *Selected Poems* (Georgetown: Demerara Publishers, 1989), 61.

30 Peter Blackman, *My Song is for All Men*, 1952, reprinted in *You Better Believe It: Black Verse in English*, Paul Breman, ed. (Harmondsworth: Penguin, 1973), 113.

31 Philip Sherlock, *Focus* (1943), 81.

32 See the Guide to further reading, p. 254.

33 Dennis Scott, "Bennett on Bennett," *Caribbean Quarterly* 14:1&2 (1968), 98.

34 On the occasion of Independence O. R. Dathorne wrote: "As yet few Guyanese writers have come to terms with their language" – "The Writers of Guyana," *The Times Literary Supplement* (May 26, 1966), 480.

35 Claude McKay, *Songs of Jamaica* (London: Gardner, 1912), 5.

36 Claude McKay, *Constab Ballads* (London: Watts, 1912), 11.

37 Brathwaite, in *Three Caribbean Poets on Their Work*, Victor Chang, ed. (Mona: Institute of Caribbean Studies, 1993), 3.

38 Erika Smilowitz, " 'Weary of Life and All My Heart's Dull Pain':
    The Poetry of Una Marson," in *Critical Issues in West Indian
    Literature: Selected Papers from West Indian Literature Conferences
    1981–1983*, Erika Smilowitz and Robert Knowles, eds. (Parkers-
    burg, IA: Caribbean Books, 1984), 25.

39 Una Marson, *The Moth and the Star*, 70, 71, 17 respectively.

40 Una Marson, *Heights and Depths*, 91–94.

41 Lloyd Brown describes the language of these poems as "Jamaican
    dialect" (*West Indian Poetry*, second edition [London: Heinemann,
    1984], 36), but such expressions as "I's gwine press my hair"
    ("Kinky Hair Blues") and "she don't got no name" ("Brown Baby
    Blues") are common in the rural American idiom that underlies
    the blues, while they would be, at the very least, unusual in
    Jamaican speech.

42 Roach, "Ballad," *Caribbean Quarterly* 4:2 (1955), 165–66; Evan
    Jones, "Song," *Bim* 20 (June 1954), 288–89; and "Lament,"
    Caribbean Voices vol. I, John Figueroa, ed. (London: Evans
    Brothers, 1966), 86–87.

43 Philip Sherlock, "Pocomania," *Focus* (1943), 80 and "Paradise,"
    Focus (1960), 49.

44 Louise Bennett, *Jamaica Labrish*, 218–19.

45 Derek Walcott, *Poems* (Kingston: City Printery, 1951), 31, 38.

46 The version of *The Sea at Dauphin* published in *Tamarack Review* 14
    (1960) has proportionately much more creole than the version
    which appears in *Dream on Monkey Mountain and Other Plays* (New
    York: Farrar, Straus & Giroux, 1970).

47 E.g. Bruce King, *Derek Walcott and West Indian Drama* (Oxford:
    Clarendon Press, 1995), 237, 273.

48 Gordon Rohlehr, "Literature and the Folk," *My Strangled City and
    Other Essays* (Port of Spain: Longman Trinidad, 1992), 68.

49 Gordon Rohlehr, "Sparrow as Poet," *David Frost Introduces Trinidad
    and Tobago*, Michael Anthony and Andrew Carr, eds. (London:
    Andre Deutsch, 1975), 84.

50 Keith Warner, *The Trinidad Calypso: A Study of the Calypso as Oral
    Literature* (London: Heinemann, 1983), 38–42.

51 Warner offers a good introduction in *ibid.*; the classic work is
    Gordon Rohlehr, *Calypso and Society in Pre-Independence Trinidad*
    (Tunapuna: author, 1990).

52 Mervyn Morris, "On Reading Louise Bennett, Seriously,"
    Jamaica Journal 1:1 (Dec., 1967), 69–74; Dennis Scott, "Bennett
    on Bennett," *Caribbean Quarterly* 14:1&2 (Mar.–June, 1968),
    97–101.

53 Ellsworth Keane, *L'Oubli* (Bridgetown: Advocate, 1950), 17; Eric

Roach, *The Flowering Rock* (Leeds: Peepal Tree Press, 1992), 90–91; Owen Campbell, *Bim* 20 (June 1954), 295–97.

54 Edward Kamau Brathwaite, "The Dust," *The Arrivants* (Oxford: Oxford University Press, 1973), 64.

55 David Dabydeen, in *Frontiers of Caribbean Literature in English*, Frank Birbalsingh, ed. (New York: St. Martin's Press, 1996), 173.

56 For a brief, non-technical account of code-switching, see Beverley Hall Alleyne, "ACIJ Linguistic Notes," *Jamaica Journal* 45 (1981), 32.

57 John Robert Lee, *Vocation and Other Poems* (Castries: UWI Extra Mural Dept., 1975), 26–28, 32–34. Each poem is accompanied by a glossary.

58 *Washer Woman Hangs her Poems in the Sun*, Margaret Watts, ed. (Tunapuna, Trinidad: Gloria V. Ferguson, 1980) 35, 36; *Creation Fire: A CAFRA Anthology of Caribbean Women's Poetry*, Ramabai Espinet, ed. (Toronto: Sister Vision and Tunapuna: CAFRA, 1990), 50.

59 Kendel Hippolyte, *Island in the Sun - Side Two* (The Morne, St. Lucia: UWI Extra Mural Department, 1980), 20–21.

60 John Agard, *Mangoes & Bullets: Selected and New Poems 1972–1984* (London: Pluto Press, 1985), 44.

61 Robert Lee, *Vocation*, 29–30.

62 *A Treasury of Guyanese Poetry*, A. J. Seymour, ed. (Georgetown: Guyana National Lithographic, 1980), 28.

63 Mervyn Morris, *On Holy Week* (Kingston: Sangster's Book Stores, 1976), 20–21.

64 John Figueroa, *Savacou* 3/4 (1971), 138–39.

65 Louise Bennett, *Jamaica Labrish*, 27–28, 28–29.

66 Anthony McNeill, *Savacou* 3/4 (Dec. 1970/Mar. 1971), 155–56.

67 Edward Baugh, *A Tale From the Rainforest* (Leeds: Peepal Tree Press, 1988), 17–18.

68 Dennis Scott, *Focus* (Kingston: City Printery, 1960), 31.

69 Opal Palmer, *Savacou* 14/15 (1979), 51, 52.

70 David Dabydeen, *Coolie Odyssey* (London: Hansib/ Dangaroo, 1988), 44, 16.

71 Derek Walcott, originally in *Trinidad and Tobago Review* (1978); *The Star-Apple Kingdom* (New York: Farrar, Straus and Giroux, 1979), 20.

72 Derek Walcott, *Collected Poems 1948–1984* (New York: Farrar, Straus & Giroux, 1986), 432–38.

73 See Helen Vendler's critical review of Walcott, "Poet of Two Worlds," *New York Review of Books* (Mar. 4, 1982), 23, 26–27, and John Figueroa's very sweet retort: "... Bwoy, you no hear wa de

lady say? / Watch di pentameter ting, man. / Dat is white people play!" in his poem "Problems of a Writer Who Does Not Quite . . ." (1982), *The Chase: A Collection of Poems* (Leeds: Peepal Tree Press, 1992), 137–38.

74 *A Treasury of Guyanese Poetry,* A. J. Seymour, ed. (Georgetown: Guyana National Lithographic, 1980), 19, 28.

75 Jane King, *Confluence: Nine St. Lucian Poets,* Kendel Hippolyte, ed. (Castries: The Source, 1988), 23–25.

76 "Foreward," [*sic*] *Savacou* 3/4 (Dec. 1970/ Mar. 1971), 6.

77 For a fuller account see Laurence A. Breiner, "How to Behave on Paper: The *Savacou* Debate," *Journal of West Indian Literature* 6:1 (July 1993), 1–10.

78 Eric Roach, "A Type Not Found in All Generations," *Trinidad Guardian* (July 14, 1971), 8.

79 Dennis Pantin, [no title], *Tapia* 21 (Oct. 3, 1971), 3.

80 Bongo Jerry, *Savacou* 3/4 (Dec. 1970/Mar. 1971), 13–16.

81 Linton Kwesi Johnson, "Five Nights of Bleeding," *Voices of the Living and the Dead* (London: Race Today, 1974), 30–32; "Dread Beat and Blood," *Savacou* 9/10 (1974), 26.

82 Michael Smith, *Savacou* 14/15 (1979), 84–86.

83 Edward Kamau Brathwaite, *Contradictory Omens: Cultural Diversity and Integration in the Caribbean* (Mona: Savacou Publications, 1974), 5; Derek Walcott, "The State of the Arts in Jamaica," UWI Radio Education Unit transcript of a Mona seminar (Mar. 14, 1965), 1.

84 Quoted in Gordon Rohlehr, "West Indian Poetry: Some Problems of Assessment" (1970), in *My Strangled City and Other Essays* (Port of Spain: Longman, 1992), 124.

6 THE RELATION TO "AMERICA"

1 Wayne Brown, "The Poetry of the Forties: Part III," *Trinidad Guardian* (Oct. 4, 1970), 9.

2 Claude McKay, "A Negro Writer to his Critics" (1932), reprinted in Wayne Cooper, *The Passion of Claude McKay: Selected Prose and Poetry 1912–1948* (New York: Schocken Books, 1973), 137.

3 Derek Walcott, *Collected Poems 1948–1984* (New York: Farrar, Straus & Giroux, 1986), 3. References to this volume will appear within the text as: (CP and page number).

4 John Figueroa, "A Note on Derek Walcott's Concern with Nothing," *Revista/Review Interamericana* 4:3 (Fall, 1974), 422–28.

5 Edward Kamau Brathwaite, "Naming," *The Arrivants* (Oxford: Oxford University Press, 1973), 217. In this chapter references to

this volume will appear within the text as: (*Arrivants*, and page number).

6 "West Indian Poetry – a Search for Voices," part 5 of a series, "The State of the Arts in Jamaica," UWI Radio Education Unit transcript of a Mona seminar (Mar. 14, 1965), 2.
7 This sense of the term derives from Claude Lévi-Strauss, *The Savage Mind* (Chicago: University of Chicago, 1966), 16–36.
8 Derek Walcott, "The Muse of History," *Is Massa Day Dead?*, Orde Coombs, ed. (New York: Doubleday, 1974), 5.
9 Brathwaite,*Bim* 12 (1950), 325–29.
10 Brathwaite, "Six Poems," *Kyk-Over-Al* 27 (1960), 83–86.
11 In Gordon Rohlehr, *Pathfinder: Black Awakening in The Arrivants of Edward Kamau Brathwaite* (Port of Spain: author, 1981), 66.
12 Brathwaite, *History of the Voice* (London: New Beacon, 1984), 31.
13 Brathwaite, "Jazz and the West Indian Novel, Part II," *Bim* 45 (1967), 39.
14 Derek Walcott, "The Muse of History," 1.
15 H. D. Carberry, *Focus* (1943), 72.
16 Eric Roach, *The Flowering Rock: Collected Poems 1938–1974* (Leeds: Peepal Tree Press, 1992), 53.
17 Anthony McNeill, *Reel from "The Life Movie"* (Kingston: Savacou Publications, 1972), 23.
18 Orlando Wong (aka Oku Onuora), *Echo* (Kingston: Sangster's Book Stores, 1977), 26.
19 Walcott, "What the Twilight Says: An Overture," *Dream on Monkey Mountain and Other Plays* (New York: Farrar, Straus & Giroux, 1970), 4.
20 Walcott, "The Muse of History," 17.
21 *Ibid.*, 2.
22 Brathwaite, "Timehri", *Is Massa Day Dead?*, Orde Coombs, ed. (New York: Doubleday, 1974), 39.
23 *Ibid.*, 42.
24 *Ibid.*, 41.
25 Walcott, *The Arkansas Testament* (New York: Farrar, Straus & Giroux, 1987), 48–51.
26 *Creation Fire: A CAFRA Anthology of Caribbean Women's Poetry* (Toronto: Sister Vision, 1990), 269.
27 Lorna Goodison, *Focus* (1983), 52.
28 *Creation Fire*, 276.
29 Frank Collymore, *Selected Poems* (Bridgetown: Coles Printery, 1971), 9. This interpretation of the poem is more fully elaborated in Laurence A. Breiner, "Is There Still a West Indian Literature?," *World Literature Written in English* 26:1 (Spring, 1986), 140–50.

30 Aimé Césaire, "Wilfredo Lam," *Cahiers d'art* (1946), as quoted in Janheinz Jahn, *Muntu: The New African Culture* (New York: Grove Press, 1961), 184.

31 Edward Baugh, "The West Indian Writer and his Quarrel with History," *Tapia* 7:8 (Feb. 20, 1977), 6–7 and 7:9 (Feb. 27, 1977), 6–7, 11.

32 Martin Carter, *Poems of Succession* (London and Port of Spain: New Beacon, 1977), 77.

33 Joseph Owens, *Dread: The Rastafarians of Jamaica* (Kingston: Sangster's Book Stores, 1976), 31.

34 Walcott, "Meanings," *Savacou* 2 (Sept., 1970), 48.

35 Anthony McNeill, *Savacou* 3/4 (Dec. 1970–Mar. 1971), 155, 158.

36 McNeill, *Reel from "The Life Movie,"* 39.

37 Mervyn Morris, *The Pond* (London: New Beacon, 1973), 18.

38 Opal Adisa Palmer, *Savacou* 14/15 (1979), 49–50.

39 For a collection of examples see Leonard Barrett, *The Rastafarians: Sounds of Cultural Dissonance* (Boston: Beacon Press, 1977), 229–37.

40 Dennis Scott, *Dreadwalk* (London/Port of Spain: New Beacon, 1982).

41 Brathwaite, *Mother Poem* (Oxford: Oxford University Press, 1977), 117.

42 Brathwaite, *Sun Poem* (Oxford: Oxford University Press, 1982), 100.

43 *Ibid.*, 97.

44 Gordon Rohlehr, "Brathwaite with a Dash of Brown: Crit, the Writer and the Written Life," *The Shape of that Hurt and Other Essays* (Port of Spain: Longman Trinidad, 1992), 231.

45 Wilson Harris, *The Guyana Quartet* (London: Faber and Faber, 1985), 335.

46 *Ibid.*, 333.

47 Morris, *The Pond*, 35–36.

48 Mervyn Morris, *Shadowboxing* (London: New Beacon, 1979), 39, 12.

49 Lorna Goodison, *Selected Poems* (Ann Arbor: University of Michigan Press, 1992), 73.

50 Goodison, *Heartease* (London: New Beacon, 1988), 24, 32, 36, 40, 42, 58.

Guide to further reading

GENERAL STUDIES OF WEST INDIAN POETRY

The best brief overview at present is the dense introduction to Burnett's *Penguin Book of Caribbean Verse* (Penguin, 1986) – the whole history of West Indian poetry deftly surveyed in forty pages. Lloyd Brown in *West Indian Poetry* (second edition; Heinemann, 1984) emphasizes themes, punctuated with full chapters on a few major authors (McKay, Walcott, Brathwaite). In fact even his historical survey chapters are generally put together out of short sections on individual authors. Bruce King's *West Indian Literature* (second edition; Macmillan, 1995) is implicitly also a history of the poetry, and the approach is comparable to Brown's, except that King has assembled chapters by a variety of scholars. J. Edward Chamberlin's *Come Back to Me My Language: Poetry and the West Indies* (Illinois, 1993), is full of insight and information, though it is not organized historically. It also provides a very extensive bibliography.

COLLECTIONS OF POETRY

The availability of works by individual poets is unpredictable, but they can be sought easily enough by name in catalogues and databases. There are a number of anthologies presenting the work of individual nations; several of these are identified in the course of chapter 2. Readers interested in a broader sample of West Indian poetry might begin with any of the four most significant general anthologies. The excellent selections in John Figueroa's *Caribbean Voices* (Evans Brothers, 1971) and Andrew Salkey's *Breaklight* (Doubleday, 1973) reflect different and complementary visions of the West Indian canon, and are themselves of historical importance. Paula Burnett's *Penguin Book of Caribbean Verse in English* is the only anthology chronologically organized. *Voiceprint* (Longman, 1989), edited by Stewart Brown, Gordon Rohlehr, and Mervyn Morris, was assembled explicitly in response to Burnett's segregation of oral and literary traditions.

For Indo-Caribbean poetry, there is Frank Birbalsingh's *Jahaji Bhai: An Anthology of Indo-Caribbean Literature* (TSAR, 1988); for women writers, Ramabai Espinet's *Creation Fire: A CAFRA Anthology of Caribbean Women's Poetry* (Sister Vision, 1990). Stephen Davis and Peter Simon's *Reggae International* (R & B, 1982) offers an excellent account of the milieu and affiliations of dub poetry; there is also an anthology, Christian Habekost's *Dub Poetry: Nineteen Poets from England and Jamaica* (Michel Schwinn, 1986). "Black British" poetry is represented in E. A. Markham's *Hinterland: Afro-Caribbean and Black British Poetry* (Bloodaxe Books, 1989), and James Berry's *News for Babylon, The Chatto Book of West Indian-British Poetry* (Chatto and Windus, 1984). For "Black Canada" see Cyril Dabydeen's *A Shapely Fire: Black Writers in Canada* (Mosaic Press, 1987).

WEST INDIAN LANGUAGE

For Caribbean English, the chief resources are S. R. R. Allsopp's *Dictionary of Caribbean English Usage* (Oxford University Press, 1997) and the Cassidy and LePage *Dictionary of Jamaican English* (Cambridge University Press, 1980). Also of interest to non-specialists are Frederic Cassidy's *Jamaica Talk* (second edition; Macmillan, 1971) and Peter Roberts's *West Indians and Their Language* (Cambridge University Press, 1988).

LITERARY STUDIES

There are still only a handful of books about individual West Indian poets. James R. Giles's *Claude McKay* (Twayne, 1976) is a good general introduction, as is Robert Hamner's *Derek Walcott* (Twayne, 1993). Rei Terada's *The Poetry of Derek Walcott: American*

Mimicry (Northeastern, 1992) is an intelligent reading of the poetry; Edward Baugh's *Derek Walcott: Memory as Vision* (Longman, 1978) is specifically a study of *Another Life*. Gordon Rohlehr's *Pathfinder* (author, 1981) is *the* magisterial study of Brathwaite's *The Arrivants*. Stewart Brown has collected essays by many hands in two valuable books, *The Art of Derek Walcott* (Seren Books, 1991) and *The Art of Kamau Brathwaite* (Seren, 1995).

Brathwaite's *Roots* (University of Michigan, 1993) contains his most important essays; Walcott's essays have not been collected, but several are included in Robert Hamner's *Critical Perspectives on Derek Walcott* (Three Continents, 1993). Extremely valuable are Gordon Rohlehr's two collections of essays, *My Strangled City and Other Essays* (Longman Trinidad, 1992) and *The Shape of That Hurt and Other Essays* (Longman Trinidad, 1992).

LITERARY HISTORIES AND CULTURAL STUDIES

A good place to start is with the observations of three West Indian pioneers: George Lamming's *The Pleasures of Exile* (Michael Joseph, 1960), V. S. Naipaul's *The Middle Passage: The Caribbean Revisited* (Andre Deutsche, 1962), and C. L. R. James's *Beyond a Boundary* (Hutchinson & Co., 1963). James's book is about much more than cricket. Anne Walmsley richly chronicles a formative period in *The Caribbean Artists Movement: 1966–1972* (New Beacon, 1992).

Finally four extraordinary books, each of which provides a different context for reading West Indian poetry: Roger Abrahams's *The Man of Words in the West Indies: Performance and the Emergence of Creole Culture* (Johns Hopkins, 1983), Antonio Benitez-Rojo's *The Repeating Island: The Caribbean and the Postmodern Perspective* (Duke University, 1992), Edouard Glissant's *Caribbean Discourse* (University Press of Virginia, 1989), and Paul Gilroy's *The Black Atlantic* (Harvard, 1993).

Index

Made in the USA
Lexington, KY
12 September 2014